**W9-AST-065**

This is a badly needed book.

— **BILL MCKIBBEN**, author of *The End of Nature*

*The Small-Mart Revolution* reveals why supporting small business makes good economic sense and how they offer the only real long-term solution for the health of our neighborhoods and our nation. It will touch your heart, while showing you how to better mind your wallet.

— **DR. NANCY SNYDERMAN**, Vice President for Consumer Education, Johnson & Johnson, and Associate Professor of Head and Neck Surgery, University of Pennsylvania

There are precious few good alternatives to the "Wal-Martization" of our communities. *The Small-Mart Revolution* not only provides an alternative analysis, it tells us how we can make it happen.

— **ROBERT GREENWALD**, director of the documentary "Wal-Mart: The High Cost of Low Price"

*The Small-Mart Revolution* is an essential resource for every local business owner, government official, and public interest citizen advocate. Michael Shuman makes a convincing case that the future belongs to the small and local. This is an authoritative, practical, and highly readable handbook on rebuilding local economies as an alternative to corporate-led economic globalization by the leading guru of local economic development.

— **DAVID C. KORTEN**, author of *When Corporations Rule the World* and *The Great Turning: From Empire to Earth Community*

*The Small-Mart Revolution* provides the most important blueprint for economic development I've ever seen. It shows how communities can prosper by putting local constituents and businesses first. The book should be required reading for local elected officials and civil servants across America.

— **LARRY AGRAN**, Mayor of Irvine, California (2000–2004)

Some of us have embraced globalization without worrying overmuch about the consequences. Others of us are fighting pointless battles against progress, technology, and capitalism. Here, Michael Shuman presents a badly needed Third Way. He says that by strengthening our local businesses and communities we'll be creating a better capitalism and a better world. And he backs it up with logic, examples, statistics, and passion! This is the kind of book that could launch a whole new social-political movement.

— **MARK SATIN**, author of *Radical Middle: The Politics We Need Now*

Michael Shuman has done it again. He shows the power of grassroots economics—not as mere theory about a future world—but as real people, today, creating an equitable economy from the grassroots up. This book will revolutionize your thinking about "development." Do yourself and all of us a favor by reading it and then acting on it.

— **KEVIN DANAHER**, Co-Director, Global Exchange

The world is about to become a larger place again. Globalism is toast. Caught up in raptures of credit-fueled discount shopping, few Americans realize how profoundly our society is about to change. We are sleepwalking into a permanent global energy crisis that will compel us to live much more locally than we have for generations. We face a desperate need to reconstruct local networks of economic relations—and we should have begun this great task yesterday. This is an invaluable guide to how we might accomplish this.

— **JAMES HOWARD KUNSTLER**, author of *The Long Emergency*

As global markets explode, Michael Shuman offers a compelling alternative for growth towards a healthier civil society. Anyone interested in the consequences of globalization dominated by multinationals should read this book.

— **MICHELE BARRY**, Professor of Medicine and Global Health, Yale University

*Going Local* became my economic development bible. *The Small Mart Revolution* is Shuman's new testament to America's progress toward genuine economic stability. Good words leading us to good jobs.
— **PAUL GLOVER**, Founder, Ithaca Hours

Shuman takes on the single-factor analysts who argue that the future lies in outsourcing our lives by showing how locally based businesses and economies are a happier, healthier solution for all. In the end, it's not how far our dollars travel that matters but how well and often they multiply near where they are earned and spent. Shuman shows how to stop local economies from being drained through the avaricious pipelines of globalization and be turned instead into deep wells serving their own communities.
— **SAM SMITH**, Editor, *Progressive Review*

Following in the footsteps of E.F. Schumacher and Jane Jacobs, who elegantly described the 'why' of local and regional economies, Michael Shuman's new book provides the much needed "how"— with compelling examples from around the world.
— **SUSAN WITT**, Executive Director, E.F. Schumacher Society

This powerfully argued book explains how small, innovative, and locally-oriented economies can undermine the power of globalized mega-companies like Wal-Mart, building healthier, wealthier, and happier local communities in the process. Even if you don't agree with all his economic arguments, his many examples of creative communities that have taken charge of their own economic, social, and cultural futures cry out for wide replication.
— **JOHN MCCLAUGHRY**, formerly Senior Policy Advisor in the Reagan White House and President, The Ethan Allen Institute

Get out of the big-box; get into your community and its economy! Shuman shows why a vibrant local economy is important, how to make it happen, and how doing so could help each of us. He offers sound analysis, and a style that emphasizes action. This book is addressed to consumers, entrepreneurs, and policy makers, and its message could not be more timely.
— **CHRISTOPHER GUNN**, author of *Third Sector Development*

Our actions as consumers, investors, and policymakers have put us in bondage to a global economy that jeopardizes the future well-being of our communities and ourselves. Shuman offers a compelling alternative vision of a more robust, more sustainable economy built around independent, locally-owned organizations. Anyone who desires to live in a free and prosperous future must read and take to heart the message in *The Small-Mart Revolution*.
— **H. THOMAS JOHNSON**, Professor of Business Administration, Portland State University

This is a terrific book. Fast-moving, full of facts and fresh analysis, a bundle of real things you can do to rebuild your own community. A practical tour-de-force. Bravo!
— **GAR ALPEROVITZ**, Lionel Re. Bauman Professor of Political Economy, University of Maryland, and author of *America Beyond Capitalism*

# the
# small-mart
# revolution

# the
# small-mart
# revolution

## HOW LOCAL BUSINESSES
## ARE BEATING THE GLOBAL COMPETITION

### Michael H. Shuman

BERRETT-KOEHLER PUBLISHERS, INC.
San Francisco

**Berrett-Koehler Publishers, Inc.**
235 Montgomery Street, Suite 650
San Francisco, CA 94104-2916
Tel: (415) 288-0260    Fax: (415) 362-2512    www.bkconnection.com

**Ordering Information**

**Quantity sales.** Special discounts are available on quantity purchases by corporations,
associations, and others. For details, contact the "Special Sales Department" at the
Berrett-Koehler address above.
**Individual sales.** Berrett-Koehler publications are available through most bookstores.
They can also be ordered directly from Berrett-Koehler: Tel: (800) 929-2929;
Fax: (802) 864-7626; www.bkconnection.com
**Orders for college textbook/course adoption use.** Please contact Berrett-Koehler:
Tel: (800) 929-2929; Fax: (802) 864-7626.
**Orders by U.S. trade bookstores and wholesalers.** Please contact Publishers Group
West, 1700 Fourth Street, Berkeley, CA 94710. Tel: (510) 528-1444; Fax (510) 528-3444.

Berrett-Koehler and the BK logo are registered trademarks of Berrett-Koehler
Publishers, Inc.

Printed in the United States of America

Berrett-Koehler books are printed on long-lasting acid-free paper. When it is available,
we choose paper that has been manufactured by environmentally responsible processes. These may include using trees grown in sustainable forests, incorporating
recycled paper, minimizing chlorine in bleaching, or recycling the energy produced
at the paper mill.

Library of Congress Cataloging-in-Publication Data
Schuman, Michael.
    The small-mart revolution : how local businesses are beating the global competition /
by Michael H. Schuman.
        p.   cm.
    Includes bibliographical references (p.  ) and index.
    ISBN-10: 1-57675-386-7; ISBN-13: 978-1-57675-386-6
    1. Small business — United States.    2. Import substitition — United States.
3. Globalization — Economic aspects — United States.    I. Title.

HD2346.U5S55    2006

338.6'42093—dc22                                                    2006040671

First Edition

11 10 09 08 07 06    10 9 8 7 6 5 4 3 2 1

*For Adam and Rachel,*
*so they understand some day why Daddy*
*would prefer not to take them to McDonald's.*

# CONTENTS

# FOREWORD

This is a badly needed book.

I say that for several reasons. The first, and most obvious, is that almost anyone who has taken the time to study the situation now knows what a death star the big box on the edge of town is. When Wal-Mart and its kind first began metastasizing across the landscape, it was impossible to say for sure what the effect would be. Perhaps people would just go there for a few items they couldn't purchase locally (in my town, small appliances) and would continue to patronize local stores for the rest. Perhaps they would so add to the general prosperity of a neighborhood that everyone's boat would be lifted on their swelling tide. As it turned out, that's not what happened. Local downtowns were depopulated—a few cars parked aimlessly by the courthouse on a Saturday morning where once there had been hundreds of people coming "into town." Jobs were lost—one and a half for every job created—and the jobs that weren't lost often paid less because now the big boys set the local wage scale. At the end of a decade, according to one thorough study, counties with the massive bargain depots had become poorer compared to those without. This is the intellectual landscape in which this book emerges—we are ready for the message.

The second reason is that fairly few people, even when they sensed these realities, could conceive of an alternative. Wal-Mart and its kin seemed to be *inevitable*, as unstoppable as a missile in flight. Michael Shuman, throughout his career, has done us the great service of dispelling that myth and showing us that these behemoths can be stopped.

And third, and by far most important, he shows us that in the end the crucial question is not stopping Wal-Mart at all. It's not about stopping anything. It's about starting something—vibrant local economies that will make our cities and towns the places we very much want them to be.

This revolution is of the first importance. It may well turn out to be one of the keys to containing global warming, for instance. (If the average bite of food didn't have to travel two thousand miles before it reached your lips; if the power for your block came from the windmill in the cul-de-sac; if the local bus was a pleasure to ride—think of the carbon that could be saved). It may, by shortening supply lines, help us ward off the worst effects of peak oil. It may also turn out to be the key to saving democracy. I mean that quite literally: a giant-sized nation of 300 million is run by those most able to dominate public life, usually because of the power their corporate wealth confers. By contrast, a town that takes real control of its economic and social life insulates itself at least a little from the corrupt decision making of the central authorities.

But it's finally important for another reason: we want and deserve the delight that comes with working communities. Wandering into a cavernous Wal-Mart is a desolate experience. Cheap, but cheap in every way. Wandering through a town where you depend on the people around you, and they depend on you—that's called living. Humans were built for it. Michael Shuman shows us how it might happen again.

*Bill McKibben*

★★★★★★★★★★★★★★★★★★★★★★★★★★★★★★★★★★★★★★★★★★

# FROM WAL-MART TO SMALL-MART

Nobody's perfect. Today is the one day each year I permit myself to be a petty thief. As my childhood shoplifter buddies used to explain, there's a thrill in being bad, plus there's cheap stuff to be had. Let me clarify—I don't plan on breaking any laws. My indulgence is perfectly legal, and many would even consider it smart shopping. But I shouldn't mince words. What I'm planning on doing ought to be called "community lifting." I'm going to make my annual summertime sneakers shopping run at Wal-Mart, even if it means snatching just a little bit of well-being from my neighbors.

Why am I doing this? Because for fifteen dollars I can get basic footwear that lasts a year. After twelve months of regular deployment, these puppies smell so bad they just might qualify as weapons of mass destruction. It's high time to bury the old pair and replace them with fresh rubber. And I don't want to spend a penny more than necessary.

Using the WalMart.com online directory, I discover that there are ten stores in the vicinity of my home in Washington, DC—not exactly your typical rural area targeted by the retailing giant. The closest one is in Alexandria, Virginia, sixteen miles away. Following directions from MapQuest, I wind my way through the region's sprawling suburbs, at one point ominously passing the reconstructed side of the Pentagon where terrorists crashed a plane in 2001. My mind flashes on the image of Mohammad Atta, leader of the 9/11 gang, caught on videotape on 9/10 buying his infamous box cutters at a Wal-Mart in Portland, Maine. Forty-five minutes later I arrive. The parking lot is jammed.

At the entrance is posted an official notice from Fairfax County indicating that the Wal-Mart Real Estate Business Trust is now seeking permission to expand the store. Business must be doing well.

Nationally, of course, Wal-Mart is one of America's greatest success stories. It began in 1962, when Sam Walton set up a chain of small variety stores in Kansas and Arkansas. For many years Wal-Marts were only selling novelties in remote rural towns. Today five thousand outlets throughout the United States and in nine other countries sell just about everything. Wal-Mart "Supercenters"—of which there are nearly two thousand in the United States—are each as big as four football fields. As Simon Head writes, "With 1.4 million employees worldwide, Wal-Mart's workforce is now larger than that of GM, Ford, GE, and IBM combined. At $258 billion in 2003, Wal-Mart's annual revenues are 2 percent of US gross domestic product (GDP), and eight times the size of Microsoft's. In fact, when ranked by its revenues, Wal-Mart is the world's largest corporation."[1]

"The secret of successful retailing," Sam Walton wrote in his autobiography, "is to give your customers what they want."

But I digress. Even though the Fairfax store seems larger than a typical National Park and few staff are in the aisles to help, I quickly find my sneakers, the exact same kind I bought last year. A perfect fit! Off to the checkout line.

As I snake my way triumphantly through the aisles, I notice a few other items I could use. We just ran out of Crispix cereal and Chips Ahoy cookies. There's a great horse toy for my daughter Rachel, two years old, and some AA-batteries to fire it up. Hmmm, now I have to come back with something for Adam, my six-year-old, who's apprehensive about beginning kindergarten. Whew, there's a *Back to School* video, featuring Franklin the Turtle. He'll also like this new Jump Start computer program to help with his math and spelling, and a new folding chair to sit at the computer. And there's the *Guinness Book of World Records* book he and I were talking about the other night—got to get that. Bill Clinton's book, *My Life*, for only twenty-two dollars? What a steal! And all this other stuff: a 120-foot extension cord to vacuum my car, a new plastic box for my loose files, a halogen reading lamp for bedside table, four new glasses for end-of-the-day drinks, a gigantic bottle of Tide, cheap bottles of Advil and Aleve for my chronic back pain that's going to get worse when I carry this load to the car. Enough!

I tag the checkout line as if it were home base and finally catch my breath. I consider asking the clerk to put me in a straitjacket so that I won't buy anything else.

It's the week before school opens, so long lines of exasperated parents and their screaming children make the nearly half-hour wait compare unfavorably to my experience squatting in a New Delhi bus station a decade earlier. My own checkout line is so long that by the time I reach the front the brain-dead clerk is relieved halfway through scanning my items. The new clerk begins by ringing me up again for the chair, a mistake to which I politely draw his attention. A bit grudgingly, he removes the extra charge. As I'm about to walk away, I look again at the receipt and discover that I have just parted with $275; I also realize that the new clerk double-charged me for the one item I came to buy in the first place—those damn sneakers!

## Bargains

What kinds of deals did I secure during my whirlwind community-lifting experience? Research shows that the "savings" from shopping at chain stores generally turn out to be vastly overestimated.[2] A 2002 survey by the Maine Department of Human Services, for example, found that local drugstores actually provided better deals than the pharmacies at Rite Aid and CVS.[3] Wal-Mart prescription prices, which fell roughly in the middle of the group surveyed, also varied significantly from place to place, depending on the degree of local competition.[4]

In the days that followed my shopping spree, I decided to do some comparative shopping at various stores in my neighborhood in northwest Washington, DC. It is true that for most of the generic items, Wal-Mart offered prices about 5 to 10 percent less than what I could find locally. Applying the upper end, I "saved" about $27.50.[5]

But recall that I was overcharged forty-six dollars on two items. Had I not caught these errors in the chaotic checkout process, I would have lost money. Okay, to be fair, Wal-Mart fixed the errors once I brought them to the irritated clerk's attention. Later, however, I learn that an NBC undercover team found that deep discounters like Wal-Mart are overcharging 10 to 25 percent of the time and that these mistakes are three to one against the consumer.[6] I had assumed that the error was not deliberate dishonesty, just poor training and low morale. But several recent academic studies have found Wal-Mart scanners yield error rates as high as 8.3 percent of the time, four times the federal standard, prompting investigations by several state attorneys general.[7]

Next, consider the time and money it took me to get to the Alexandria store. That year the Internal Revenue Service allowed businesses to write off about 40.5 cents per mile for auto wear and tear, gas, insurance, and other incidentals. The thirty-two-mile round trip thus cost fourteen dollars. I spent ninety minutes driving round trip and thirty minutes in a checkout line. Assuming I'm worth at least a living wage of ten dollars per hour, that's twenty dollars of my time. The transaction cost of this trip was thirty-four dollars, again, greater than my savings.

When I returned home my wife, whose instincts for taste and quality are far more trustworthy than my own, took one look at my four discount scotch glasses and told me that she was promptly dispatching them to the local recycling facility. She declared the reading lamp too ugly to gain admittance into our bedroom. Rachel's horse toy lasted about a week before it broke, and the pieces scattered to the far corners of the house. The cheap 120-foot extension cord turned out to lack the third safety prong most of our appliances now require, so it now sits on a shelf in the basement gathering dust.

What about the pure joy of shopping, of gliding from department to department while humming Muzak versions of old Top 40 hits? Not. Rather than bump into my neighbors and trade some gossip, I wound up shopping in a sea of strangers who were all as agitated as I was and unwilling to kibitz.

And the biggest loss was this: I never expected to buy most of this stuff in the first place. I came to buy $15 sneakers, and wound up spending $275 on a half-dozen bags of junk. Caught up in the superficial frenzy of discounts and deals, I wound up spending nearly twenty times more money than I intended, much of it on goods of shoddy quality in a shopping excursion that wasted two hours of my time and gave me an enormous headache. Even more embarrassing, the sneakers I came to buy, which wound up not having a price tag, actually cost twenty-six dollars, about the same price I would have paid at a dozen other stores in Washington.

Yes, crime doesn't pay.

## The Dark Side

Why use terms like "crime" and "community lifting"? Why should I feel bad about doing what millions of Americans do every day with no reservations whatsoever? Because the reality is that every dollar I decide not to spend at my local businesses and instead surrender to Wal-Mart saps just a little bit of vitality from my community, all for bargains that turn out to be largely illusory. Had I spent my $275 at locally owned stores like Rodman's or Strosniders, many more of my dollars would have remained circulating in my local economy and boosting the area's income, wealth, and jobs. My personal gain, which proved illusory, was my neighbors' loss.

But doesn't Wal-Mart at least provide a bunch of decent jobs for my neighbors? In fact, the average pay of a sales clerk at Wal-Mart is $8.50 per hour. The company keeps many employees working in part-time positions to avoid paying health care and other benefits. So many workers live below the poverty line that in 2004 Wal-Mart workers qualified for $2.5 billion in federal welfare assistance, according to a recent congressional report.[8] The U.S. government is shelling out as much as $2,103 per employee for children's health care, low-income tax credits, and housing assistance. State welfare agencies are making similarly steep outlays. One in four Wal-Mart employees in Georgia has a child in the state's program for needy children.[9] This crazy quilt of public policies means that every taxpayer, including those businesses paying their workers decent wages, is effectively footing the bill for Wal-Mart's low prices.

A recent lawsuit revealed that the night crew is occasionally kept locked in the store past closing and receives no overtime. Issued to every store manager is a booklet called the "Manager's Toolbox to Remaining Union Free." When a renegade meat-cutters' department in a Texas Wal-Mart voted to unionize in 2000, Wal-Mart shut down the department and fired the employees.[10]

Wal-Mart is arguably the greatest destroyer of communities on the planet. Vampirelike, it sucks retail transactions out of existing businesses and decimates once-vibrant downtowns. Kenneth Stone of Iowa State University is one of a handful of scholars to study systematically the impact of Wal-Mart's spread on independent retailers.[11] Between

1983 and 1996, at a time when chain stores like Wal-Mart increased their sales by 42 percent, he found that overall retail sales in Iowa plummeted in small towns: by 17 percent in towns with 2,500 to 5,000 people, by 30 percent in towns with 1,000 to 2,500 residents, and by 40 percent in towns with fewer than 1,000 residents.

But dwelling on Wal-Mart is, frankly, a distraction. The only real difference between Wal-Mart and thousands of other chain stores is its degree of success and its take-no-prisoners tactics. I begrudge its methods and mission, not its success. The fundamental challenge for communities struggling to revive their economies is not to destroy Wal-Mart, because a Target or a Sears or a hundred other chains stand ready to take its place. The challenge is, instead, to find ways to nurture competitive local alternatives to Wal-Mart that can revitalize our local economies and our communities.

## The Small-Mart Revolution

When you think about Small-Marts, the first things that come to mind are the mom-and-pops and neighborhood stores that have been struggling and disappearing in recent years. Through business tactics that have been, depending on your perspective, brilliant or ruthless, chain stores like Costco and major Internet retailers like Amazon have steamrolled almost every community's homegrown businesses. Five supermarket chains sell 42 percent of all our groceries, Home Depot and Lowe's account for 45 percent of hardware and building supplies, and Barnes & Noble and Borders control half of all bookstore sales.[12] "Most striking of all," writes Stacy Mitchell, a researcher for the Institute for Local Self-Reliance and an astute observer of these trends, "Wal-Mart now captures nearly 10 percent of all U.S. retail spending. Wal-Mart is the largest grocer in the country, the largest music seller, the largest jeweler, the largest furniture dealer, and the largest toy seller."[13]

The increasing visual and financial presence of these powerful chains on our streetscapes, however, can be misleading. Retail is just one of the many sectors that produce wealth for a community, typically representing only about 7 percent of a local economy, and chain stores just half of that. Every box of corn flakes contains the labor and resources of farmers who grow the corn, manufacturers who produce the flakes, accountants and lawyers who support corporate management, utility dispatchers who provide the power and lights, wholesalers who connect the retailers with the manufacturer, and shippers who bring the cereal to the store. The Small-Mart Revolution is about supporting independent and local businesses in *all* of these sectors.

Just as the American Revolution of 1776 was not merely a revolt against the tyranny of the king of England but also a watershed for democracy and freedom, the Small-Mart Revolution is about much more than fighting chain stores. If you spend your shopping hours each week making sure that not a single screw on your workbench comes from Home Depot while your mortgage sits in Wells Fargo Bank, in dollar terms you've made one baby step forward and a hundred-mile leap backward. If your limited time and energy are exhausted in opposing big-box malls, you may have little left to build a community-friendly economy. If you blow your political capital on erecting controversial zoning and trade barriers against businesses you detest, you'll be ill-equipped to implement the policy reforms needed to level the playing field that currently tilts against small business.

In other words: what the Small-Mart Revolution is *for* is more important than what it's *against*. The Small-Mart Revolution aims to improve the prosperity of every community, here and abroad, by maximizing opportunities for locally owned businesses. And since "place-based" businesses already make up more than half of a typical community's economy, the Small-Mart Revolution, for the most part, means doing more of what we already know how to do pretty well. In that sense, it's not terribly radical. But sometimes it's the subtle changes in our lives, in our buying and investing habits, in our business practices, and in our public policies that are the hardest to realize.

The Small-Mart Revolution *is* against one thing—the vast web of laws and public policies that directly disadvantage small and local businesses. Currently, nearly all business subsidies in this country go to nonlocal firms. These exceed $50 billion per year at the state and local level, and $63 billion per year at the national level.[14] The capital markets, as we'll see, also are heavily rigged against small business. Just these two factors alone have suffocated what could have been the Small-Mart Revolution over the past decade. Despite all the hype about globalization, if we manage to level the playing fields in subsidies and capital access, the next decade might well see a Small-Mart Renaissance.

When the Berlin Wall fell after the Velvet Revolution more than a decade ago, a young political scientist named Francis Fukuyama captured the spirit of the moment in an article audaciously titled "The End of History."[15] Fukuyama argued that now that capitalism had triumphed over state socialism, only a few minor questions about the future of humanity remain. Even if Fukuyama's thesis turns out to be right—and a decade later, with Chinese Communists still ruling a fifth of humanity and thriving as Wal-Mart's biggest suppliers, his pronouncements seem a bit premature—he erred in a more fundamental way. We are now witnessing an epochal struggle between two dramatically different visions of capitalism, the outcome of which will define many interesting and important years of history to come.

One vision can be summarized by former British Prime Minister Margaret Thatcher's declaration that "there is no alternative" to globalization and its neoliberal tenets of free markets and free trade.[16] All over the world, conventional economic developers have embraced the logic of "there is no alternative"—or TINA—in the form of two imperatives: get Toyota to locate in your backyard, and export your goods as far and widely as possible. These ideas are so widely accepted by politicians, economists, and policymakers across the political spectrum that even to question them is tantamount to heresy.

There *is* a capitalist alternative gaining acceptance across the United States and throughout the world: economic development rooted in local ownership and import substitution, or LOIS for short. Local ownership means that working control of a business resides within a geographically defined community. And import substitution means that, whenever it's cost-effective to produce goods and services locally, a community should do so. Together these principles suggest—as such intellectual pioneers as E. F. Schumacher and Jane Jacobs have argued over the last two generations—the virtues of an economy that takes full advantage of local talent, local capital, and local markets.

Why should it matter exactly who owns a business? And why should we care whether a business serves local or global markets? After all, don't all businesses contribute to a community's well-being, no matter what their ownership and no matter where their markets? Sure, nearly all kinds of businesses offer a community the benefits of jobs, tax dollars, charitable contributions, and local economic stimulus. As we will see, however, LOIS firms deliver these benefits more reliably, more robustly, and more sustainably than the nonlocal alternatives do. That means our choices—as consumers, as investors, as entrepreneurs, as policymakers—can make a huge difference in how well our communities prosper.

Few of us believe the old saying that what's good for General Motors is good for America, because too little of GM remains in America, too many shares of GM stock are publicly traded worldwide, too few Americans actually work for GM (fewer every day it seems), and too many of the benefits are distributed in so many unexpected ways (in hidden Cayman Island bank accounts, for example). The little goodwill we might have once had for the automotive giant has been largely exhausted by its Neanderthal attachment to gas-guzzling SUVs that have resulted in poor sales, plant closures, and massive layoffs. Most of us suspect—correctly it turns out—that local businesses in our community are more directly connected to our well-being. The assets of these small firms are, by definition, sited in the community and owned by people residing there. They almost exclusively hire neighbors. The benefits of their success and the fallout of their failure are experienced directly by residents.

The term "Small-Mart," as I use it in this book, refers to many different kinds of LOIS business. Most Small-Marts are privately run small businesses, principally sole-proprietorships and partnerships. Some are privately held corporations, and a few are even publicly traded stock companies (though the shares must only be tradable locally). The term also is meant to include nonprofits, cooperatives, worker-owned businesses, public enterprises, public-private partnerships, and anything else anchored to a community through ownership.[17] While I use "Small-Marts" and "small businesses" interchangeably, I should clarify the relationship between the two. Small-Marts don't have to be small, but nearly all are. "Smallness" only matters because most small businesses tend to be locally owned. There are certainly some very large companies, like the Hershey Chocolate Company (as we explore in chapter 2), that are locally controlled and would qualify as Small-Marts as well. Similarly, a few small businesses have owners living thousands of miles away and would not qualify as Small-Marts. Common sense suggests that these are the exceptions that prove the rule.

## Small-Mart Nation

If the Small-Mart Revolution succeeds in seeding, growing, and spreading LOIS businesses, how might your life be different? Let's look ahead twenty-five years, and see what a Small-Mart world looks like.

**Your Economy.** The first thing you'll notice is how many of your neighbors are running their own businesses, many out of their own homes. Almost everyone else is working for these local firms, enjoying shorter commutes and more time with their families. The idea of a one-company town is obsolete. Even rural communities with a few thousand residents now have twenty-five, fifty, or a hundred companies. Most of these businesses serve local needs, but some also have robust export markets. All these businesses, physically anchored through local ownership, have become powerful gushers of wealth as well as resilient hedges against the kinds of disasters that used to occur when a major, distantly owned employer, moved—or threatened to move—overseas.

**Your Purchasing.** You're now spending most of your hard-earned money on competitively priced and locally produced high-quality goods and services, where each dollar gets recycled many times within your community. You're buying fresh fruits, vegetables, and chickens grown by nearby farmers, shopping at a small market or co-op (some of which home deliver), and eating out at locally owned restaurants. You're driving less and filling the tank with locally made biodiesel or hydrogen. You own your home, rent from a local landlord, or hold a mortgage from a local bank. Your residence is built from locally available stone and lumber and filled with locally made furniture and household accessories like locally made flatware, plates, and plants. You're using electricity generated by local windpower, hydropower, or solar cells, and bringing down your municipal utility bill through local efficiency measures. (In fact, you may be making money from some of these energy devices by selling surplus power to your neighbors.) You're donating to local churches and charities. You're sampling emerging local fashions, jewelry, shoes, art, theater, newspapers, books, music, beer and wine, shampoos, and soaps. You're seeing local doctors, dentists, and therapists, using local lawyers and accountants, supporting local schools and public services. Thanks to information distributed by a Local First Campaign, you're confident that very little of this costs more than the nonlocal alternatives and ebullient that some of these choices are actually saving you money. The only real cost is the extra time and attentiveness required to shop carefully, to filter out the allure of false bargains from chain stores, and to deprogram yourself from the appealing but misleading bombast of global advertising.

**Your Investing.** Some of your savings sits in a local bank or credit union, the only entities you are confident will loan out or reinvest this money locally. If you have extra money, you might invest in a neighbor's business you're excited about. Or you might buy stock in one of the many local companies being traded on your local stock exchange. Most of your retirement sits in an IRA, SEP, 401(k), or other vehicle run by a local mutual fund with a diversified portfolio of local businesses. And no matter what your income, you're enjoying the local benefits of a totally revamped Social Security system that places responsibility for trust fund management in state and local hands.

**Your Entrepreneurship.** For those who ever dreamed of running their own business, this is one of the most exciting moments in U.S. history. The changes in everyone's purchasing habits, outlined above, are opening up all kinds of new niches for locally produced goods and locally provided services. You and other entrepreneurs in the community are now working together to maintain your competitive edge against global giants through local business alliances and national producers' cooperatives that undertake joint advertising, procurement, warehousing, and distribution. You might take advantage of a new generation of "incubators" that support local start-ups with training and capital, or you might accept local credit and debit cards that promote local purchasing.

**Your Policymaking.** The era of wasting millions of local dollars on luring outside businesses is thankfully over. Your community doesn't stand in the way of nonlocal retailers or manufacturers coming in, but in the name of the free market, *you no longer pay them any financial tribute*. One reason the small businesses in your community are thriving is that your city government has systematically eliminated dozens of laws and policies concerned with zoning, policing, schools, business practices, government procurement, and pension investment that were once tilted toward nonlocal business. Those few dollars spent on business development are now focused, laser-like, on supporting various elements of the Small-Mart Revolution, like entrepreneurship training and local stock markets.

**Your Community.** Years earlier, the Small-Mart Revolution got rolling when key members of your community decided to participate in a year-long "visioning" process. They pinpointed unnecessary "leaks" of dollars from your local economy, identified promising local business opportunities that could plug those leaks, and mobilized consumers, investors, entrepreneurs, and policymakers to support those businesses.

**Your World.** Even though the Small-Mart Revolution began in your backyard, your community and thousands of others like it around the world have gradually come to appreciate that their well-being depends on the participation of every community in every country. The revolutionary step, you realized, was not to increase global trade per se, but to increase global self-reliance. You now generously and freely share technology, business designs, and public policies with partners in the world's poorest communities. A growing number of communities worldwide producing more of their own goods and services means a significant growth in global wealth, investment, and spending, with fewer environmental problems. Paradoxically, global trade is expanding in absolute terms, even as trade is becoming a diminishing percentage of every community's economy.

This glimpse of the future defines the logical arc of this book. In the pages that follow, you'll find arguments, in two parts, on the virtues and the vision of the Small-Mart Revolution. Part I explores the struggle between LOIS and TINA: how TINA is wrecking local economies (chapter 1); why LOIS is a far better basis for economic development (chapter 2); and eight global trends that are making LOIS more competitive (chapter 3). Part II moves from theory to practice and explores what various constituencies need to do to accelerate the Small-Mart Revolution. The key players are consumers (chapter 4), investors (chapter 5), entrepreneurs (chapter 6), and policymakers (chapter 7). The most effective Small-Mart initiatives, however, are those that bring all these players together as a team of community builders (chapter 8). The final chapter outlines a new philosophy of globalization implicit in the Small-Mart Revolution.

## Origins

*The Small-Mart Revolution* is a direct descendent of my last book, *Going Local: Creating Self-Reliant Communities in a Global Age*, in which I argued that local ownership of business and self-reliance of a community were critical requirements for a prosperous and sustainable local economy.[18] The most enthusiastic readers of that book, initially at least, were the antiglobalization activists recently energized by the Battle for Seattle, where they had all but stopped a meeting of the World Trade Organization (WTO). As months and then years passed by I found many pockets of interest among policymakers, politicians, and community developers, but conspicuously AWOL were those who had the most to gain from the arguments—the proprietors of small business.

Just after *Going Local* went on sale, I traveled to the San Francisco Bay Area, where I had gotten my undergraduate and law degrees and had lived for nearly fifteen years. I was eager to see how the book was doing at one of my favorite locally owned bookstores in Menlo Park. The owners had recently placed signs in the outside windows decrying the dangers that chains like Borders and Barnes & Noble posed to independent bookstores and to the entire publishing industry. Here, I optimistically thought, was the kind of venue where *Going Local* would thrive. I looked for copies on the shelves, found none, and assumed the book was selling briskly. I asked a clerk if she had more copies in the back, and she returned to report that, apparently, after the book had sat on a remote shelf for a few weeks with no sales, the store dutifully sent back its three consignment copies. Even local bookstores fighting for their lives didn't see the relevance of a book that made arguments about why consumers should buy local. But this was my failure, I concluded, not theirs.

I puzzled over how to broaden my audience. On the evening of September 10, 2001, a group of colleagues gathered in a hotel room in Washington, DC, to discuss our participation in an upcoming conference of the Social Ventures Network (SVN), a group of progressive business leaders. Among those attending were Hazel Henderson, one of the intellectual pioneers of a community-and-nature-centered vision of economics, and Edgar Cahn, the architect of Time Dollars. The time, we thought, was ripe to recruit visionary entrepreneurs for this cause.

The next morning, of course, the new century burst into fireballs at the Pentagon and the World Trade Center. By the time SVN conference participants gathered the courage to board transcontinental jetliners several weeks later, they seemed to have a new seriousness of purpose. Stripped of the usual comforts of American security and keenly aware of how fragile life suddenly had become, attendees seemed unusually receptive to our collective message: that the future of small business, the future of community vitality, even the future of humanity depend on a fundamentally new approach to our local economies. At the end of the four-day conference, nearly fifty people stayed another half day to discuss next steps, and out of the intensive discussions was born the Business Alliance for Local Living Economies, or BALLE.

BALLE was not the first organization to organize locally owned business—the American Independent Business Association (AMIBA) had been formed several years earlier—but it brought a new and exciting vision that linked networks of small businesses with the mission of local economy building. The agenda included challenging some of the core assumptions in the economic development community, demanding that politicians stop giving away precious local resources to lure nonlocal business, rethinking public policies that disadvantage small businesses from top to bottom, and building a new movement of businesses and consumers that would train, hire, invest, and buy local. BALLE has since grown to two dozen chapters around the country collectively representing several thousand small businesses. Over the past four years I've visited and spoken to most of these chapters and learned about cutting-edge businesses all around the country. It is their stories, thinking, and lessons that lie at the heart of this book.

I have written this book, however, not just for small businesspeople, but also for ordinary citizens like you and me who are trying to figure out what to do about our daily choices in shopping, investing, and politics. This is not a tome for policy wonks, though I've added numbers, tables, and footnotes here and there for those so inclined. It's also not an academic book, though I certainly hope students and professors alike will find a few things to learn. It's a book designed for personal awareness and personal action, to guide readers in their inevitable roles as consumers, investors, breadwinners, and voters.

## A Vision, Not a Religion

The central argument here is that LOIS businesses are the key to a community's economic future. The more we nurture and support Small-Marts, the more likely we will bring prosperity to all Americans—rich and poor, black and white, male and female, rural and urban, young and old. With greater prosperity for so many diverse groups, we also have a better shot at solving hundreds of other knotty problems bedeviling our society. If we are smart enough to globally share everything we learn about how LOIS businesses can succeed and modest enough to learn about successful LOIS business designs and strategies elsewhere, we can make major strides toward relieving global poverty and saving global ecosystems.

Despite this grand (but hopefully not grandiose) vision, I want to underscore that LOIS can only be a modest part of any serious agenda of social change. Put in the language of formal logic, LOIS is a necessary but insufficient condition for many needed global reforms. LOIS is a tool, not a panacea. It provides a set of guiding principles, not answers to every complex question concerning economics and policy.

Readers looking for a hidden agenda, for an all-encompassing ideology, for an answer to every thorny question, will be disappointed. I am deeply suspicious of grand theories about people, history, society, politics, and economics. I distrust those who are incapable of seeing virtues in arguments for differing or opposing viewpoints. My own views are an amalgam of thinking from the right, left, and center.

At the core of my worldview is a belief in *subsidiarity*. That is, I believe that individuals and communities should have enough freedom and autonomy to solve their own problems. To the extent that I embrace collective action, whether public or private, I believe it should

be done as locally as possible, where affected individuals can participate fully in the decision making and can truly know the faces of those
touched by their choices. I distrust anything that is not, in the author
Kirkpatrick Sale's terminology, "human scale:" big business, big labor,
big government, big armies, big charities, big UN agencies, and Big
Brother.[19] Government responsibility, power, and budgets should be
primarily local, which means it will be smaller at the state level, smaller
still at the national level, and only incidental at the global level. Only
when there is a very good reason to move power up to a higher level—
if, for example, a community is belching smoke across a half-dozen
states—should we permit larger political jurisdictions to get involved.
I believe that most centralized institutions today, whether the IRS or
the WTO, should be slimmed down and have the bulk of their powers
and responsibilities returned to communities.

Conservatives will be pleased that I believe deeply in personal freedom, free markets, and local control, with an absolute minimum of
federal rules, regulations, and interventions. Much of my writing has
been on the virtues of devolution, small business, patriotism, and for-
profit business.[20] They will be delighted to find in these pages my calls
to abolish business taxes, nurture entrepreneurship, and cut wasteful
federal spending.

Progressives will be relieved, though, to learn that I believe in markets as tools, not as magic wands. I recognize that markets can neither
solve every problem nor deliver every opportunity. Moreover, there are
so many imperfections in the typical marketplace that public initiative,
guided by strict adherence to the precautionary principle, is still
needed to counter or undo them. I am therefore an enthusiastic
believer in strong governments and governance, provided these are
primarily local. I also embrace the liberal vision of trying to help every
human being on Earth achieve decent community, and favor aggressive global antipoverty and environmental protection initiatives, led
however, not by large-scale government, UN, or World Bank programs,
but by grassroots groups and communities.[21]

Some will conclude I'm just sloppy or opportunistic in allowing so
many seemingly disparate thoughts to live in my head. But the more I
travel across the United States and share these ideas, the more I believe
there is coherence to this worldview, even if it lacks a clear name or

organized party. I have no idea how to situate my views in the current cramped political climate in the United States. You could say that I support progressive ends with conservative means. Color me, neither red nor blue, but purple. With the fastest-growing political faction in the United States being independents, I'm confident that most readers share my aversion to getting pigeonholed by the extremes. I believe that today's deep divisions, widened by radio shock jocks, direct mailers, lobbyists, and interest groups who have anything but our best interests in mind, do not reflect serious divisions of philosophy, but nevertheless freeze opportunities for constructive social action.

I hope the ideas espoused in this book offer fertile common ground for left and right to come together. And maybe, just maybe, in the process of working together to build robust, viable, homegrown economies, even the most uncompromising partisans will begin to see the virtues in their opponents' views, and we, as a nation, as a society, as a civilization, as a species, can begin to make progress on the other issues that divide us.

★★★★★★★★★★★★★★★★★★★★★★★★★★★★★★★★★★★★★★★★★

# PART ONE  THE GATHERING GALE

★★★★★★★★★★★★★★★★★★★★★★★★★★★★★★★★★★★★★★★★★

The next gale that sweeps from the north will bring to our ears the clash of resounding arms! Why stand we here idle? . . . Is life so dear or peace so sweet as to be purchased at the price of chains . . . ? Forbid it, Almighty God. I know not what course others may take, but as for me, give me *community* or give me death!

—PATRICK HENRY
*(with one minor revision)*

★★★★★★★★★★★★★★★★★★★★★★★★★★★★★★★★★★★★★★★★★★

# one

# WRECKONOMICS

Jack J. Shuman, my father, never had it easy, but compared to his parents, immigrants from Russia who had to cope with Czarist oppression, exhausting ocean voyages (two, in my grandmother's case), anti-Semitism, and the Great Depression, life was sweet. After World War II, he completed a master's degree in mechanical engineering and soon found a job working for Western Electric, the major parts and equipment supplier for the nation's telephone system. He worked his entire professional life for Ma Bell and even wound up retiring a few years earlier than planned after a court-ordered breakup of the telecom monopoly in 1984. The deal was simple: work hard and stick with the company, and we'll give you a decent middle-class salary for the rest of your life with periodic raises, decent health care, and a generous pension. The family settled in North Massapequa, New York, where the public schools were good, tract housing affordable, and mass transit to Manhattan fast and reliable.

Today, this lifestyle seems so alien that it might as well have existed in the Middle Ages. Almost no one expects to hold a job for a lifetime anymore. Companies hire and fire employees at will, and even top executives pack parachutes and expect to bail every few years. Workers, even those few still represented by a union, know that they are increasingly on their own and that they must be prepared to move nomad-like from job to job. For most Americans weekly take-home pay in wages, once inflation is factored out, has grown by remarkably little over the past generation.[1] Employer health care plans are being pruned every year and increasingly charged directly to workers, and more than forty-six million Americans lack any health insurance whatsoever.[2] Company pension plans have gotten smaller and less reliable, requiring Americans to save what they can through individual retirement accounts and other private vehicles. Taxes seem continually to go up as public services go down. Mass transit systems and public schools are a mess—where I live, in the District of Columbia, public schools rank dead last in the country, and even the best of the lot have their occasional playground shootings—pushing middle-class families to exhaust their savings on private schools.

The American Dream is fast shriveling up. My family's security is far shakier than my parents', and I fear what lies ahead for my children.

I suspect I am not alone. How about you? How secure do you feel? Are you satisfied with your job, your health care coverage, your family's well-being, your schools, your community? What does the future portend for your children?

One of the central paradoxes of contemporary American life is that despite so much wealth and progress, we have never been so insecure. Millions of middle-class Americans have taken advantage of low interest rates and borrowed their way to short-term stability, but we know that sooner or later this will come crashing down. The trigger could be a bursting real estate bubble, the collapse of the U.S. dollar, high inflation driven by skyrocketing energy prices, a dirty bomb set off by terrorists—or all of the above. Many of us are no further than one layoff, one major illness, or one national calamity away from plunging into a personal economic tailspin.

The causes underlying our insecurities are many and varied, but there is no question that a primary culprit is a set of forces we have come to call globalization. The United States emerged from World War II as the most powerful economy on the planet, its corporations the dominant players in every product line imaginable, from Lincoln Continentals to Sunbeam toasters, from Coca-Cola to Chase Manhattan Bank. One by one, however, other nations caught up: first the Western Europeans and the Japanese; then the "Asian Tigers" like South Korea, Malaysia, and Singapore; and now the population giants, China and India. Competition has forced American companies to become brutally attentive to the bottom line, and the luxuries of job security, health care, and pensions once enjoyed by our workers have been steadily whittled away, a process further hastened by those ideologically dis-

posed toward dismantling organized labor and other public protec-
tions of worker rights. (The executives of many of these companies
have never had it better, but that's another story.)

One important way U.S. companies have decided to become more
globally competitive is by relocating offices, factories, and headquarters
to countries where the costs of production are lower. Scarcely a month
goes by when we don't read in the local papers that a firm employing
hundreds, even thousands, of our neighbors is moving overseas. The
departure of these old stalwarts of our community has been devastating, leaving craters in our local economies that once depended on
them. The sage advice of economists and policy experts to communities has been to redouble our efforts to hold on to and lure back global
business. Anxious to bring any new jobs to counter the loss of old
ones, communities have enthusiastically welcomed chain stores, big-
box malls, airports, tourist traps, and casinos, seemingly unconcerned
that these new firms are coming with lower wages, part-time jobs, no
health care, and flaky pensions.

Insecurity, we are told, is a necessary price for prosperity. *New York
Times* columnist Thomas Friedman insists that globalization is "making it possible for . . . corporations to reach farther, faster, cheaper, and
deeper around the world" and is fostering "a flowering of both wealth
and technological innovation the likes of which the world has never
before seen."[3] Similarly, local economic developers, who see their mission as orchestrating private and public decisions to maximize local
business activity, have looked at the reality of globalization and concluded that *there is no alternative* (TINA). Change is painful, but the
new mission of a community, as they see it, is to take full advantage of
the cornucopia of global opportunities while minimizing the regret-
table side effects. And that's why we must embrace TINA.

## The Iron Lady

I have plenty critical to say about TINA, but let me try, at least in this
one section, to play the devil's advocate and state its case as dispas-
sionately as possible. It goes something like this: In the new go-go
global economy, every community must run faster to become more
competitive. The best way to do this, according to the early economist

David Ricardo in his theory of comparative advantage, is to find a handful of industries in which to specialize, and to market world-class products. Exports from our best industries, like prescription drugs from New Jersey or country music from Tennessee, bring new earnings that we can then spend on supplies, parts, and technology for related industries. Clusters of similar firms then coalesce, and their constituent businesses spur one another to innovate, become more productive, and strengthen a community's global niche.

As competition from every nook and cranny of the planet intensifies, the most successful enterprises, the eight-hundred-pound gorillas anchoring and driving these clusters, will be the most globally minded, ambitious, and nimble, and the scale of these firms—the Microsofts, the Mercks, the Bank of Americas—is necessarily large. They may not need to have an office in every country or a million employees, but they do require a critical mass of finance, technology, and talent that no small business can possibly muster. If you live in a community lucky enough to have such a firm already, the priority is to retain it. The vast majority of communities, however, must lure them to anchor new clusters. And if your community can't snare a firm's global headquarters, then it should at least go for a major branch office, a factory, a warehouse, a service center, or, heck, even a sales outlet will do.

Economic developers sometimes distinguish between businesses of primary and secondary importance. They consider manufacturing primary because historically it has provided more jobs that are higher paying and longer lasting. The other sectors of the economy—like food, energy, education, and various business and household services—are seen as secondary since they seem to grow around the primary sectors.

A good example of this logic is South Carolina's decision, more than a decade ago, to pony up $130 million to attract a two-thousand-employee automobile plant owned by BMW. Some years after this deal was consummated, BMW hired the Moore School of Business at the University of South Carolina to perform an "independent" evaluation of the deal. "Undeniably," the researchers concluded, "the BMW location decision represented a major achievement in South Carolina's promotion of economic development."[4] By their calculations the plant has led to the creation of 16,600 jobs in the state and $4.1 billion in additional annual output.

Since economic developers frequently cite this deal to show how beneficial TINA subsidies can be, we will examine the study in a little more detail shortly. For now, let's just observe the logic of TINA thinking. The Moore School explains how the deal flowed from the rigorous application of the principles of mainstream economic development: "Economic theory clearly states that regional growth and development depends on developing an export base." Why exports? Because "manufacturing operations bring new money flowing into the state from outside. . . . The money is not recycled from one sector of the state's economy to another—*it is almost all an economic gain for the state's citizens*—providing money that can be used to purchase goods and services from other regions and countries."[5]

A decade ago economic developers saw "incentives" like those South Carolina offered as their most important tools for expanding export businesses. These took many forms, including grants, low-interest loans, loan guarantees, industrial development bonds, tax breaks, zoning preferences, training programs, new streets and sewers, you name it. But economic development has increasingly focused on creating a favorable "business climate." "Regulatory reform" seeks to reduce burdensome red tape, which means weakening public standards related to health, labor, environmental protection, and product safety. "Infrastructure" initiatives put in place roads, utilities, airports, telecommunications, and high-speed Internet facilities that can serve export-focused firms. "Workforce development" seeks to mobilize education and employment systems to provide higher-quality employees for these companies. And a diverse assortment of land-use tools like industrial parks, enterprise and empowerment zones, downtown development districts, and historic preservation create magnets for enterprises and consumers alike.

While the primary drivers of a TINA economy are big, globally oriented businesses, smaller businesses are important as partners in a cluster or as secondary suppliers of goods and services purchased by workers employed in that cluster. That's why TINA loves LOIS, locally owned and import-substituting businesses. Every chamber of commerce praises small businesses, mindful that they create the vast majority of new jobs in the community (and also loyally contribute most of the chamber dues). Every economic developer waxes eloquent that small businesses serve as the backbone of the local economy. Every

politician rushes for a photo op with the most successful local entrepreneurs. The International Economic Development Council (IEDC),
in its primer on economic development, begins: "Even though working
with existing businesses and assisting their growth never makes head-
lines, local firms already have a local commitment and are a far more
reliable method of job growth than the headline-grabbing attraction
efforts."[6]

"Through economic development activities," the IEDC handbook
continues, "existing businesses are nurtured and expanded, new businesses are attracted to an area, and new enterprises are created." Like
children in a healthy family, all businesses are to be loved equally
because "each of these activities leads to job creation, an increase to the
tax base, and improvement of the overall quality of life within a community—all adding to the wealth of the community."[7]

TINA advocates cheer for all business: big and small, new and old,
local and nonlocal, clean and dirty, free market or prison, anything
that produces jobs. But to understand the real contours of the economic development politics of TINA advocates, we must look not at
what they say but at what they do.

## Wreckonomics 101

For more than fifty years the Maytag factory in Galesburg, Illinois,
manufactured refrigerators.[8] No longer. In 2004 the company gave
pink slips to its last sixteen hundred employees and moved operations
to Mexico. When the first rumblings about the departure were heard,
economic developers in Galesburg desperately mobilized $8.6 million
from local sales taxes and state grants to retrofit the plant. They abated
property taxes for ten years that otherwise would have gone to public
schools. Maytag did stick around a bit longer, but ultimately the lure of
cheap labor south of the border was too great. The granddaddy of the
incentives package, Jeff Klinck, now admits: "Maytag's leaving town
has devastated our community."[9]

Fifteen hundred miles to the southeast, economic developers in
Putnam County, Florida, gave $4.5 million in cash and tax breaks to
Sykes Enterprises to build a call center.[10] Sykes came, thanked the com-
munity for the gift, operated for five years, then moved its center over-

seas. Timothy Keyser, a local lawyer, says, "It's universal blackmail out there, with corporations all playing the same game."[11]

Economic developers in Indiana paid $320 million in taxpayer money to United Airlines to build a state-of-the-art aircraft maintenance center at the Indianapolis International Airport. The company had promised to employ five thousand well-paid mechanics and invest $500 million of its own capital, but in the end the center never employed more than twenty-five hundred.[12] In 2003, having not made good on even half of its promised investment, United shut down the center and outsourced the work to cheaper private contractors down South.

According to an article in the *St. Petersburg Times*, economic developers in Florida pumped $49 million of tax breaks and gifts into a microchip plant originally run by AT&T after it threatened to move to Spain. Today, employment is about a third of what it was in the year 2000, and much of the equipment in the plant has already been shipped overseas. All of Florida's economic development programs between 2004 and 2005 cost the state government $900 million. That same article astutely observed: "The nearly empty factory could be a symbol for the flaws that beset what government and business leaders call 'economic development.'"[13]

According to Good Jobs First, a small think tank dedicated to identifying and eliminating corporate pork, Wal-Mart also has received more than $1 billion in state and local government support over the last ten years in 244 separate deals.[14] Nearly a dozen communities paid from $19 to 46 million each to attract one of the world's wealthiest companies to set up a distribution center.

There are literally hundreds of these stories from every part of the United States and they all are practically identical.[15] Convinced that TINA firms will make or break a region, economic developers insist on lavishing them with taxpayer money to persuade them to come or to stay. Alan Peters, an urban planning professor at the University of Iowa who has studied these deals, says, "It seems like almost every state is giving away grandmother, grandfather, the family jewels, you name it, everything."[16]

And for what? The company rarely fulfills its pledges entirely, and sometimes not at all, and sooner or later it moves elsewhere. Some state and local officials have learned by now that these deals are likely to be losers, but economic developers ominously warn—*there is no alternative*. Peters and his colleague, Peter Fisher, estimate that public payments to TINA, nearly all made in back rooms with no public scrutiny, now cost the American taxpayer an estimated $50 billion per year.[17] And that's just state and local money.

Many economic developers respond that they've learned from the mistakes of the past and no longer place so much emphasis on these deals. Nonsense. Eye-popping bribes in the range of $10,000 to $30,000 per promised job that were paid to attract auto manufacturers in the early 1980s now seem modest.[18] Alabama, South Carolina, Michigan, and Mississippi spent from $59,000 to $193,000 per job to attract or retain various auto plants in the 1990s.[19] In the mid-1990s Kentucky lavished two Canadian steel producers with $350,000 per job. Governor Pataki in New York recently gave IBM $500,000 per job as an inducement not to move out of the state. Governor Jeb Bush of Florida dispensed $1,000,000 per job to attract the Scripps Biological Research Center. Governor Gary Locke of Washington paid a whopping $2,500,000 per job to prevent Boeing from removing the remnants of its operations in the state (Boeing management had already fled to Chicago).[20] The anecdotal evidence suggests that the bidding wars for TINA businesses are actually escalating.

Governor Joseph E. Kernan of Indiana regrets what happened with United Airlines. He laments that one locality snatching jobs from another does nothing to improve the national economy and concedes that these subsidies probably don't have very much influence on TINA business decisions anyway. "But," he adds, "Indiana, like virtually every other state, is not going to unilaterally disarm."[21] After all, *there is no alternative*.

## Elephant-Mouse Casserole

Contrasting the balanced rhetoric of economic developers with their singular focus on TINA is like trying to walk straight in a hallway of fun-house mirrors. Their even-handedness with respect to large and small business can be compared to the even-handedness of cooks baking a proverbial elephant-mouse casserole. Add one elephant and one mouse, mix vigorously, then savor the diverse flavors. Not. Just as elephant-mouse casserole tastes pretty much like pure elephant, TINA-LOIS economic development looks pretty much like pure TINA.

While no national studies have sorted out exactly what percent of economic development monies are going to TINA versus LOIS, common sense suggests that nearly all of it is going to TINA. The purpose of the $50 billion taxpayers spend each year is to attract or hold on to companies that are, by definition, not anchored to the community, not locally owned, not focused on local markets. If there were similar bags of money being distributed to LOIS businesses, then maybe they would not be competitively disadvantaged. In fact, the playing field is tilted like a double black diamond ski slope against LOIS. Economic developers apparently assume that LOIS businesses can never be major manufacturers or the primary drivers of a local economy and that they can never anchor a cluster. Moreover, because the long-term commitment and loyalty of LOIS businesses to a community can be taken for granted, the locals get very few incentives at all. Sure, a few programs here and there are deployed to help small business with microloans, training, incubation, and so forth, but even these often favor TINA wannabes.

But isn't there at least a modest case to be made for TINA subsidies? Wasting money on deals that don't go well may make no sense, but that's twenty-twenty hindsight. Aren't there examples of some TINA firms that have taken the money, stayed, and contributed to the economy and made the risk of the incentives package worth it? What about South Carolina's investment of $130 million in BMW? What possible LOIS investment could produce more than sixteen thousand jobs and $4.1 billion in additional annual output? Perhaps if we could just improve the reliability of TINA deals by doling out the subsidies slowly as promises are met (and not in advance), by making the companies commit in writing to stay for a reasonable length of time, or by punishing subsidy abusers with treble damages for breaking an agreement.

This kinder, gentler vision of TINA still doesn't make much sense. Subsidies beyond $480,000 per job—like those recently paid out by Florida, Washington, and New York—can *never* be justified. At that point, state and local government might as well put the money in a low-risk U.S. savings bond and pay a household a living wage in perpetuity, without ever needing to mess around with the risky intermediary of a corporation.[22] Because so little of the earnings of TINA companies is retained by host communities (as detailed in chapter 2), the economic benefits of just leaving the annual proceeds in the hands of a beneficiary family may well be higher.

But what about smaller subsidies like those to BMW? According to the Moore School study, government gifts came in at a modest $81,479 per job (in 2001 dollars). Best I can tell, no one has critically reviewed the Moore School's work, and, in fact, a comprehensive review is almost impossible because much of the data analyzed (what the purchasing patterns of BMW are, for example) is proprietary. But here are a few reasons to treat its claims with skepticism.

First, consider what gets counted. The $130 million in subsidies magically materialize and over the next seven years produce jobs and wealth. But where did the $130 million come from? What kinds of jobs might have been produced had that same money been invested in schools seven years earlier? What would have been the outcome had that money been given to the state's most promising small businesses? What if it had stayed in consumers' pockets? These and a thousand alternative scenarios are what economists call *opportunity costs*. And like almost all economic developers, the Moore School ducks the issue.

Here's what we do know: According to another study by Clemson University's Strom Thurmond Institute, lost state and local taxes from deals like these will cost South Carolinians $2.7 billion over a decade.[23] Some of the shortfall has been made up with increased taxes on sales, telephones, restaurants, road uses, and vehicle and boat registrations—and, stunningly, with increased taxes on LOIS businesses. According to Alfred W. Stuart, a geography professor at the University of North Carolina at Charlotte, who surveyed local businesspeople affected by the BMW plant for the Greenville Chamber of Commerce, "Many of them were really pissed off about it. . . . They said, 'I've been in business for years, been paying taxes, and they're not doing anything for me. And now they're shelling out for this German company.'"[24] "It's a feeding frenzy," complains Mat Self, chair of Greenwood Mills, an old South Carolina textile manufacturer. "You've got $57 billion in infrastructure needs in the state (according to a state legislative commission), and you're reducing taxes?"[25]

A few years earlier, at the annual convention of the American Council of Chamber of Commerce Executives, I debated Wayne Sterling, one of the architects of the BMW deal, who recently had moved to head Virginia's Public/Private Partnership, with the hopes of landing for Virginia as big a deal as he had for South Carolina. I asked him whether he or anyone else had ever examined the opportunity costs and he fumed no, adding that it should be obvious that small businesses could never produce these kinds of benefits.

In fact, it's not obvious at all. At the heart of the Moore School analysis is an economic model called the Minnesota IMPLAN System. It is based on the assumption that if you enter data on the number of new jobs or additional payroll going into a local economy, you can then predict two things coming out. One is the number of *indirect* jobs generated by local purchasing. The other is the number of *induced* jobs generated by the expenditures of the new employees (both direct and indirect). The Moore School analysis basically said that BMW employed 4,300 people in 2002, which created 6,712 indirect jobs and 5,652 induced jobs.

There are three explanations of these superficially impressive results. The first is that BMW pays higher salaries than are typical in South Carolina. But many local businesses pay higher salaries, too. Had South Carolina announced that $130 million in subsidies would be available to *any* firm that pays average wages above, say, twenty-five dollars per hour, there's little doubt that hundreds of small businesses would have applied.

A second key to the success of the BMW deal was that the company is now buying inputs locally. The Moore School study pointed out that "27 new automotive suppliers have clustered close to the Greer-area plant, while 6 additional pre-existing local suppliers have obtained supply contracts." Maximizing local linkages, which is a key characteristic of a successful cluster, is a goal for nearly all economic development projects. South Carolina lucked out here, because there is a substantial body of evidence (reviewed in the next chapter) that for every dollar of operation, TINA businesses spend less locally than LOIS firms do. Had the new suppliers not located in the state, or had they located in the neighboring states of North Carolina or Virginia, the indirect jobs would have been substantially fewer.

The third reason the BMW deal performed well was that the company stuck around and grew. Initially the company promised only two thousand jobs. The company and many locals liked the deal, and BMW gradually expanded its South Carolina operations. But it has only been a decade. Will BMW be in South Carolina for twenty, thirty, or fifty years? Or will it—like AT&T, Sykes, and United—decide to move on? Who knows? The important point is that *the decision is no longer in South Carolina's hands.* As a publicly traded company, BMW's decisions about which plants to open and close will be driven 100 percent by its bottom line, not South Carolina's. And for the next generation, every time BMW hints about departing, South Carolina will have to dig up fresh incentives. What are the projected costs of these? If BMW departs, what will be the economic, environmental, or social costs? How much will South Carolina have to pay to the workers in unemployment and welfare? How will it cope with communities whose tax bases are decimated and no longer can pay for their schools, police, or basic services? A glimpse at Detroit today—with vast tracts of abandoned, burned-out buildings that are all that remain of a once-vibrant automobile-manufacturing sector—offers plausible clues to what South Carolina could face down the road.

The best that can be said about TINA deals like South Carolina's with BMW are that they represent a roll of the dice. If everything goes right, if the incentives don't break the bank, if the company grows, if it buys from local suppliers, if it sticks around for a generation or two, if it diversifies the region's economy before it departs, then, yes, a TINA subsidy can pay reasonable dividends. But the more likely fate is that which befalls any compulsive gambler—the poorhouse.

Moreover, to continue the casino analogy: If you can win without laying down a bet, why gamble at all? What evidence does the Moore School study offer that the subsidy had anything to do with BMW's decision to site the plant in South Carolina in the first place? Well, none. The authors observe that "the state has a set of fundamental assets" including a qualified work force, accessible ports, roads, and railroads, "public-private, pro-business partnerships," and ready access to BMW's primary U.S. markets.[26] On top of that "there are low unionization and labor costs in South Carolina relative to other possible sites." Hmmm, so what exactly was the role of the subsidy? *"Although not the fundamental location determinant,"* demurs the Moore School study, "incentives add to the attractiveness of a site. . . . All recent auto-motive plant opening have been supported by state incentives." In other words, South Carolina had to do it, because *there is no alternative.*

As it turns out, the bulk of the evidence suggests that TINA projects almost always will proceed without the incentives. Even very large sub-sidies, compared to ongoing costs of a TINA firm's operations, repre-sent a tiny portion of the bottom line. When Deloitte & Touche, a con-sulting firm with expertise in helping businesses with their location decisions, analyzed five years of data to weigh the importance of vari-ous factors, it found that tax breaks, one of the principal subsidy tools, were a "low priority" and had "minimum cost impact."[27] What really matters are the basics of a given location, such as the costs and talent of the workforce, the presence of shipping facilities, the proximity to markets, and the overall business friendliness of a community (more on this, shortly). Incentives really only come into play when two loca-tions seem roughly equal in their fundamentals, which is rarely the case. Even then, a jurisdiction playing fast and loose with incentives may also be revealing its profligacy with public funds and its unrelia-bility in delivering basic public services. Reviewing all the literature on incentives, Peters and Fisher, the two University of Iowa professors, conclude that "the standard justifications given for incentive policy by state and local officials, politicians, and many academics are, at best, poorly supported by the evidence."[28]

Some economic developers defend subsidies by saying that there are simply not enough job-creating opportunities available from LOIS businesses. In rural or inner-city communities, where there are few businesses at all, this seems at least superficially true. But, then again, how can anyone possibly know? Was a public request for proposals—known as an "RFP process"—announcing that $1 million in business support is available and that the government is now taking bids to see who can provide the most jobs for the fewest dollars, ever formally published in the newspaper? Were the LOIS possibilities ever system-atically compared with the TINA possibilities? Economic developers actually have no idea what kinds of LOIS proposals and plans might be out there. Proponents of TINA, who laud the virtues of free markets, appear unwilling to subject their theories and pet projects to real market tests.

The final refuge for sloppy economic development thinking may be the renewed assertion, little more, that public policy must be supportive of all jobs. If we support every LOIS job possible, doesn't it still make sense to stimulate TINA jobs? Sure, but only if you've first exhausted the full universe of LOIS possibilities. And without a true bidding process, you cannot possibly know whether this is true.

The study of economics is largely about how to manage scarcity. How can society combine limited numbers of workers, dollars, resources, buildings, gizmos, and ideas in a way that will produce the greatest happiness for the greatest number of people? It is astonishing when economic developers simply claim that they wish to support all kinds of business, equally, without ever setting priorities. Like every other human activity, economic development requires the careful allocation of finite time, energy, and money, especially in poor communities where development is most urgently needed. And the decision to favor TINA businesses, hidden in a rhetorical fog of fairness and served in elephant-mouse casserole, means that LOIS gets unfairly disadvantaged.

The more plausible explanation of the prioritization of TINA can be found not in economics but in politics. Presenting the public with one deal providing one thousand jobs seems to have greater payoffs than presenting one hundred deals with ten jobs each. Politicians would rather be photographed cutting a ribbon once on page A-1 than having to schlep around to a hundred places, on a hundred different days, always for page D-6 announcements in the business section. Economic developers also can more easily prove their worth—and justify getting a nice raise and budget bump—with one large, well-publicized deal. Their gain, however, is the community's loss.

## TINA's Reign of Error

The above criticisms of TINA suggest that the worst these economic developers can be accused of is wasting money on the wrong kinds of businesses and making it more difficult for small businesses to compete. But inefficiency, bias, and waste are hardly the only malfeasances of those who promote the TINA model. The deeper problem is that economic developers are systematically undermining the possibilities for establishing sustainable and prosperous communities.

The core difference between a TINA business and a LOIS business is this: A TINA business is much more likely to move to cut costs, increase sales, and maximize profits. The roots of LOIS businesses in the community run deeper, the costs of departing are greater, and they therefore tend to stay put.[29] While there are some trends that ought to persuade TINA managers not to "go offshore" (see chapter 3), most today see only competitive advantages in leaving the United States. Put yourself in the shoes of a corporate captain, and you too might dismiss all the old reasons for sticking around:

- *Do you depend on a special technology only available in the United States?* The old argument justifying higher wages for American workers was that our technology made them more productive. Now, however, you can easily move the same technology to any factory location where labor is cheaper because, increasingly, the technology is not heavy equipment or machinery but the electrons of software, which can be transported halfway around the planet almost instantly as an attachment to an email.
- *Is it too expensive to tear down your existing factory and build a new one?* The capital costs of most businesses are becoming only a tiny fraction of the overall expense of doing business. And if another community is willing to provide you land and buildings for free, why hesitate? Plus, the U.S. business tax code allows you to write off the cost of moving and then treats new taxes you might have to pay to a foreign country as a tax credit. Heck, moving might even result in Uncle Sam paying you!
- *But isn't our work force too skilled, too unique, too important to abandon?* Forget about it. As Thomas Friedman argues, millions of highly educated Indians and Chinese are prepared to take over your job for a tiny fraction of your current wage.[30]

It may take years for TINA managers to understand the full risks and costs of leaving the United States, so for the moment, the pull toward mobility dominates their imagination The mobility mindset means that the odds of a community rolling the incentives dice just right, of achieving even the kind of qualified success South Carolina achieved with BMW, are getting smaller every day. If TINA business support means that the enlarged and empowered firms move elsewhere in the world, then the entire universe of "economic development" can be thought of simply as extravagant gifts to the global TINA establishment at the expense of community.

But if we're *really* generous with our business support year after year, TINA advocates might counter, why would beneficiary businesses possibly leave? Because every community is playing this game, and someone, somewhere, is prepared to up the ante. We're in the midst of a subsidy arms race in which every community is ultimately a loser. The only possible "winners" are those communities with the worst labor and environmental standards. Communities competing to provide the best business climate are increasingly inclined to bust unions, lower wages, and weaken ecological standards. That was a big reason BMW embraced South Carolina. Even though BMW paid better wages than were typical in South Carolina, in the first five years of the deal manufacturing wages in the state actually shrank in real terms while they grew nationally.[31] Not a single new piece of labor and environmental legislation can be proposed at any level of government without critics pointing out the adverse consequences for retaining or attracting businesses. *And the criticism is correct.* It is increasingly difficult for a community following the TINA model to achieve prosperity and a high quality of life.

Sure, there are ways to tinker with this ruthless equation. As Richard Florida, the business school professor who popularized the concept of the "creative economy," has argued, managers and entrepreneurs are part of a creative class that is searching for certain community values as part of its location calculus.[32] Some would prefer to have good schools, trendy shops and restaurants, plentiful movie theaters and museums, thriving artistic communities, and diverse residents. Fun, cool, rewarding—all these things matter to the globe-trotting professional. But under closer scrutiny, most of the companies that make up the creative economy are locally owned anyway. And the captains of a TINA company attached to a community because of lifestyle are easy pickings for takeover sharks.

## Whose Destiny?

A community made up primarily of TINA businesses has essentially given up control over its future. Like the old mining company towns in West Virginia, TINA-dominated communities are operated by managers who are distant, remote, and often insensitive to local needs. Outsiders determine what the prices of goods should be, who should be hired, when layoffs should occur. And by wielding the threat to leave and exerting influence on local politicians (often through campaign contributions), these companies effectively can veto any piece of local legislation they do not like. Communities embracing TINA quickly find that have made themselves vulnerable to the erosion of self-governance and to the weakening of participatory democracy.

When economic relationships are more personal, they usually become more humane. When we work for, buy from, or invest in people we know, we tend to exercise a greater degree of care and responsibility. Shopkeepers take more time with each customer, craftspeople are more attentive to details, business associates share intimate details about one another's children, hobbies, and passions. If a customer forgets her wallet, a seller who knows her will still make the sale and apply credit. A bank lender who knows a potential borrower will give more weight to factors like his family and reputation.

The steady erosion of these human connections makes us more distrustful, more fearful about what "they" might do to "us," coarser in our treatment of faceless business partners, buyers, sellers, and investors. Would a small business owner declare bankruptcy to liquidate pensions held in trust for her workers? Perhaps, but the public censure that owner might have to bear around town arguably deters such behavior. Larger companies, like United Airlines, have had no such compunctions.

Economists, developers, and politicians repeatedly tell us that the replacement of these once-intimate relationships with anonymous ones will make us wealthier. To take advantage of these opportunities, we must set aside all our old, local, and small-minded ways of doing things. We should stop shopping at our favorite local stores because the prices at the chains are cheaper. As business people, any preference for people we know will, in the end, deny us access to the world's best talent, resources, and technology. The globe is now not only the relevant marketplace but also the only community that should matter.

The TINA mindset is that price trumps place—*always* (in the Wal-Mart vernacular). More specifically, cheap goods and services are more important than endangered species, beautiful wilderness, local democracy, historic preservation, downtown aesthetics, even more important than religion. How likely is it that a community in our current consumer culture could reenact Blue Laws to limit commerce on Sundays?

Around the country, communities proclaim that their single greatest priority is the safety, the morals, the education, and the success of their children, and economic development policies are often couched in terms of serving future generations. But how can a community embrace policies that rob schools of millions? The *St. Petersburg Times* has noted that Florida's annual TINA gifts "could pay for nearly 11,000 new teachers, pre-kindergarten classes for 150,000 4-year-olds and all of next year's tuition increase for more than 250,000 university students."[33] South Carolina, the top dog in TINA subsidies, has just about the lowest SAT scores in the nation. When basketball coach Rick Barnes decided to desert Clemson University (based in Pickens County, where many BMW workers work) for Austin, Texas, he admitted that he and his wife had concluded that "the schools are horrible."[34]

For Dorothy in *The Wizard of Oz* there is "no place like home," yet it is home that is exactly what TINA advocates ask us to sacrifice. In a community-friendly world, every place would develop a diversity of businesses that met the residents' basic needs but also took advantage of local resources, climate, culture, and history. If some residents were unemployed, others would work with them to develop new businesses to employ, engage, and integrate them. In the TINA mindset, in contrast, the unemployed are simply excess capacity to be shipped to another community. We're told to keep our bags packed so we can migrate at a moment's notice to another job hundreds or thousands of miles away. Forget about your friends and neighbors. Tell your kids to let go of their silly attachments to teachers and friends. Put away all those memories around your house. Community is just another obstacle to progress.

★★★★★★★★★★★★★★★★★★★★★★★★★★★★★★★★★★★★★★★★★★★★

# two

# THE LOIS ALTERNATIVE

The Hershey Chocolate Company in Hershey, Pennsylvania, is not your typical LOIS business. Its stock is publicly traded, which normally makes local ownership impossible, but a local charity, the Hershey Trust, keeps ownership local by controlling 77 percent of all voting shares.[1] Unlike most LOIS businesses, it is hardly small. In 2001 about sixty-two hundred employees were on payroll, many living in the Hershey area. The company not only saturates local chocolate demand but also sells worldwide to the tune of $4.6 billion per year.

The Hershey Trust is effectively the heart that pumps monetary blood throughout the regional economy. It owns 100 percent of the shares of the Hershey Entertainment and Resorts Company, which employs another fifteen hundred locals (plus five thousand seasonal workers) in its amusement parks, stadiums, campgrounds, country clubs, and numerous other enterprises. On top of that, the Trust runs a school for twelve hundred underprivileged kids, grades K through 12. Milton Hershey put all his stock in the Trust in 1918 to underwrite the academy in perpetuity.

In 2002 the Hershey Trust did what 99.9 percent of all corporate boards do: it decided that it would be wise to diversify its investments and that it would entertain offers to sell off its shares. The announcement sent waves of panic throughout the community as residents whose lives depended on the company contemplated the prospect of new owners gradually moving the company overseas. Local politicians, community leaders, and the unions pled with the Trust to reconsider. Pennsylvania's attorney general, Mike Fisher, went into court to stop the sale.

A TINA company would have ignored the local rabble, fought the lawsuit, and kept its focus on profitability. The stakes were huge. The Chicago-based Wm. Wrigley Jr. Co. put a $12.5 billion buy-out on the table, and Nestlé and Cadbury Schweppes were reportedly prepared to offer as much as $15 billion.[2] But something miraculous happened. The Hershey Trust's board changed its mind. It reaffirmed its commitments to the community and even said that it wouldn't revisit the issue without approval from the Dauphin County Orphans Court. The Trust, of course, could change its mind again and convert the company into a TINA business (local owners always can sell out). But for the moment its decision showed how the logic governing LOIS businesses is fundamentally different from that governing TINA, fundamentally more humane, fundamentally more community-friendly.

Everything we know suggests that LOIS businesses are substantially more beneficial for a local economy than TINA businesses. This doesn't mean that TINA businesses are necessarily bad. Many sell a wonderful range of products, pay decent wages, and donate generously to local charities. But dollar for dollar of business, TINA firms contribute less to a community's well-being than LOIS firms do.

## 'Local' Is What Goes Around

The temptation, when attempting to define a qualitative word like "local" in quantitative terms, is to resort to Justice Potter Stewart's famous definition of pornography: "I know it when I see it."[3] But let's try to do obetter. Perhaps the most critical element of local is proximity—both physical and geographic—because every person's purchasing choices are driven, in part, by the convenience, familiarity, and comfort of nearby stores, restaurants, professionals, and so forth.

Think of yourself as the center of your own consumption solar system, emanating rays of purchasing power. Most of your purchases are made close by—the local bank that carries the mortgage, the local clothing shops, local filling station, local charities. Travel a little outside your community and the number of purchases diminishes. Maybe it's that special trip to a mega-mall an hour away, or a consult with a medical specialist three towns over. Venture even farther out and you'll find a few purchases you make on Amazon for a book or on eBay for some rare Pokémon cards.

Each purchase you make triggers purchases by others. For instance, a dollar spent on rent might be spent again by your property owner at your local grocer, who in turn pays an employee, who then buys a movie ticket. This phenomenon is what economists call "the multiplier." The more times a dollar circulates within a defined geographic area and the faster it circulates without leaving that area, the more income, wealth, and jobs it generates. This basic concept in community economics points to the importance of maximizing the number of dollars entering a community and minimizing their subsequent departure.

The multiplier obviously diminishes with geographic distance. The farther from home you go to make a purchase, the less of the multiplier comes back and touches your community. Buy a radio down the block, the multiplier is high; buy it ten miles away, the multiplier weakens; buy it mail order, and your community gets practically no multiplier whatsoever.

There is one boundary beyond which part of the multiplier drops precipitously—that of a tax jurisdiction. A rough definition of "local," then, might be the smallest jurisdiction with real tax authority. For some this will be a town, for others it will be a city or a county. Since every purchase leads to a variety of taxes—sales taxes, wage taxes, property taxes, and business taxes—making a purchase even one village over can significantly diminish the taxes that might have gone to your own local government. For example, the savings Massachusetts consumers enjoy when they make long drives to New Hampshire malls to avoid sales taxes wind up being huge losses to the Bay State.

A business can only be considered locally owned if those who control it live in that community. That could mean the ownership is held by the sole proprietor who lives and works in the same town. It could also mean that residing in the community are more than half of a firm's partners (through a partnership, limited liability partnership, or S-corporation), shareholders (C-corporation), workers (worker cooperative or employee stock ownership plan company), or consumers (consumer cooperative). It could also refer to a nonprofit tied to the community either through its board, its mission (like a community development corporation), or through a local membership with voting rights. And it could refer to the business activities of local public agencies and public-private partnerships. There are differing consequences of each ownership structure—some, for example, are more vulnerable to a TINA takeover than others—but all offer robust benefits that stem directly from the localness of ownership and control.

There are still further complications when defining a business as local or not. Consider franchises. On paper a proprietor can own most of the outlet's capital, claim most of the profits, and yet still, by the terms of contracts and licenses, enjoy very little control. The specifics matter here. If a Subway sandwich shop is technically owned by an individual, but is largely controlled by the national chain, it cannot really be considered a LOIS business.

Or consider the residence of a proprietor in a metropolitan area. Suppose you live in Miami. Under the definition above your locality might be the city limits. Finding a local lawyer is easy. If a lawyer lives and works in Miami, she is indisputably local. But suppose she works in Miami but lives farther north in Boca Raton. Is she still local? Or what if she lives in Miami but works in Boca Raton? In either case, some of the lawyers' expenditures now leak out of Miami.

Or consider a computer purchase. You are careful to go to a locally owned electronics store but are dismayed to discover that most of the computers on display were assembled in Asia. After careful research, you finally find one model that's assembled locally and sold in the assembler's small shop. But when you crack open the machine, you realize all the components still come from Asia.

The truth is that these details matter enormously when it comes to the local multiplier. Yet few of us have time to do so much homework before every purchase. These complexities highlight why efforts to promote LOIS business involve far more than exhortations to buy or invest locally. Significant research is needed to help consumers identify goods and services with the highest degree of local content and control, and with the greatest likelihood of producing the greatest benefit for a community. The principle is easy, but its application can be difficult.

## The Local Majority

Local business actually constitutes the lion's share of the U.S. economy. The U.S. Small Business Administration (SBA) defines small businesses as firms having fewer than five hundred employees, and these actually account for half of private sector employment in the country and 44 percent of private payrolls. A more restrictive definition of small business—as a firm with fewer than one hundred employees—still accounts for about a third of private employment and private payrolls. By either definition, more than 99 percent of all firms in the United States are small businesses.[4] Put another way, footloose global businesses dominate our imagination, get showered with subsidies, and monopolize our capital markets, but actually occupy only about half of the economy. Firms with more than five hundred employees constitute only about 0.3 percent of all firms. They account for 56 percent of private payrolls, but supply fewer than half of all private jobs.

The private sector, moreover, is only part of the U.S. economy. Nearly a quarter of the nation's income, measured by the GDP, comes from household employers, nonprofits, and various government entities.[5] All of these categories are place based, in the sense that none of them considers setting up shop in China. Large firms turn out to be responsible for no more than 42 percent of the economy, and place-based jobs account for at least 58 percent. *We can say, therefore, that Small-Marts are responsible for most of a typical community's economy.*

This observation becomes even stronger when you consider what's left out of these tallies. Businesses with no employees, millions of which Americans increasingly run out of their homes (many as their second or third jobs), are excluded. Another gap in the official data is unpaid household work, still done primarily by women. Were housework paid at market rates, some estimate this additional income would account for as much as a quarter of the economy.[6] If the volunteers serving senior citizens were paid a wage of eight dollars per hour, the total value of the services would exceed the actual cost of formal home health care and nursing home care.[7] The value of all volunteer efforts in the country, of course, is greater still. Another gap, according to Edgar Feige of the University of Wisconsin, is the underground or black economy, mostly homegrown, valued somewhere between $500 billion and $1 trillion.[8] As law professor Edgar S. Cahn writes, "A wide range of estimates—from Gary Beck to Nancy Folbre—finds that at least 40% of our country's productive work goes on outside of the market economy."[9] Nearly all of these missing pieces are local, which means that a better accounting system would most likely show that *at least three-quarters of our economic activity is currently place based.*

We must also remember that the Small-Mart sector is unevenly distributed throughout the country; in some regions its participation is significantly higher than the overall average. In a quarter of the states, firms with more than five hundred employees account for less than half of private payrolls. Move into suburban and rural areas, and the role of small businesses gets larger still. In Montana and Wyoming only four out of ten payroll dollars come from large firms, suggesting that the Small-Mart portion of their economies, in conventional accounting terms, probably hovers around 70 percent.

But don't small businesses represent the backwater of business, the inefficient remnants of the old economy? Hardly. According to the SBA, small firms generate 60 to 80 percent of all new jobs and produce thirteen to fourteen times more patents per employee than large firms.

What about the high failure rate of small business? The SBA reports that a third of small business start-ups shut down within two years, and half within four years. These figures are sometimes tossed around to suggest how unreliable Small-Marts are, but the real story is much more interesting. The failure rates only refer to start-ups, not existing small businesses. Owners of a third of the closures, moreover, actually pronounce their ventures successful (for example, an entrepreneur who operates a home-based catering business for a few years that then serves as a launching pad for a new restaurant).[10] And here's another surprising fact: for almost every one of the last ten years the birth rate of small businesses has exceeded the death rate, while for large firms the death rate has been greater than the birth rate. Between 2000 and 2001 for example, 553,000 small businesses closed but 585,000 opened, with a net increase of 32,000 firms.[11] The total universe of existing small business was about 5.6 million firms, which means that in any given year, about 90 percent of existing small businesses continue to compete effectively. During the same 2000 to 2001 period there was a net loss of about two hundred large firms.

How has globalization changed the role of small business? Over the past decade, while globalization was becoming a household word, a shift in favor of larger businesses has occurred, but arguably only a modest one. Between 1990 and 2001 about 4 percent of the jobs shifted from very small to large firms. Firms with 100 to 499 employees remained steady.

These data lend themselves to several different interpretations. On the one hand, you could conclude that the mighty gales of global "creative destruction," in the famous phrase of economist Joseph Schumpeter, caused surprisingly little change in the composition of the economy. After all, fewer than four out of a hundred workers were affected, and more than 96 percent of the size structure of the economy remained stable (and again, a shift that is even smaller when one considers home-based, non-employee, and unpaid workers). On the other hand, you could see this as proof that TINA-style globalization has taken a serious toll on the smallest businesses in the United States and that if the next several decades look like the previous decade, small businesses could become as rare as the spotted owl.

Whichever view you choose, the question of why TINA did slightly better than LOIS during those years remains. Most economists would say that these trends prove the greater efficiency and superior performance of TINA firms. Global companies, taking advantage of economies of larger scale as well as lower wages and looser environmental standards abroad, are now producing the cheapest goods and supplying the most cost-effective services, undercutting an increasing number of local businesses. This interpretation omits, however, myriad "imperfections" in our market economy that uniformly favor TINA.

Consider two other important stories about the relative strength of LOIS versus TINA businesses that are mutually contradictory. (See appendix A for details.) One story is of massive consolidation. Between 1998 and 2002 the sector that experienced the greatest degree of consolidation was the securities industry, reflecting the decision of Congress to remove the regulatory barrier between banking and securities.[12] Broadcasting and telecommunications, another industry undergoing massive deregulation, was second. Hospitals have also become more centralized—a direct result of the health care crisis—and the growth of chain stores has contributed to the consolidation of retailing of clothing, electronics, and sporting goods. Each consolidating industry could receive a dissertation's worth of scrutiny of the people, technology, innovations, and laws responsible for the shift in scale.

But an equally important story is that almost as many sectors in the economy are actually decentralizing. Investment advising for trusts and estates has gone local. Minimills for steelmaking are doing well. Utilities are shrinking in size. Even as some textile, clothing, and transportation equipment manufacturing moves overseas, smaller plants in these sectors are expanding.

Which story is right? Well, both are. And they suggest that for every piece of bad news for Small-Marts, there's good news as well. In many sectors Small-Marts are innovating, taking advantage of cutting-edge ideas in marketing and technology, and making inroads against larger business. And looking ahead (as we do in chapter 3), the most important trends in the global economy actually favor the expansion of Small-Marts. That doesn't mean that the Small-Mart Revolution is inevitable, especially if the current pro-TINA biases in subsidies, capital markets, and economic-development practice are not undone. The Small-Mart Revolution requires dramatic changes in the behavior of consumers, investors, entrepreneurs, and policymakers.

But let's return to a more basic question: Why should we favor LOIS and join the revolution at all?

## Swing LO, Sweet Business

However we define local ownership, it turns out to be an essential condition for community prosperity for at least five reasons, spelled out below. The first four flow from the inherent difference between LOIS and TINA firms: most local entrepreneurs form their businesses in a particular place because they love living there. For a few sophisticated LOIS entrepreneurs, other factors like taxes, workforce quality, and clusters may come into play, at least in their initial decision about where to set up the business. But once a LOIS enterprise is up and running, the entrepreneur's family, workers, and customers are woven into the fabric of the community, and as a result, he or she has relatively little interest in moving to Mexico or Malaysia.

**Local Ownership Advantage #1: Long-Term Wealth Generators.** Because their entrepreneurs stay put, LOIS businesses are more likely than TINA ones to be cash cows for communities for many years, often for many generations. The Hershey Chocolate Company has brought tens of billions of dollars into the community over its lifetime and will do so for the foreseeable future.

**Local Ownership Advantage #2: Fewer Destructive Exits.** The anchoring of LOIS businesses minimizes the incidence of sudden, calamitous, and costly departures. For about a century, the economy in Millinocket, Maine, was built around the Great Northern Paper Company, which was one of the largest and most advanced paper manufacturers in the world. During Christmas of 2002 the owners of the company living "away" decided that operations would be better based elsewhere, and the last fourteen hundred workers were laid off. For the next year the unemployment rate hovered at about 35 percent, higher than what the country endured during the Great Depression. This kind of death spiral—a sudden departure followed by massive unemployment, shrinking property values, lower tax collections, deep cuts in schools, police, and other services, which throws still more people out of work, and so forth—is far less likely in a regional economy made up primarily of LOIS businesses.

**Local Ownership Advantage #3: Higher Labor and Environmental Standards.** A community made up mostly of LOIS businesses can better shape its laws, regulations, and business incentives to protect the local quality of life. A TINA-dependent community is effectively held hostage to its largest TINA companies. While not shy about lobbying politicians, locally owned companies usually do not threaten to leave town. A community filled primarily with locally owned businesses can set reasonable labor and environmental standards with confidence that these enterprises are likely to adapt rather than flee. For example, on Maryland's Eastern Shore, two powerful poultry companies, Tyson and Perdue, have successfully fought legislative efforts to raise their workers' wages or clean up the billions of pounds of chicken manure they dump into the Chesapeake Bay ecosystem by deploying one powerful argument: regulate us and we'll move to more lax jurisdictions like Georgia or Arkansas. (See chapter 6 for more on this story.)

**Local Ownership Advantage #4: Better Chances of Success.** In November 2003 I debated Jack Roberts, the head of Lane County Metro

Partnership, the principal economic development organization in the region surrounding Eugene, Oregon. Like other developers in the state, Roberts handed out tax abatements to businesses as an incentive to either move to the area or expand. Consistent with the elephant-mouse casserole, about 95 percent of his abatements were used to lure six TINA companies to move in, while the other 5 percent were given to dozens of LOIS businesses. Ultimately, according to an investigative report in the local newspaper, the cost to the community in lost taxes was about $23,800 per job for the TINA firms and $2,100 per job for the LOIS firms.[13] Why were the TINA jobs *more than ten times* more expensive? Roberts argued that it was just bad luck. The firms recruited were mostly high tech, and when investors lost faith in the tech sector around 2000 and 2001, management cut costs by shutting down the plants. What Roberts' argument overlooks, however, is that business cycles are *always* oscillating, and during inevitable down periods a TINA business will be prone to consider moving a factory to a lower-cost region. In fact, even during up periods, a TINA business will consider moving if the rate of return on investment can be ratcheted a notch or two higher. Why keep a factory open in Eugene, earning a 10 percent return, if it can earn 20 percent in Bangalore? To a LOIS entrepreneur, in contrast, these community-destroying options are off the table.

**Local Ownership Advantage #5: Higher Economic Multipliers.** In the summer of 2003, a consulting group of economists called Civic Economics studied the impact of a proposed Borders bookstore in Austin, Texas, compared with two local bookstores.[14] They found that one hundred dollars spent at the Borders would circulate thirteen dollars in the Austin economy, while the same one hundred dollars spent at the two local bookstores would circulate forty-five dollars—roughly three times the multiplier. In 2004 Civic Economics completed another study of Andersonville, a neighborhood in Chicago. The principal finding was that a dollar spent at a local restaurant had 25 percent more economic impact than a chain. The local advantage was 63 percent more for local retail, and 90 percent more for local services.

This last point, largely unfamiliar to economic developers, is worth further elaboration. A study of eight local businesses in the towns of

Rockland, Camden, and Belfast found that they spent 45 percent of their revenue within their local counties, and another 9 percent state-wide. The aggregate level of in-state spending was nearly four times greater than that from a typical chain store. Other studies in the United States and abroad also have found that local businesses yield two to four times the multiplier benefit as comparable nonlocal businesses.[15]

Skeptics complain that these multiplier studies are flawed. They claim that the economic models used are filled with uncertainties, especially when a small locale is under study; that the multipliers stud-ied are always specific to a location, so generalizations are difficult; and that the TINA and LOIS businesses being compared are really so dif-ferent that it's like comparing apples to goldfish. They also contend that the results are unreliable because the researchers have only partial information on the chain firms' expenditures.

Whatever the merit to these objections, the skeptics overlook three points. First, the authors of these studies, unlike some of their TINA-scholar counterparts, are honest enough to point out the flaws in their own methodology. Second, these flaws differ little from the flaws of the pro-TINA studies, like the Moore School's puff piece on South Caro-lina's investment in BMW. Third and most important, the underlying reason why local businesses have higher multipliers is obvious and unlikely ever to change: *they spend more locally*. In the Austin analysis, local bookstores, unlike Borders, have local management, use local business services, advertise locally, and enjoy profits locally. These four items alone can easily constitute a third or more of a business's total expenditures. That LOIS businesses almost always spend more locally means that they almost always yield a higher multiplier.

To recap all these advantages, look at the National Football League. All but one franchise is owned by a single (usually obnoxious) individual, and these modern moguls have threatened to split town if demands for hundreds of millions of dollars for new stadiums and salary increases are not met. When Cleveland refused, Art Modell, owner of the Browns, took *his* team to Baltimore. The one exceptional franchise is the Green Bay Packers, a community-controlled nonprofit, whose shareholder-members are primarily citizens of Wisconsin.[16] Because its fans will never allow the team to leave town, the Packers have become a critical source of wealth and economic multipliers for Green Bay, one that will be around for generations of Cheesehead fans to come. Being locally controlled means the team cannot suddenly depart and punch a hole in the economy, even if its rate of return might be higher somewhere else. If the city ever passed a living wage ordinance, the Packers would learn to adapt, since fleeing is not an option.

If local ownership of a football team can confer all these benefits, doesn't it make sense to insist on local ownership of farms, factories, and banks?

## What the Meaning of IS Is

Here's a quick recipe for local prosperity: create a diversity of locally owned businesses, design them to use local resources sustainably, and make sure that together they are fully employing residents and producing at least enough goods and services to satisfy residents' needs. For those needs that cannot be met through local production, export enough goods and services to provide residents with the income to buy needed imports. To understand this formula, consider two ways how *not* to create a thriving local economy.

Suppose your community were completely self-reliant. You and your Robinson Crusoe brethren might build houses out of local wood and stone, grow food in the community greenhouses, draw water from rooftop rain collectors, and so forth. This kind of primitive economy can work, provided you're willing to forgo all the products and technology originating from elsewhere on the planet. For most us this is inconceivable. Even those of us who embrace lives of "voluntary simplicity" have many clothes on our back, couches in our living rooms, and computers on our desks that come from elsewhere. We need to sell something to buy these goods. Absolute self-reliance won't work.

Next, suppose your community met only other people's needs—that is, your businesses were 100 percent dedicated to exports, like the Mexican maquiladoras that line the southern border of the United States. Now you're making money, but you're also a sitting duck that can be blown away by outsiders' economic shotguns. If you followed economists' advice to find your special niche in the global economy, you might be exporting one or two products, and your well-being would be totally dependent on the stability of those global markets. Lose your lead, as Detroit did with automobiles and Youngstown did with steel, and your economy collapses. Plus, you're vulnerable to all kinds of nasty surprises because you're importing everything else, even your most basic needs, which now must come in the form of canned food and bottled water. The best example of this is the U.S. economy's dependence on foreign oil, which ties us—like a damsel in a bad melodrama—to sudden OPEC-orchestrated spikes in global petroleum prices and requires a foreign policy weighed down by increasingly expensive and bloody military involvements in the Middle East.

A better alternative is to blend the two extremes. The healthiest economy is both self-reliant *and* a strong exporter. Meet as many of your own needs as possible, *then* compete globally with a diversity of products. By being relatively self-reliant, you're far less vulnerable to events outside your control. By having global sales, you're not closing off your economy to outside goods and technology. Meanwhile, you're conducting as much business as possible with both local and foreign consumers, which brings wealth into the community and pumps up the multiplier. Cut back on *either* self-reliance or exports, and you lose income, wealth, and jobs.

This may seem contradictory. If every community in the world became more self-reliant, wouldn't the aggregate level of imports shrink and make it difficult, if not impossible, for communities to increase their exports? In the short term, yes. But over the long term, import substitution would enable tens of thousands of communities worldwide to stop wasting precious earnings from exports on imports they could just as easily produce for themselves, and encourage them instead to reinvest those earnings in industries that could truly fill unique niches in the global economy. It's a mistake to view any economy, especially the world's, as a zero-sum game where one player's gain is another's loss.

The relationship between any two communities in the global economy is not unlike a marriage. As couples counselors advise, relationships falter when two partners are too interdependent. When any stress affecting one partner—the loss of a job, an illness, a bad-hair

day—brings down the other, the couple suffers. A much healthier relationship is grounded in the relative strength of each partner, who each
should have his or her own interests, hobbies, friends, and professional identity, so that when anything goes wrong, the couple can support one another from a position of strength. Our ability to love, like
our ability to produce, must be grounded in our own security. And our
economy, like our love, when it comes from a place of community, can
grow without limit.[17]

If it's important to develop strong exports and to be self-reliant
through import substitution, should both strategies be implemented
simultaneously or should one be prioritized over the other? The pre-
vailing view among state and local economic development experts is to
prioritize exports. That's why they spend millions of dollars to lure
and keep TINA businesses. Only through export earnings, as the
Moore School scholars argued about South Carolina's decision to give
millions to BMW (see chapter 1), can a community enjoy the potentially unlimited fruits of *new* dollars.

But the argument is flawed. How does a dollar brought into the
community from export sales differ from a dollar retained in the community's economy through local sales? From a multiplier standpoint,
there's no difference whatsoever. One academic analysis of eight southeastern states, looking at the relationship between local services and
nonlocal non-service industries like manufacturing and mining, found
both dimensions of the economy equally important. After reviewing
this data, Thomas Michael Power, chair of the economics department
at the University of Montana, observes: "Growth in service activities
played a very important role in determining overall local economic
growth. Manufacturing and other export-oriented activities were not
the primary economic forces. Others have also found evidence that
'local' economic activities may drive the overall economy rather than
just adjust passively to export activities."[18]

Even though development through import replacement and development through exports propel one another, there are many compelling reasons to favor the former from a public policy standpoint.
Import substitution involves shifting purchases from businesses outside the community to those inside, which usually means from businesses owned by outsiders to those owned locally. All the benefits of

local ownership are therefore reinforced through import substitution. Every time a community chooses to produce its own apples rather than import them, assuming that the prices of all apples are roughly equal, it boosts the economic well-being of its own apple farmers, as well as all the local suppliers to the farmers and all the other local businesses where the farmers spend their money.

Export-led development means opening yourself up to many otherwise avoidable dangers. Importing oil leaves the fate of our economy in the hands of OPEC ministers, Latin American strongmen, and Arab sheikdoms. Importing Canadian beef invites outbreaks of mad cow disease. Importing chickens puts you on the front lines of the avian flu pandemic.

Import substitution also turns out to be one of the smartest ways of strengthening homeland security. Terrorists are keenly aware that the types of infrastructure most vulnerable to a catastrophic collapse are centralized structures such as the electricity grid. Nuclear power plants were actually on the 9/11 hijackers' short list of potential targets, no doubt to terrorize the surrounding populace by simultaneously wiping out critical energy supplies and raining radioactive debris over them Chernobyl-style.[19] The water grid in California could be shattered by a disruptive blow to the Tehachapi pumping station that brings water from the northern rivers to desert lawns in Los Angeles. The natural gas grid could be destroyed through sabotage of liquefied natural gas ports and other key pipeline interchanges. Centralized food supplies could be used to spread rapidly meat contaminated with mad cow disease and other microorganisms.[20] To the extent that communities can make themselves more self-reliant—on their own electricity, water, fuel, and food—they will be far less vulnerable to terrorist attacks. The *Wall Street Journal* understood this point eight weeks after 9/11 when it published the following observation in an article on the front page of the "Capital" section: "Even before terrorists leveled the World Trade Center, economic and technological forces were combining to decentralize the economy. Sept. 11 will only reinforce these centrifugal forces. . . ."[21]

Supporting the development of diverse enterprises—enacting import-substitution policies—enhances the skill base of a community and acts as a kind of insurance policy, an investment in the people, know-how, and technology that can enable you to take full advantage of the "next big thing" in the economy. A generation ago a Boeing-dependent Seattle could not have possibly known that its future lay, not in aerospace, but in software and coffee. You never can know, and it is only by having a diversified economy, as Seattle did, that you can have the skills to seize whatever opportunities arise.

Paradoxically, import substitution also turns out to be the best way to create a healthy export sector. An unhealthy approach to exports is to do what Millinocket, Maine, did, which, as noted earlier in this chapter, put all its economic eggs in the basket of paper production. Similarly, when economic developers attempt to divine what your community's one or two great "niches" might be in the global economy, they are essentially playing a dangerous game of Russian roulette. If your niche suddenly becomes obsolete, you're dead. A far smarter approach is to invest in dozens of local small businesses, all grounded in local markets, knowing that some will then develop a variety of healthy export markets. A multiplicity of export linkages is the most powerful and safest way to compete globally.

Suppose North Dakota wished to replace imports of electricity with local wind-electricity generators. Once it built windmills and became self-reliant on electricity, it would then be dependent on outside supplies of windmills. If it set up a windmill industry, it would become dependent on outside supplies of machine parts and metal. This process of substitution never ends. But it leaves North Dakota with many strengthened local industries—in electricity, windmills, machine parts, and metal industries—that not only can meet local needs but also can take advantage of export opportunities.

Even if import replacement leads to more exports, the distinction between this process and export-led development is much more than simply a matter of semantics. Had South Carolina followed an import-replacing development strategy, it would have used the same money it paid BMW—or much less—to nurture hundreds of existing, locally owned businesses, some of which would have then become strong exporters. Development led by import replacement rather than export promotion diversifies, stabilizes, and strengthens the local economy, while allowing the best exporters to rise on their own merits. As Thomas Michael Power says, "Export-oriented economies remain primitive, suffer through booms and busts, and go nowhere. It is only when an area begins making for itself what it once imported that a viable economic base begins to grow."[22]

This touches on a final advantage of import-substituting development. Which is easier: for governors, mayors, and economic developers to learn a foreign language like Japanese, travel abroad to snag some new global company, steal tens of millions of dollars from the taxpayers to provide the necessary incentives, and then have to defend the decision a decade later when the company moves on; or for the same folks to speak in plain English with their own business community, work together on nurturing homegrown enterprises, and enjoy the fruits of their efforts when they retire? The excitement officials and civil servants feel when they travel to exotic lands and rack up the frequent flier miles is understandable, but it should never be done on community time.

## Myriad Benefits of LOIS

A community economy rooted in LOIS businesses will enjoy many other benefits because LOIS fits hand in glove with other theories about what constitutes a successful, healthy, and vibrant community.

LOIS, for example, is a natural cousin of "smart growth" or anti-sprawl policies. Promoters of smart growth envision, for example, the redesign of a community so that residents can walk or ride bikes from home to school, from work to the grocery store. They want to scrap old zoning laws and promote multiple uses—residential, commercial, clean industrial, educational, civic—in existing spaces. They believe it's better to fully use the town center than to build subdivisions on green spaces on the periphery. Because LOIS businesses tend to be small, they can fit more easily inside homes or on the ground floor of residences. Because they focus primarily on local markets, LOIS businesses place a high premium on being easily accessible by local residents.

Not every LOIS business is a model environmental citizen—one can certainly point to small-scale manufacturers and local dry cleaners that release carcinogens—but an economy made up largely of LOIS business is more likely to be green. Local ownership provides an important form of ecological accountability since the owner must breathe the same air and drink the same water, and his or her family must ultimately live side by side with the rest of the community. Moreover, many LOIS businesses are service related, and these usually are labor intensive and have fewer environmental impacts. As noted earlier, a community with primarily locally owned businesses—businesses that will not consider moving to Mexico or China—can raise environmental standards with greater confidence that these firms will adapt, a circumstance that tips the political balance in favor of tougher environmental regulations.

A TINA-dependent community, in contrast, is likely to suffer several kinds of environmental hazards. Box stores, for example, are characterized by gigantic parking lots, which cover vast tracts of land with concrete that drain off oil, gasoline, and other toxins into the water table, often in torrents that can lead to flooding. When national chains move on, these huge spaces are neglected, become eyesores, and lower property values. Nationwide Wal-Mart has three hundred vacant stores, and most are less than a mile away from the Supercenter that took the predecessor store's place.[23]

The relative immobility of LOIS businesses also serves the rights of labor, though this argument contradicts the historic hostilities union organizers and old-school lefties harbor toward small business. Their concern has been that, compared to larger businesses, small businesses pay lower wages, provide fewer benefits, and are less susceptible to union organizing. There is evidence, to be sure, that businesses with more than five hundred employees pay about a third more on average than businesses with fewer than five hundred employees. But one recent statistical analysis of the relevant academic literature found that between 1988 and 2003 these differences, in both wages and benefits, shrank by about a third.[24] If this trend continues—especially as many of the once high-paying larger firms continue to move factories overseas and as low-wage retailers like Wal-Mart continue to displace existing small business—these differences could disappear altogether.

TINA businesses that once offered fabulous worker benefits are now chopping them away, as more and more managers struggle to contain ballooning health care costs and place responsibility for pension contributions directly on the employee. The growing incidence of TINA firms declaring bankruptcy (including United Airlines, a company controlled by its supposedly enlightened workforce) as a strategy to escape long-standing health plans and pension benefits should give pause to anyone who thinks that big business is the ticket to economic security. The real solutions for all Americans to have better health care and retirement—and not just those employed or employable—must come, as they do in almost every other industrialized country, from smarter public policy (much of it, as discussed in chapters 5 and 7, state and local). In fact, public policies that do a better job of ensuring these benefits for all workers may eliminate one of the big reasons some choose to work for TINA firms and expand the number and quality of people eager to work in small business.

Small businesses may be less easy to unionize than large ones, but that doesn't necessarily make them less sensitive to labor rights. Some of the most socially responsible entrepreneurs in this country are the small business pioneers who are members of organizations like BALLE and SVN and who believe that high wages and decent benefits are not just good motivators but also moral imperatives. The closeness of the relationships between the people on the top and the bottom of these small firms also can be a powerful force for empathetic management. And it seems ludicrous for labor to favor TINA businesses when nearly all of them, by now, cannot wait to purge their businesses of unions by moving production overseas.

Sooner or later, the labor movement in the United States will recognize that TINA enterprises have become dead ends for vindicating the rights of workers. Labor should embrace small business, unionize it where it can, and encourage worker ownership, participation, and entrepreneurship where it can't. Meanwhile, higher community standards through living wages (discussed in chapter 7) and serious health care reform are probably the most effective ways of helping all workers, irrespective of the size of their employer.

Another sign of a prosperous community is how well it preserves its unique culture, foods, ecology, architecture, history, music, and art. LOIS businesses celebrate these features, while chain stores steamroll them with retail monocultures. Austin's small business network employs the slogan "Keep Austin Weird." Outsider-owned firms take what they can from local assets and move on. It's the homegrown entrepreneurs whose time horizon extends even beyond their grandchildren and who care most about preserving these assets. And it's the local marketers who are most inclined to serve local tastes with specific microbrews and clothing lines. "Weirdness" is what attracts tourists, engages locals in their culture, draws talented newcomers, and keeps young people hanging around. As Jim Hightower writes, "Why stay at the anywhere-and-nowhere Holiday Inn when we've got the funkily-refurbished Austin Motel right downtown, boasting this reassuring slogan on its marquee: 'No additives, No preservatives, Corporate-free since 1938.'"[25]

Richard Florida's arguments about the importance of a "creative class" for economic success, mentioned in chapter 1, also tend to support LOIS businesses. Florida argues that among the key inducements for a creative class to move to and stay in a community are its civic culture, its intellectual bent, its diversity, and its sense of self—all attributes clearly enhanced in a LOIS economy. A LOIS economy seeks to celebrate its own culture, not import mass culture through boring chain restaurants and Cineplexes. A LOIS economy seeks to have more residents engaged as entrepreneurs, and fewer as worker bees for a Honda plant. Myriad ideas and elements of a culture can best emerge through myriad homegrown enterprises.

What about a community's social well-being and political culture? In 1946 two noted social scientists, C. Wright Mills and Melville Ulmer, explored this question by comparing communities dominated by one or two large manufacturers versus those with many small businesses. They found that small business communities "provided for their residents a considerably more balanced economic life than did big business cities" and that "the general level of civic welfare was appreciably higher."[26] A congressional committee published the study, and in the foreword, Senator James E. Murray wrote:

> It appears that in the small-business cities is found the most favorable environment for the development and growth of civic spirit. A more balanced economic life and greater industrial stability is provided in the small-business cities. There the employment is more diversified, the home-owning middle class is larger, and self-employment greater. Public health is greater . . . the study reveals that a baby has a considerably greater chance to sur-

vive in his first year in the small-business city than in the one dominated by a few large firms.[27]

Thomas Lyson, a professor of rural sociology at Cornell University, updated this study by looking at 226 manufacturing-dependent counties in the United States. He concluded that these communities are "vulnerable to greater inequality, lower levels of welfare, and increased rates of social disruption than localities where the economy is more diversified."[28]

We know that the longer residents live in a community, the more likely they are to vote, and that economically diverse communities have higher participation rates in local politics. Moreover, Harvard political scientist Robert Putnam has identified the long-term relationships in stable communities as facilitating the kinds of civic institutions— schools, churches, charities, fraternal leagues, business clubs—that are essential for economic success. As one group of scholars recently concluded after reviewing the social science literature: "[T]he degree to which the economic underpinnings of local communities can be stabilized—or not—will be inextricably linked with the quality of American democracy in the coming century."[29] A LOIS economy with many long-term homegrown businesses is more likely to contribute to such stability than the boom-and-bust economy created by place-hopping corporations.

But perhaps the most important benefit of spreading LOIS businesses is that it allows a community to rehumanize the economic relationships among its residents and reassert control over its destiny.

## The Challenges of Social Responsibility

Just as LOIS is a necessary but insufficient condition for building a prosperous community economy, LOIS is also a necessary but insufficient condition for making businesses socially responsible. To understand why, it's helpful to look at the three-stage evolution of the concept of socially responsible business.

The first phase was characterized primarily by Fortune 500 companies trying to improve their social performance, often in small ways with large public relations budgets. Perhaps the classic example is

Share Our Strength, a campaign to end hunger whose sponsor, American Express, spent more on promoting its good deeds than on the deeds themselves. Many executives in these companies continue to share "best practices" in environmental and labor performance through Business for Social Responsibility (BSR), which got started in 1992.[30] And, yes, it's undeniably laudable when huge chain stores like Costco pay higher wages, or when the SUV-addicted Ford Motor Company announces its commitment to higher-mileage vehicles, or even when Wal-Mart teams up with noted green designer Bill McDonough to improve the energy efficiency of its stores.

A second phase was led by small- and medium-sized firms whose proprietors were more eager to align themselves and their companies with social causes, and whose CEOs collaborate through organizations like the Social Ventures Network (SVN). It's hard not to applaud the Body Shops, the Ben & Jerry's, and the Benettons of the world, each of which manufactures decent products, comports (however imperfectly) with reasonably responsible labor and environmental standards, and piggybacks snippets of consumer education in its advertising.

No one should confuse these small steps, however, with the promise of the Small-Mart Revolution. Kinder, gentler, friendlier, and greener TINA businesses can only go so far in reforming themselves before the brutal logic of globalization precipitates a move abroad that undoes all of this progress. How much credit do you get if you give your workers better wages and health care benefits this year, and then shut down the plant next? Or if you reduce your energy use, like Wal-Mart, while encouraging millions of purchasers to skip nearby downtown stores and drive literally billions of additional miles per year to the Supercenters?[31]

At the end of the day, any business that sacrifices its bottom line in the name of responsibility leaves itself vulnerable to a hostile acquisition by another TINA firm that has got the mettle to make such "hard choices." That's what happened to Ben & Jerry's, which was gobbled up by Unilever. Alternatively, the heads of socially responsible TINA businesses sooner or later want to cash out and move on, and it becomes very hard to say no to lucrative offers by mainstream TINA companies, which is what happened when PepsiCo bought out Odwalla Juices and Groupe DANONE (makers of Dannon yogurt) acquired Stonyfield

Yogurt. (How such owners can exit without sacrificing the local character of their company is discussed in chapter 5.) A commitment to social responsibility is just one more inefficiency the new TINA managers will try to wring out of these companies.

These dynamics underscore why social responsibility must include local ownership. And why it's so disheartening to see a proliferation of nonprofits, books, green directories, conferences, and declarations proclaiming social responsibility without ever a mention of the issues of ownership or control. In early 2003 California State Senator Alarcon introduced a bill in the California state legislature (SB 974) that would have awarded 5 to 10 percent bidding preferences on state and local government contracts whenever a business achieved ten of thirteen criteria for social responsibility. It duly recognized corporations paying living wages, providing health insurance and retirement plans, promoting recycling, implementing job retention, and respecting consumer safety. But what about ownership? Except for a vague criterion encouraging "worker involvement or worker ownership," there was no mention of *local* ownership whatsoever. Yet it also needs to be said that the criteria of the Alarcon bill are important and that they do not automatically flow from local ownership. No company structure, on its own, can guarantee that managers always do the right thing. Corporate responsibility requires LOIS but also two kinds of supplements.

First, a prosperous community requires healthy local governance so that reasonably high labor and environmental standards are set for all business. The "High Road" in economic development, as Dan Swinney, a sharp Chicago-based organizer, calls it, inevitably demands that public bodies set speed limits, rights of way, and traffic signals for commerce.[32] For example, enacting a living wage ordinance as did the city of Santa Fe, New Mexico, raised labor standards significantly.[33] An economy made up mostly of LOIS businesses may make it politically possible to enact a living wage, though it does not follow that LOIS businesses automatically will embrace it (many didn't in Santa Fe). They will, however, adapt to it over time, because moving is not an option and shutting down is not in their interest.

A second mechanism is to nurture more enlightened shareholders. Some owners of LOIS businesses—family members, partners, friends, colleagues, and other investors—can be just as brutal in demanding that managers pay attention to the short-term bottom line as the face-less stockholders of publicly traded companies. A healthy LOIS econ-omy ultimately requires activist shareholders who are capable of bal-ancing the interests of the company with those of the community so that when a living wage ordinance is passed, they don't react by shut-ting down.[34] Because the shareholders live in the community and pre-sumably know, appreciate, and even honor many of their neighbors, they are more likely than absentee owners to make more community-friendly choices—but they won't do so automatically. Public education and peer pressure must remind shareholders that their responsibility is to discharge their duties to *both* the company and the community in a balanced way.

The private and public spheres of a community are intimately related, and the tone and activities of one influence the other. An econ-omy comprising mostly LOIS enterprises can weave together peer rela-tionships among businesses, and between businesses and others, that facilitate communication, discourse, reason, even empathy, all of which are necessary for good governance and high stakeholder awareness.

Many economists concede that, *in theory*, a community rich with LOIS businesses will prosper. Yes, a community made up of locally owned businesses will enjoy more engines of wealth, over many more years, with less worry about catastrophic departures, and with greater multipliers for every dollar of business. And a self-reliant community will be more secure, better able to tap a deeper pool of labor skills, ben-efit from a wider range of connections to the global economy, and cel-ebrate that its economic development programs, now shorn of outra-geous incentives and extravagant junkets, are cheaper and more cost effective. *But*, insist these dismal social scientists, we are in an era where bigger is better. The most competitive goods and services can only come from larger TINA firms, and the consumer advantages they confer outweigh any potential community advantages from LOIS firms.

Were this dilemma real, if we had to choose between competitive goods and services from community-destroying TINA firms and un-competitive goods and services from community-friendly LOIS firms, picking the right future would be agonizingly difficult. Fortunately, LOIS firms are far more competitive than almost anyone realizes.

# three

★★★★★★★★★★★★★★★★★★★★★★★★★★★★★★★★★★★★★★★★★★★★★★

# AMAZING SHRINKING MACHINES

Paleontologists millions of years hence might describe our time as the Era of the Gigantic Bankasaurs. Their digs might turn up fragments from 1998, when Citicorp took over Travelers, Bank One nabbed First Chicago NBD, and NationsBank gobbled up Bank of America (while assuming the latter's name).[1] Or they might find signs of Wells Fargo combining with Norwest, or of Bank of America spending $47 billion to acquire FleetBoston Financial in 2003. All these fossilized remains would suggest that only the biggest creatures could survive.

Well, not quite. Despite all the hoopla, researchers at the Federal Reserve in Minneapolis have quietly concluded that "after banks reach a fairly modest size [about $100 million in assets], there is no cost advantage to further expansion. Some evidence even suggests diseconomies of scale for very large banks."[2] Larger banks pay less on savings accounts, charge more on checking, pay higher overheads, and suffer greater default rates. The Financial Markets Center, a financial research and education organization, has found that, compared to banks with far-flung portfolios, those that concentrate lending in a geographic region are typically twice as profitable and wind up with fewer bad loans.[3] Sooner or later, consumers will wake up and smell the locally brewed coffee.

Banking, it turns out, is hardly the only area where bigger is less competitive. Consider the following examples:

- Despite corporate consolidation of supermarkets, with Wal-Mart now the top food seller in the country, there has been a huge growth in local food systems, everything from farmers markets to community-supported agriculture.

- Local recycling operations increasingly are providing cheaper metal, glass, and paper than the global producers who extract and process virgin resources.

- Over the next generation, most Americans will get the cheapest electricity, not from centralized coal- and nuclear-dependent utilities, but from local windmills and rooftop photovoltaic cells, which are now the world's fastest growing energy supplies.[4]

Scale, as economists are quick to point out, could crush LOIS. No matter how valuable LOIS businesses are for local multipliers and economic well-being, the goods and services they produce must still be competitive with those produced by larger firms. Many economists believe that larger companies are more efficient because they can spread their fixed costs (such as management, tax filings, and office expenses) over more units of production. If this is true—as proponents of globalization claim and as opponents fear—then community economies are truly in trouble.

But there is a growing body of evidence that economies of scale in many business sectors, after several generations of modest growth, are beginning to shrink. As any first-year economics student learns, firms lower average costs by expanding, *but only up to a point*. Beyond that point, according to the law of diminishing returns to scale, complexities, breakdowns, and inefficiencies begin to drive average costs back up. The collapse of massive state-owned enterprises in the old Soviet Union and the historic bankruptcies of Enron and New York City are notable reminders of a lesson we should have learned from the bankasaurs' ancestors: don't bet on big.[5]

A closer look at the issues of scale suggests two surprising conclusions. The first is that there are competitive models for LOIS business in almost every sector of the economy. These models, if studied, replicated, and improved upon, can provide every community in the United States, big and small, major opportunities to become more self-reliant. A second conclusion is that a number of significant global trends are emerging that are shrinking economies of scale. Global reach is weighing down TINA firms with dramatic new inefficiencies in both production and distribution, and the rising price of oil will intensify both. As people grow wealthier, they tend to spend proportionally less on goods and more on services that are inherently local. The best and the brightest young people are increasingly drawn to small business. The abolition of corporate welfare and the steady decline of the U.S. dollar also bode well for the Small-Mart Revolution. Ultimately, of course, many factors unrelated to efficiency shape the economy. The continuing proliferation of mergers, driven not by economies of scale but by short-term profiteering, is a reminder that efficiency is not destiny. It therefore remains essential for mindful and committed consumers, investors, entrepreneurs, and policymakers to lead the Small-Mart Revolution.

## Many "Right" Scales

Policymakers and business planners tend to think about economies of scale as God-given. In their minds a smooth curve charts the efficiency of firms in any given industry; by following that curve, from a base-ment operation to a global corporation, the exact point of greatest prof-itability can be found. The universe of business possibilities, however, turns out to be not so simple—and much more interesting.

For any given business, there is never one but many economies of scale. No one design works for all firms, in all environments, for all markets. Part of the challenge of localization is to refocus every com-munity's ingenuity on creating efficiency and quality at a much smaller scale. Once the appropriate scale is chosen, innovation within that scale can bring down costs and increase profits.

If you are an entrepreneur seeking to create a LOIS business in a particular industry, it doesn't matter if your industry is filled with large competitors; it only matters that you are able to find small-scale firms in the industry that are competitive or, failing that, design one yourself.

The U.S. Census Bureau regularly publishes details about more than one thousand kinds of business, categorized by what is called the North American Industry Classification System, or NAICS. If you rank these categories by the probability that any firm in that category will be large, you find that the third "largest scale" industry is "Guided Missile & Space Vehicle Manufacturing." If ever there was a natural niche for big business, it would be one with an intergalactic mission. And yet, of the ten firms in that category nationally, three have fewer than one hundred employees. While it's impossible to know exactly which firms NAICS is counting (the raw data are confidential), two likely candidates are Scaled Composites and Environmental Aerospace Corporation (EAC). Scaled Composites, located in the Mojave Desert, is a limited liability corporation founded in 1982 by Burt Rutan that is designing an orbital passenger spacecraft called SpaceShipOne. In 2003 *Scientific American* named Rutan as one of its top fifty technology leaders. EAC, based in South Florida, was incorporated in 1994 and has developed the Hyperion I series of sounding rockets for the National Aeronautics and Space Administration. *For the particular niche they are serving, these companies are organized at just the right scale.*

Here's another interesting exercise: recall that the Small Business Administration defines small business as having fewer than five hundred employees. In how many of the thousand-plus categories are there more large firms than small? The answer is, stunningly, only seven, including the rocketry category. So let's concede, for argument's sake, that LOIS firms probably cannot do very well at running central banks or nuclear power plants, mining phosphate rock, or manufacturing pipelines or cyclic crude. Big deal. *More than 99 percent of the other thousand-plus categories have more small firms than large ones.* Any community interested in starting an import-substituting business in just about anything else will, with a little homework, be able to find plenty of viable small-business models.

Okay, I can hear the nit-picks. Yes, I agree that not all firms as large as five hundred employees are locally owned. But even if we use one hundred employees as our proxy for LOIS firms, the business categories where there are more large firms than small ones grows from seven to twenty-two. We can add to our list of unlikely industries for LOIS success pulp, newsprint, and paperboard mills, various kinds of hospitals, power plants burning fossil fuels, and the manufacturers of sugar beets, carbon black, refrigerators, glass jars, tire cords, and ferroalloys. Plenty of viable smaller firms exist in each of these categories, but they happen to be less numerous than the large firms.

(For those of you eggheads interested in more a detailed analysis of this point, check out appendix B, which performs the above analysis on the basis of payrolls.)

Inside each business category, of course, are fascinating specifics. The single least localized type of manufacturing is "transportation equipment," which refers to firms making cars, planes, trains, and the like. This suggests why reducing our dependence on automobiles is an important goal, not only to reduce our dependence on foreign oil and limit the environmental damage cars and oil burning cause, but also for the sake of localization. (If you can't make vehicles locally, at least use them less!) Other categories containing relatively few LOIS firms are the manufacturers of food, beverages, tobacco, textiles, paper, petroleum and coal products, chemicals, primary metals, computers, and appliances. What's interesting is how many of these items can be produced locally through environmentally friendly innovations already under way (see chapter 6 for details). LOIS recycling can begin to replace the TINA textile, paper, and primary metal industries. LOIS biofuel and biochemical firms can provide substitutes for petroleum and coal products and for chemicals. Reuse and repair can reduce the demand for virgin computers and appliances. A coherent localization strategy means helping not only entrepreneurs seize emerging small-business opportunities but also consumers choose a more localizable mix of goods and services.

The intriguing bottom line is this: there are exemplary smaller-scale businesses in almost every industry. Even in the few categories where, on balance, TINA is succeeding more than LOIS, the differences are not big enough to suggest that the right LOIS firm cannot succeed. For any business the ingenuity, drive, and quality of its managers or workers and the quality of its products and services matter more than the sheer size of an operation. A smart LOIS entrepreneur in almost every industry has a shot at success. And "smart" means taking full advantage of emerging global trends that are making TINA less competitive.

## Eight Deglobalizing Trends

TINA is in trouble. Despite being run by the best business minds in the world, despite the usual advantages of operating on a larger scale (plus the unusual ones, like being monopolists), despite $113 billion in subsidies each year, despite spirited promotion by the world's most influential economists, journalists, and politicians, TINA-style globalization may soon start losing ground. At least eight trends are now shrinking economies of scale and making LOIS increasingly competitive.

## 1. INEFFICIENCIES OF GLOBAL-SCALE PRODUCTION

Can you imagine mass-producing most of your electronics, toiletries, and canned goods locally? Probably not. Indeed, almost everything mass-produced these days, from toothpaste to socks, is being done in low-wage countries like China, where unskilled workers and robots perform routine assembly-line tasks at high speed and low cost. When it comes to mass production, we understand intuitively the labor-cost advantages enjoyed by global-scale producers. What we forget, however, is that all these goods must be designed and sold to narrow niches of consumers, and that consumer tastes differ enormously from place to place. In a September 2005 *Harvard Business Review* article aptly entitled "All Strategy Is Local," Bruce Greenwald and Judd Kahn argue that the most successful firms these days are "'local,' either in the geographic sense or in the sense of being limited to one product or a handful of related ones. The two most powerful competitive advantages, customer captivity and economies of scale—which pack an even bigger punch when combined—are more achievable and sustainable in markets that are restricted in these ways."[6]

The idea of "customer captivity" is that once consumers get comfortable with and attached to a certain product, changing to another substitute is difficult. As the old cigarette commercial used to say, "I'd rather fight than switch." Over the past ten years I've grown accustomed to my Mach 3 razor, and it would take quite a splashy marketing campaign to persuade me to try something new. Suppose a private school hires a local manufacturer to make uniforms, all with certain specifications and designs. Contracting another manufacturer is possible but costly since it requires working out a whole new supplier relationship. Why bother?

A smart producer would rather be a barracuda in a small market than a guppy in a large one. Greenwald and Kahn show that regional grocers have deployed this strategy to achieve much greater levels of profitability than national chains (including Wal-Mart). The most successful telecommunications firms have been the Baby Bell branches of the former telephone monopoly that had strong regional positions, like Verizon, SBC, Qwest, and BellSouth, not the global players like WorldCom and Global Crossing. The profitability of newspaper companies grounded in local markets has been nearly double that of the media giants like Time-Warner, Viacom, Disney, and the News Corporation.

Managers perform more effectively when they know their markets intimately, master one or two products, and dominate their local niche. Greenwald and Kahn meant "local" in the sense of focusing on a single national market or a large region within a country, but the logic applies with equal force to smaller geographic units as well. After all, the tastes, rules, business practices, and cultural norms of Seattle are quite dissimilar to those of Kansas City, Dallas, or Bangor. Once a local producer dominates these markets, it's very hard for an outsider to break in.

The HEB supermarkets have grown market share in their native Texas, even competing well against Wal-Mart, by carefully stocking their stores with goods narrowly tailored to their market.[7] Residents of the Rio Grande Valley who cannot afford air conditioners find on HEB's shelves low-cost rubbing alcohol mixed with skin moisturizers, which they can use to cool down. Special ovens in the store churn out hot tortillas and fresh chips. The 304 stores each have an enormous produce department that features thirty different kinds of olives. In Hispanic neighborhoods, HEB sells metallic "discos" that the locals use to cook brisket. In Houston's Asian neighborhoods, the stores carry tanks of live fish and shellfish. In an effort to get her employees to put themselves into the customers' shoes, Suzanne Wade, HEB's president of food and drugs, gave them each twenty dollars and asked them to try feeding their family on it for a week. The result was a new storewide emphasis on rice and beans.

In principle a global-scale producer can wield its vast resources to produce many different products for many different local tastes. But in practice a local producer is better situated to intuit, design, manufacture flexibly, and deliver just-on-time appropriate products.[8] Consumers can better communicate their needs to local producers, either directly or through local retailers. General Foods probably will never be able to persuade New Yorkers to replace their locally baked bagels with Minnesota-made generics (though it might be able to acquire bagel-makers). Microbrewers have flourished throughout the United States and the United Kingdom because each caters to highly specialized local tastes. The increasing discrimination of the palates of Bay Area consumers, toward inclusion of more varieties of locally grown fruits and vegetables, has more than tripled the region's agricultural economy by 61 percent between 1988 and 1998 and now translates into $1.7 billion of additional agricultural activity in the local economy each year.[9] Community food systems could potentially generate the same wealth in every region of the country.

One reason regional and local banks perform more efficiently than their national and global counterparts is that they actually know their borrowers. Personal knowledge of an individual taking out a loan—about his or her family, trustworthiness, personal ties, previous business efforts, and so forth—leads to better risk assessments than a mechanical review of income and credit history.

The great conservative economist Friedrich Hayek argued that state socialism was doomed because knowledge is too complex, too subjective, and too dependent on particular circumstances of time and place for even the smartest, best-intentioned bureaucrats to comprehend. Big Brother's natural inclinations to average, simplify, generalize, and abstract necessarily filter out critically important facts that make national policymaking inherently insensitive to local needs. The same problem afflicts global-scale corporations.

A producer with laser-beam focus on a local market will build a factory in it or close to it, sized only large enough to meet that demand while keeping inventories low. It will embrace the concepts of *flexible manufacturing* and *economy of scope*. Paul Kidd, author of *Agile Manufacturing*, writes:

> We are moving towards an environment in which competitive products need customer-specific tailoring and high quality. At the same time new trends are shortening the product's life cycle, making the number of repeat orders smaller and reducing batch sizes, while adding variety. . . . While economies of scale is based on mass manufacturing and the idea that it is always more profitable to produce a large quantity of goods in large batches, econ-

omies of scope relies on the principles that machines should be used to make a wide range of product lines with small batch sizes. Economies of scope is the ability to convert fixed capital from one purpose to another.[10]

Decentralized production thus increasingly makes sense to manufacturers. Some 40 percent of U.S. raw steel production—and its most profitable sector—is made up of minimills that reprocess scrap steel with electric arc furnaces, each located close to its consumer market. Toyota is clearly not a LOIS company, but some of its innovations suggest new possibilities for regional auto manufacturing. High costs of inventories and production bottlenecks, where a glitch in one part of the centralized assembly line can cause a shutdown of the entire plant, led Toyota to build small plants with shorter production cycles sited closer to specific markets, each capable of just-in-time delivery of automobiles. Professor H. Thomas Johnson of Portland State University School of Business was stunned to discover, after studying Toyota for more than a decade, that the company considered its 90,000-unit-per-year plant in Melbourne, Australia, as efficient as the 500,000-unit-per-year plant in Georgetown, Kentucky.[11] Futurist Peter Schwartz, cofounder and chair of the Global Business Network, speculates on the possibility of a new generation of regional car manufacturers, each producing special models that would take advantage of the natural fuels available locally and that would embody size, durability, fashion, and other characteristics of a region.[12]

Consumers with increasingly discriminating tastes are driving these trends. Local producers are inherently in the best position to recognize these tastes and respond to them with just the right products, at just the right time, in just the right way.

### 2. INEFFICIENCIES OF GLOBAL DISTRIBUTION

Even where global-scale production is cost-effective, global-scale distribution increasingly isn't. In fact, in a growing number of sectors distribution costs are substantially greater than those of production, opening huge opportunities for LOIS business to economize.

Consider food. In 1910, for every dollar Americans spent for food, forty cents went to farmers and the rest to marketers and providers of inputs like seeds, energy, and fertilizer; now eight cents go to farmers, nineteen cents to input providers, and seventy-three cents to mar-keters.[13] These seventy-three cents are largely unrelated to the end product consumers really want—fresh, nutritious, tasty food. They're wasted on packaging, refrigeration, spoilage, advertising, trucking, supermarket fees, and middle-people. The Leopold Center for Sustain-able Agriculture at Iowa State estimates that the primary ingredients that make up a strawberry yogurt travel 2,216 miles before getting to an Iowa consumer's plate.[14] If farmers were directly linked with nearby consumers, a significant portion of these costs could be wrung out. Food prices could come down or farmers' meager incomes could go up. Maybe both.

This helps to explain the spectacular growth of community-based food systems in recent years. More than one thousand community-supported agricultural or horticultural operations are now operating in every state, linking farmers directly with household "subscribers." Between 1994 and 2004 the number of farmers markets in the coun-try more than doubled to 3,700.[15] Almost everywhere today are exam-ples of food-buying clubs and cooperatives, farm-to-school programs, roadside stands, direct delivery services, slow-food groups, and online farm directories, all facilitating direct links between consumers and farmers.

Many restaurants now routinely emphasize local ingredients. Alice Waters at Chez Panisse in Berkeley popularized this movement, but it's no more original than a fresh apple pie. The Chefs Collaborative involves more than a thousand of the top American chefs who are pro-moting improvements in food quality through the use of local ingre-dients. A "Slow Food" movement emphasizing the social importance of higher-quality food and eating occasions, which started in Italy, is now spreading across the United States, and even morphing into a "Slow Cities" movement.[16]

Tod Murphy, founder and owner of the Farmers' Diner in Vermont, prides himself on using eggs, meats, fruits, and vegetables produced within seventy miles of the restaurant. More than sixty-five cents of every dollar spent at the restaurant stays local.[17] Murphy is also devel-oping direct distribution systems for the farmers in his network with high-end grocery stores, hotels, and food-service channels. He outgrew his initial diner and is moving operations into a new one three times bigger. He now plans to license and spread the concept elsewhere in the country.

It's easy to see how rural communities, most of which have some farming traditions, can localize their food systems. The key is for farmers to move from growing one or two crops *en masse* for commodity markets to growing a wider range of smaller crops for local consumption. Many farmers who have gone this way have breathed new life into their business and increased their income by more than half.[18]

But what about the cities and the suburbs? In fact, more than a third of fresh vegetables, fruits, livestock, poultry, and fish produced in the United States comes from metropolitan areas.[19] The most recent survey of the American Community Gardening Association, in 1996, found more than six thousand community gardens in the thirty-eight cities surveyed, and that the city with the highest number of gardens per capita was Newark, New Jersey.[20] The National Gardening Association estimates that one out of five American households grows some edible produce,[21] and several surveys have found that the typical participating family saves between one hundred and seven hundred dollars per year in food expenses.[22]

The impressive performance of urban farms around the country suggests the broad potential for this movement. In *On Good Land: The Autobiography of an Urban Farm,* Michael Abelman documents his fifteen-year effort to create an economically viable farm in Goleta, California, a suburb of Santa Barbara.[23] Today, Fairview Gardens is a twelve-acre organic farm, surrounded by suburban sprawl, shopping malls, housing developments, and highways. The farm grosses over $350,000 per year and produces milk, eggs, free-range chickens, goats, and more than one hundred varieties of fruits and vegetables for its five hundred member families.

Several trends suggest that this kind of model can be replicated elsewhere. First, municipalities have serious unmet demands for food. As Mohammed Nuru, founder of the San Francisco League of Urban Gardeners (SLUG), has written, "In cities like San Francisco, many communities are cut off from access to fresh foods and from information about proper nutrition. In some communities, corner markets and fast-food establishments are the dominant food supply businesses, offering mostly liquor and processed food."[24] A survey of food stores in three zip codes in Detroit with particularly low income levels found that fewer than one in five carried foodstuffs that would meet the U.S. Department of Agriculture's (USDA) definition of a "healthy food basket," and even these items tended to be spoiled, stale, and overpriced.[25] In part because food is both costly and inaccessible to inner-city residents, the Economic Research Service of the USDA estimates that 5.7 million households with children in metropolitan areas are "food insecure," which means that residents are either hungry or at risk of hunger.[26] Developing new, accessible, and affordable sources of healthy nutrition for these young people is a practical and moral imperative for their future—and ours.

Second, inner cities have among the highest unemployment rates in the country. In principle, much of the work required for urban farming could be done by those currently unemployed. No advanced degrees in agriculture are necessary. In practice, some support is helpful, especially to overcome psychological barriers city dwellers have about becoming farmers. But once newcomers start to work the land, few give it up, despite the backbreaking labor.

Third, more land is becoming available for urban farming. Most U.S. cities are spreading out over larger geographic areas, while their populations are remaining stable or declining. Between 1980 and 1990, for example, the population of metropolitan Chicago grew only 4 percent while the city government gained authority over 40 percent more land. The exodus of industry and people has left more than 31,000 vacant lots in Philadelphia, and 70,000 in Chicago; in Trenton an estimated 18 percent of its land mass is vacant; and the U.S. General Accounting Office (GAO) says that as many as 425,000 brownfields (heavily contaminated industrial sites) could be cleaned up and converted into food-growing sites.[27] Clearing these parcels of garbage, toxins, and abandoned buildings can require up-front costs as well as technical skills, both of which municipal governments could provide. Even when brownfield sites cannot be cleaned cost effectively, they can nonetheless be used for growing ornamental plants or trees, or they can provide the plots for raised beds with clean, imported soil.

Over time, farming on city structures themselves—on rooftops, balconies, walls, and decks—might become economically attractive. Rooftops alone account for nearly a third of a typical city's surface area.

The biggest difficulty with rooftop gardening is the weight that soil places on buildings. To address this challenge, Paul Mankiewicz, of New York's Gaia Institute, has developed Solid State Hydroponics, which uses lightweight shredded Styrofoam instead of sand and provides water to edible plants through a latticework of tubes.[28] He also has designed a lightweight greenhouse that replaces heavy glass with thin plastic films. Mankiewicz argues that these innovations might enable a large apartment house to grow enough fruits and vegetables for four thousand people per year. The jury is still out on whether high-tech hydroponics compromises the tastiness, healthfulness, or genetics of produce, but certainly such experimentation should be welcomed.

Food is not the only industry where inefficiencies in distribution have ushered in the Small-Mart Revolution. Another is the sale of electricity. Historically, electric utilities built a relatively small number of large central generating stations because larger units were more cost-effective than smaller units and because the cost of transmission and distribution to the end user was trivial. Neither of these assumptions is true any more.

During each of the four decades prior to the 1990s, U.S. utilities ordered an average of 268 power plants.[29] Their orders in the decade of the 1990s fell to 22. That didn't mean that new generators were no longer being built because of over-regulating bureaucrats, but rather that all the building had moved into the private sector. Companies outside utilities more than quadrupled their net capacity between 1990 and 2001, with most new plants smaller than one hundred megawatts (less than a tenth the size of the old nuclear plants). In the year 2000 the Caterpillar Company sold sixty thousand diesel generators, with output equivalent to nine Hoover Dams.[30] Another fast-growing source of electricity is privately controlled windpower, which accounts for nearly seven gigawatts nationwide. The Europeans are building their decentralized wind capacity even more aggressively and by the end of 2004 pushed worldwide capacity to forty-six gigawatts.

Smaller electricity generators have become cheaper, according to Amory Lovins and his colleagues at the Rocky Mountain Institute, for many reasons—207 to be precise, according to a telephone-book-length analysis of the industry they recently completed.[31] For example, big power plants, which require many years to build and work their way through multiple regulatory processes, can become huge financial burdens for a company, especially if demand projections are off. Decentralized electricity devices, in contrast, can be mass produced, bought in lots small and large, added exactly as and where needed, and usually involve environmental reviews that are no more demanding than for, say, a lawnmower or snow blower.

Meanwhile, the price of fixing an increasingly rickety national electricity grid has become unaffordable. In August 2003 a major blackout crippled the Northeast United States and adjacent parts of Canada, affecting some fifty million people. According to a Cambridge-based consulting firm called the Brattle Group, damages from the blackout—primarily from lost business—were about $6 billion.[32] Plans are currently being floated to invest more than $100 billion to improve the reliability of the national grid. These expenditures would be foolish when, as Lovins argues, "nearly a dozen other technological, conceptual, and institutional forces are . . . driving a rapid shift towards the 'distributed utility,' where power generation migrates from remote plants to customers' back yards, basements, rooftops, and driveways."[33]

It is telling that the communities largely unaffected by the Northeast blackout, as well as another blackout in the Pacific Northwest a few years earlier, were self-reliant municipal utilities districts. In California these were also the communities able to avoid the multibillion-dollar, price-gouging shenanigans of Enron.

To generalize: Whenever the cost of production is low relative to distribution, there are new economies of smaller scale that can be gained by linking local producers directly with nearby consumers. This is the Achilles heel of globalization. And it seems likely to infect many more global industries, beyond food and electricity, as the next trend kicks in.

### 3. RISING ENERGY PRICES

Perhaps the single biggest factor threatening global distribution today is the rising price of oil. Obviously, petroleum is not the only form of energy Americans use, but historically it has been the most portable, convenient, stable, and inexpensive. A huge rise in oil prices necessarily inflates the cost of all goods shipments and all personal transit, thus affecting the entire economy.

For many years, economists would try to show how smart they were

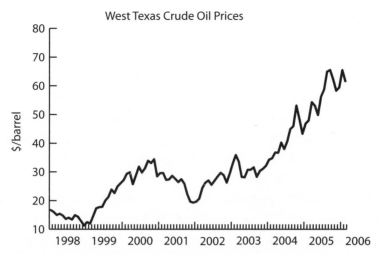

FIGURE 1. Spot prices of West Texas intermediate crude oil.
*Source:* Historic monthly data is available from EconMagic.com, at
www.economagic.com/em-cgi/data.exe/var/west-texas-crude-long.

by proving that oil prices were actually falling since OPEC came onto
the global scene in the 1970s. And, indeed, if you selected just the
right beginning and ending years for your calculations and factored out
inflation, you could show a stabilization or even a modest decline in oil
prices. This cute game is now over.

Figure 1 shows the rising cost of a barrel of West Texas intermediate
crude oil since 1998. No matter how cleverly beginning and end points
are chosen, a reasonable analyst must concede that the price of oil has
tripled or even quadrupled over the past six years. Only a fool would bet
with certainty where the price will be in five, ten, or twenty years. But
only an even bigger fool could fail to see that the price of oil will rise
and, in all likelihood, quite dramatically. The laws of supply and
demand simply cannot be repealed through wishful thinking.

The United States peaked in its own oil production in 1970 at about
eleven million barrels per day. Today we're producing closer to five
million barrels a day. To meet our daily consumption, fifteen million
barrels must be imported. This requires the United States to deploy its
military might in the Persian Gulf to "secure" oil-producing countries,
to turn a blind eye to Saudi Jihadists and the Madrassas training the
next generation of terrorists, and to prop up debt-ridden oil producers

like Mexico. No one, left or right, is happy about the consequences of these messy entanglements.

Global oil production is about to begin a long precipitous decline. The North Sea and Norwegian oil fields that eased the world's supply after OPEC came onto the scene are running dry, and new discoveries worldwide are getting fewer and fewer. Some analysts, like the International Energy Agency, believe that world oil production will peak between 2013 and 2037.[34] Others believe the peak could come within the next five years.[35]

In April 2005 Matthew Simmons, a Wall Street energy investment CEO and advisor to President George W. Bush, told a meeting of the world's top energy analysts that one of the big unknowns, the size of oil reserves in Saudi Arabia, may be much smaller than everyone thinks: "There is a big chance that Saudi Arabia actually peaked production in 1981. We have no reliable data. . . . I suspect if we had, we would find that we are over-producing in most of our major fields and that we should be throttling back. We may have passed that point."[36]

With expected increases in global population and per capita consumption, the U.S. Energy Information Administration projects that demand for oil worldwide will grow by forty million barrels a day by 2025, a 50 percent increase over demand in 2002.[37] The result— inevitably, inexorably—will be higher oil prices. Oil price hikes in the short run will hurt many Americans: commuters with long drives to work; truckers who haul heavy goods around the country; the poor who depend on oil for heat during the winter. But it ultimately could be a godsend to local economies, in three significant ways.

First, price hikes will make local production for local consumption relatively cheap. All those brilliant industrialists who built low-wage factories in China may suddenly find themselves saddled with transportation-cost increases that surpass the labor savings. Those investments are precarious anyway because they depend on the continued Communist Party repression of labor in the name of "the people." One wonders how Mao Zedung would react if he knew that low-paid, nonunion Chinese labor were responsible for nearly a tenth of the products sold at Wal-Mart.[38] When a billion of the world's worst-treated workers begin to liberate themselves from *these* chains, the global production line is in for serious trouble.

Second, oil price hikes will transform suburban sprawl from an unpleasant and unaesthetic lifestyle into an unaffordable one. No one likes to sit for hours each day in traffic jams while commuting to work, driving the kids to school, running (well, crawling) to the supermarket. We've gradually learned to ease our suffering with a cell phone plugged in one ear and XM radio blaring into the other. But rising gasoline prices may force us to revisit the possibility of locating work, school, play, and shopping all within a reasonable walking distance of home. The scrapping of many old-fashioned zoning laws that keep these functions segregated will open every neighborhood to new opportunities for corner stores, household businesses, and community gardens.

Third, the rising cost of energy will lead to more aggressive conservation. Only hands-on inspection, conducted house-by-house or business-by-business, can uncover which walls and ceilings need to be insulated, which appliances need to be replaced, which energy-using habits need to be altered. Some energy-efficiency devices such as compact-fluorescent light bulbs, superefficient windows, or reflective materials for rooftops may need to be manufactured in large, centralized plants. But the installation of these devices can be done best by a local workforce, intimately familiar with the local terrain, architecture, and business culture.

Already, the changing economics of energy efficiency has enabled a whole new industry of local "energy-service companies," or ESCOs, to take root. A recent study by Lawrence Berkeley Laboratory documents that in the 1990s more than one hundred ESCOs have saved between $17 and $20 billion by providing energy-efficiency hardware, software, and services.[39] The typical ESCO is a small- or medium-sized company that oversees energy conservation projects for a period of seven to ten years. It signs a contract with a business, school, or public agency, promising to save a set amount of energy and energy expenditures. It conceptualizes, implements, and finances the project and receives payment based on achieving or surpassing the efficiency targets.

Rising oil prices open up all kinds of new local business opportunities. The skyrocketing cost of pumping water hundreds of miles in desert regions, like Southern California, could spawn a new generation of Water Efficiency Companies, or WASCOs. Mass transit options will look increasingly attractive, especially if flexible light-rail and jitneys are prioritized over exorbitant underground rail systems. Artificial fertilizers that require intensive inputs of petroleum will lose ground to organic soil amendments from local composting and manure recycling operations.

To be sure, if cheap alternatives to petroleum are developed, global distribution will be able to continue business as usual. For the moment, however, this cheery scenario seems highly implausible as the other conventional fuels—natural gas, coal, and nuclear—also become more expensive.

Almost no credible projection of natural gas prices, for example, foresees a drop in the near future. A recent report from the National Petroleum Council concludes: "There has been a fundamental shift in the natural gas supply/demand balance that has resulted in higher prices and volatility in recent years. This situation is expected to continue. . . ."[40] Between now and 2025, "[s]upply and demand will balance at a higher range of prices than historical levels."[41]

Electricity from coal burning and uranium fission could expand since we have plentiful domestic supplies of both fuels, but the costs of building these power plants—not to mention operations—is more costly and financially risky, as we've seen, than building decentralized generating capacity.[42] These capital costs are likely to remain high, especially if coal emissions are appropriately cleaned up and the myriad environmental challenges of nuclear power, like waste disposal, are satisfactorily solved. (The one horrendous problem of nuclear power that can never be solved—the spread of technology and materials that terrorists can use to set off twenty-first-century Hiroshimas and dirty bombs—should persuade decision makers attentive to homeland security to veto the option.[43])

Some of the leaders in an emerging movement of citizens concerned with "Peak Oil" go one step further and argue that *no* alternatives will substitute for oil, and that the United States will face, in the words of Jan Lundahl, a "Petro-Apocalypse," a postmodern Stone Age.[44] Fortunately, the most dire predictions are unlikely.[45] Even if energy is more expensive, it won't be unavailable. Myriad technologies already exist that can substitute for oil, albeit at a higher price. For our fleets of automobiles, there are new generations of cars using new-generation batteries, fuel cells, ethanol, and photovoltaic cells. For household heating, the leading technologies are passive solar design, heat pumps, active solar water heating systems, and biomass burning. Solar systems also are capable of generating very high-grade heat for industrial processes, though because the sun is intermittent, industries may still favor on-site burning of biomass fuels or the use of electricity. Also remember that coal will still be around for such applications for several hundred years. As for electricity generation, existing technologies that tap river, wind, solar, and geothermal power are likely to be improved and mass-produced, and they will soon be joined by cutting-edge technologies that generate electricity from waves, tides, even locally contained tornadoes! All of these technologies, of course, become more feasible if every effort is made to minimize the end-use demands for mobility, heat, or electricity.

Peak-oil activists counter that biodiesel and ethanol from biomass will never substitute for oil. They point out that the heavy subsidies given to producers over the past generation has led some producers to grow specialized, fertilizer-intensive crops and to convert the corn or other biomass in very inefficient processes. Besides overlooking the subsidies that have been lavished on the conventional sources that the alternatives have been competing against, these skeptics don't realize that most of the less efficient technologies and techniques are being discarded.[46] After reviewing several studies by U.S. national laboratories, the Rocky Mountain Institute calculated that by 2025 a quarter of the nation's oil needs could be met through the conversion of biomass "without large impacts on the current agricultural system."[47] In addition, they found that "[r]ecent advances in biotechnology and cellulose-to-ethanol conversion can double previous techniques' yield, yet cost less in both capital and energy. Replacing fossil-fuel hydrocarbons with plant-derived carbohydrates will strengthen rural America, boost net farm income by tens of billions of dollars a year, and create more than 750,000 new jobs."[48]

Unimaginable? In just three decades the Brazilians replaced a quarter of their gasoline use with ethanol and biodiesel fuels derived primarily from sugar-cane waste.[49] The program now supplies blended biofuels to four million cars, and Brazil is contemplating an expansion to export ethanol. In 2003 the Europeans produced seventeen times more biodiesel than the United States did. What's in short supply is not a viable energy alternative but the common sense to adapt to higher energy prices through the Small-Mart Revolution.

## 4. PERSONALIZED SERVICES

Another piece of good news is the shift in modern economies from the manufacture of goods to the delivery of services. One reason is that technological advances have brought down the prices of many manufactured goods.[50] The first calculator I used in high-school physics from Hewlett-Packard cost about two hundred dollars. The calculator sitting on my desk today, substantially more powerful and operating on a solar cell, cost less than 2 percent that price (factoring out inflation). As Americans spend less to acquire calculators, refrigerators, and toasters, they are free to spend more on health care, education, and leisure. Plus, once an American family has five cars, fifteen electric toothbrushes, and a radio in every bathroom, the propensity for more stuff—thankfully—begins to drop. In a sense, the global economy, by helping bring about these price drops and saturating certain consumer demands, has laid the foundation for its own demise.

In 1960 U.S. consumers spent four of every ten "personal consumption" dollars on services, and the rest on goods.[51] In 1980, 48 percent of our consumer dollars went to services; in 1990, 55 percent; and in 2003, 59 percent. These changes, economist Paul Krugman argues in *Pop Internationalism,* are moving the U.S. economy inexorably toward localization: "A steadily rising share of the work force produces services that are sold only within that same metropolitan area. . . . And that's why most people in Los Angeles produce services for local consumption and therefore do pretty much the same things as most people in metropolitan New York—or for that matter in London, Paris and modern Chicago."[52]

Few services can be mechanized or delivered from afar via the Internet. Have you ever gotten a massage over the World Wide Web? Okay, a few folks like their intimacy electronic, but most of us prefer a real person rubbing our backs. No matter how many terrific courses are available online, good teaching will still require, as it has for millennia, real humans working side by side with the students to facilitate learning through discourse, empathy, and support. Many services—

whether health care, teaching, legal representation, or accounting—
demand a close, personal, trusting relationship.

Community banks are realizing that one of their competitive advantages is in their personalized customer service. The following item
recently appeared in the journal of the American Banking Association:

> Ron Reinhartz, president and CEO of the Bank of Santa Clara, an
> eight-branch bank south of the San Francisco Bay Area . . . says
> his big-bank competitors are in his market all the time, sending
> in sharp, well-spoken types who visit his small-business cus-
> tomers, pull out laptops, crunch some numbers, then offer the
> customers unsecured lines of credit for very decent amounts of
> money. Many are dazzled and delighted to go with the big bank.
> But six months or a year later, many of those customers are back
> with his bank. How come? Because the customers often have a
> hard time finding someone at the big bank to answer a question
> or fix a problem quickly.
>
> "That's our salvation," Reinartz says. Of his twenty-two thou-
> sand customers, he estimates that some eighteen thousand are
> known to his staff by their first names.[53]

The temptations of even LOIS companies to outsource services will
remain, as *New York Times* columnist Thomas Friedman's latest book,
*The World Is Flat*, reminds us.[54] But the supposed trend has been wildly
overstated. In 2004 the United States imported about $302 billion
worth of services, a number that has been rising somewhat faster than
national income but now represents just over *2 percent* of our national
income, a tiny part of our economy, a fifth of the value of goods
imported.[55] The United States actually runs a trade surplus in services,
which means we are exporting more than we are importing, and this
surplus has remained steady over the past decade.[56]

Some companies that outsourced services, moreover, now regard it
as a colossal error. Not a few computer companies have been dismayed
to discover consumer revolts against the outsourcing of the "tech support" divisions to Bangalore, where well-trained troubleshooters must
follow regimented scripts that take twice as long and yield half the
results.[57] After a mountain of complaints, Dell moved its tech support
back to Texas. Thomas Friedman writes enthusiastically about how

many U.S. accounting firms send their work overseas each evening to low-paid number crunchers.[58] What he doesn't say is how many clients of these firms would take their business elsewhere, in utter disgust, if they knew of the often covert practice.

That Americans are consuming fewer goods and more services is sometimes portrayed as a sign of our economic decline. Employing the logic of TINA, some economists suggest that the only way localities can really prosper is through a massive revival of large-scale manufacturing. This amounts to a nostalgic longing for an era that is all but gone. Those high-wage jobs are disappearing everywhere, as TINA firms move their manufacturing units from one low-wage country to another. As Bruce Greenwald and Judd Kahn observe in the *Harvard Business Review*:

> With the globalization of manufacturing has come an increase in competition, along with decline in profitability. Companies and countries that ignore this reality and try to compete in global markets for manufacturing face stagnation and poor performance, not to mention the challenge of going up against billions of capable, low-wage Chinese and Indian workers. The countries that have tried to follow this path—most notably Japan, Germany, and France—are suffering the consequences of low economic growth and underemployment.[59]

As oil prices rise, much of the manufacturing we need still can and will return home, but to smaller LOIS firms. We should be careful not to wish, willy-nilly, that Americans just consume more goods, because many of these firms, irrespective of their location, provide far fewer jobs and far lower wages than they used to. From an environmental perspective, we might also rejoice that we are producing more wealth through our expertise rather than through the production of stuff that requires energy and resources and usually leaves a huge trail of pollution and waste. Services often require little more than a home office, a computer, and listing in the Yellow Pages, and offer huge opportunities for growing economies in even the smallest of communities.

### 5. THE GROWING IRRELEVANCE OF LOCATION

While many services demand personal delivery and many goods become cheaper with local production and distribution, much of the rest of the economy is becoming totally unhinged from place. This is a boon for local economies, though it also poses special challenges. The nightmare scenario is that a bunch of low-wage super-regions could increasingly produce everything for everyone (though the rest of the world would then be destitute and unable to buy these products). More likely, a growing number of businesses with global markets will be able to conduct their work in just about any location at just about any scale. One implication is that every U.S. community will have huge new opportunities for homegrown enterprise.

The most competitive communities in the United States will be the smartest, not the largest. Size does not limit a community in the skills it can develop, the knowledge it can retain, or the technology it can acquire. Nor, as many college towns demonstrate, does size determine the quality of local research or public education.

From the vantage point of professional opportunities, place matters less. Technical revolutions are making it increasingly possible for anyone to do almost anything economically from almost anywhere. More than twenty million Americans (including me) do some work at home, a number that is sure to grow.[60] This is an extraordinary development. From another perspective, it means we can choose places to live in on the basis of everything else we value in community—beauty, culture, music, art, traditions, religion, family, and friends. Find a place you love, *then* put together your ideal job. A stockbroker can work on horseback; urban planners can write studies from the tops of the Rockies; a family farmer can design a new food product on a transcontinental flight. These radical changes rip apart all the old assumptions about the comparative advantages of cities.

But isn't a certain critical mass of workers, managers, innovators, and firms necessary to achieve competitiveness? The regional planning literature is filled with theories about "agglomerations" of many businesses, people, capital, and technology in a particular place. The proximate siting of related and interrelating firms is believed to create certain economies of scale.[61] Whatever the virtues of agglomerations and clusters, it seems equally true that these advantages are disappearing. Information technologies, linked in an expanding World Wide Web, are bringing more and more individuals, companies, and innovations within our personal and professional orbits at the click of a mouse. A skilled computer user arguably performs more efficiently by filtering out the noise of office life—the gossip, the management disputes, the wacko coworkers. Why take your chances with someone else's geographical agglomeration when you can strategically pick and choose the exact personal agglomeration, physical and virtual, that best fits your own needs?

Manufacturing once depended on special places that were close to inputs from farms, mines, and forests, or that had access to assets like universities, libraries, harbors, ports, roads, rivers, and telecommunications. But increasingly the biggest input for manufacturing is information. Scholars at Princeton's Center for Energy and Environmental Studies have documented that Americans and Western Europeans consume fewer raw materials as GDP rises.[62] U.S. steel use per dollar of GDP in 1990, for example, had dropped to the same level it was at in 1880.[63] Similar declines can be observed in our consumption of most basic materials including cement, ammonia, chlorine, and aluminum. The central reason for this is that advances in technology have liberated products from bulky materials. Cars, for example, are increasingly made with composite materials that are stronger, lighter, and cheaper than steel. As oil prices rise, these will increasingly come from plant-based biomaterials.

The truth is that location just doesn't matter nearly as much as it used to, provided you have access to state-of-the-art telecommunications technology, as most communities now do. Which is why, once again, it's brains, not brawn, that matters. To be sure, places confer certain natural advantages for a few businesses. Ski resort entrepreneurs will continue to fare better in Aspen than in Nantucket. A location's natural endowments—forests, coal deposits, rivers, caribou herds—will allow smart entrepreneurs to spin specialized goods and services. And yet, overall, every community has many more options that are not dependent on these resources.

It needs to be said that the driving force for the growing irrelevance of place—electronic communication—is not a uniform blessing for community economies. The most powerful Web-based businesses, like Amazon and eBay, emphasize global markets rather than local ones. These players, essentially electronic Wal-Marts, not only do not replace imports but also increase a community's dependence on outside goods and services. And for the next few years at least, e-companies will remain deadbeats with respect to the public sector since they tiptoe around local sales taxation.[64] Still, the Web and e-commerce ultimately facilitate the best deals, and to the extent that the Small-Mart Revolution is about spreading information about competitive local goods and services to more consumers, they will remain valuable tools for localization. In fact, many LOIS businesses use Amazon and eBay as platforms for local commerce. And the Web is also seeing a wonderful proliferation of tools for finding local businesses. The Delocator (www.delocator.com), for example, helps you find a local coffee house, and plans to expand its search engine for other types of local businesses.

## 6. WORKFORCE EFFECTIVENESS

Another diseconomy of global-scale firms is that they tend to show less loyalty to their workforce and more inclination to compete through wage cuts, outsourcing, and plant relocation. Jim Kelly, former chair and CEO of United Parcel Service, has noted the average corporation now replaces its entire workforce every four years.[65] Research suggests that this begets all kinds of nasty boomerang effects, including lower worker morale and productivity. Wal-Mart's skimping on its employees means, among other things, poor training, which leads to the kinds of infuriating overcharges reported in the introduction.

The insecurity of TINA workers actually contributes to a number of inefficiencies. One study found that, among unionized shops, absenteeism in large firms (with one thousand or more employees) was 133 times greater than it was in smaller firms (with one to twenty-five employees).[66] LOIS firms that value personal ties between management and the workforce and that don't entertain the possibility of moving facilities overseas are better equipped to keep worker morale and productivity high. Other research suggests that the best way to communicate a major change in a corporation is through small, face-to-face meetings.[67] Large companies, by either necessity or habit, tend to convey information—poorly—through auditorium-sized meetings, videotapes, or newsletters. Eric Chester, author of *Getting Them to Give a Damn* and founder and CEO of Generation WHY, suggests, "By the very nature of their size, big companies tend not to communicate as in-depth with their front lines as smaller companies do, leaving front-line talent at larger companies to feel lost in the shuffle."[68]

The emphasis on personal rather than bureaucratic ties is perhaps what makes LOIS businesses more reliable innovators. Half of all the drugs big pharmaceutical companies bring to market these days turn out to be licensed from small research companies, and the latter's role seems to be growing.[69] Thomas J. Peters and Robert H. Waterman Jr. note in their bestselling book, *In Search of Excellence*: "A researcher concluded recently that research effectiveness was inversely related to group size: assemble more than seven people and research effectiveness goes down. Our stories of ten-person 'skunk-works' out-inventing groups of several hundred are corroborative."[70]

According to *Workforce Management Online*, the three criteria that define what college graduates are looking for in a job are "a job that fits with their skills, professional development opportunity, and company reputation and ethics."[71] All of these give LOIS businesses an edge. Employees at smaller companies, according to a recent Harris Interactive poll, are more likely to agree that top management "displays integrity or morality" or "is committed to advancing the skills of employees." Another characteristic of the class of 2005, says *Workforce Management Online*, "[is that] they want to work to live, not live to work." A TINA business with little job stability and with the prospect of moving around from place to place is not what most young people have in mind. They would rather pick a city or region for its amenities, stay put, and raise a family.

## 7. KOSHER PUBLIC POLICY

More good news for community-scale business is that time may be running out for corporate pork. A remarkable left-right consensus is gaining political clout to undo the vast fabric of subsidies that make large-scale production artificially cheap and small-scale production artificially expensive. The 2003 report of the Green Scissors Coalition, spearheaded by the National Taxpayers Union Foundation, a conservative antigovernment group, and Friends of the Earth, a liberal environmental group, has identified $58 billion of annual government subsidies to mining, logging, fishing, farming, arms, and energy-production industries that are simultaneously wasteful of taxpayer dollars and destructive to the environment.[72] Nearly all the beneficiaries of these programs are TINA companies, either directly—such as corporate farmers, big timber companies, nuclear reactor manufacturers, or oil and gas companies—or indirectly—monies for highways or waterways that boost TINA by making the long-distance shipment of goods relatively cheap, and local production for local consumption relatively expensive.

The subsidization of TINA is one of the dirty secrets of globalization. Recall that TINA enjoys at least $50 billion a year in state and local subsidies in the form of business incentives. Moreover, the $58 billion identified by Green Scissors is just part of all corporate welfare doled out at the national level. The libertarian Cato Institute estimates that the federal government annually gives corporations $87 billion per year.[73] The World Resources Institute calculates that the annual federal subsidy to cars and trucks may be as much as $300 billion a year.[74] These are staggering numbers, even for a $12 trillion economy.

The politics of pork, to be sure, stand in the way of reform. TINA companies lobby politicians at all levels of government and generously give to their campaigns to secure these subsidies. The McCain-Feingold campaign finance reforms signed into law in 2001 have done little to change our legalized system of bribery.

Ultimately public revulsion could become the decisive factor, especially as new taxes or budget cuts become necessary. As of this writing, the country is looking at a projected federal deficit of more than $400 billion per year, and a total national debt of about $8 trillion (nearly $27,000 per American).[75] A majority of the nation's cities are trying to keep their heads above a rising tide of red ink.[76] Something must give. How many Americans, if genuinely given the choice, really would want to pay higher taxes to continue feeding all the TINA piggies?

## 8. THE DECLINE OF THE DOLLAR

The end of the U.S. dollar's dominance of the global economy is another trend that seems likely to propel the Small-Mart Revolution forward. The dollar is currently the world's "reserve currency," which means, for example, that oil sales by OPEC are made in dollars, and most central banks hold their reserves in dollars. If any other country had racked up debt at the rate of $1 trillion per year, as the United

States did in 2004 (adding together its national debt and trade deficit), its currency would collapse, because no one wants to hold a sinking asset. But the status of the U.S. dollar provides a measure of stability, despite our profligacy.

This special role seems unlikely to continue forever as countries and private institutions weigh the rising cost of holding a slumping currency. Major U.S. creditors, like Japan or China, could decide to dump their dollars. OPEC could follow the recommendation of Iran that it switch to another reserve currency, like the recently appreciating Euro. Activists around the world, perturbed at various policies of the Bush administration, such as the war in Iraq and its refusal to sign the Kyoto accord on global warming, also could begin to urge their governments to get rid of dollars. These fears are shared by conservative insiders. Paul Craig Roberts, who was the Assistant Secretary of the Treasury under President Ronald Reagan, believes that these are possible because "the policies of the Bush administration have undermined America's world leadership and isolated the U.S. One result could be that oil producers abandon the dollar as a means of payment."[77]

A nosedive by the dollar will affect many sectors of the economy in complicated ways. Exports will rise. Foreign tourism will flock to the new affordable American destinations, while many of us will decide that foreign trips are beyond our budgets. Foreign investors will buy up more U.S. assets. But most importantly for our communities, the prices of imported goods, including many of those sold by chains, will rise. This will give new impetus to import substitution and local production.

## Why the Urge to Merge?

These eight trends do not mean that economies of scale are shrinking for every good and service. Ultimately the scale of a business reflects a set of choices—by entrepreneurs running the business, by investors underwriting it, and by consumers buying its wares. Moreover, as Hershey's Chocolate Company shows, bigger does not necessarily have to extinguish local ownership.

Still, one other trend that seems to undercut the argument of this chapter is the proliferation of mergers and acquisitions. If economies of scale are really shrinking, shouldn't these be rarer? Smart entrepreneurs, as well as their investors, would presumably avoid creating bigger and bigger firms if bigness were ruining performance. Contrary to this presumption, however, is the reality that what's good for managers and shareholders is not always what's good for the business.

The reason why the bankasaurs, for example, are getting bigger has nothing to do with efficiency. A recent review of the literature on mergers by Paul A. Pautler of the Federal Trade Commission (FTC) found that these deals actually depress stock value 45 to 70 percent of the time.[78] Consider just a few recent debacles: CSX's stock fell 20 percent after its merger with Conrail (Scribner). Five years after the $4.7 billion Sony-Columbia Pictures in 1989, the company wrote off $2.7 billion.[79] AT&T acquired National Cash Register for $7.5 billion in 1991, and spun it off in 1996 for $3.4 billion. The AOL-Time Warner deal wound up shrinking the combined stock worth of the two companies by $200 billion.

Perhaps the best explanation for merger-mania is an odd coincidence of personal interests between the acquiring and acquired firms. The acquiring company is willing to pay shareholders of the acquired company a nice, short-term premium to gain control of the company. Meanwhile, the CEO of the acquiring company usually gets a handsome raise and bonus. The Federal Reserve of Minneapolis observes about banking consolidation: "The data suggest that, regardless of bank profitability, the bigger the bank, the bigger the compensation package its top managers receive."[80] Complaining about Gillette's merger with Procter & Gamble, the vice chair of the board wrote in an open letter, "Thousands of Gillette's employees will soon receive pink slips. Their 'leader' (CEO James Kilts) will receive $170 million."[81] Richard T. Bliss and Richard J. Rosen, both business professors, analyzed mergers between 1986 and 1995, and found that the typical deal boosted executive compensation by 20 to 30 percent. Moreover, for every million dollars of increased company size, those executives who expanded company size through real growth received, on average, only 54 percent of the wage increase that an executive deploying a merger did.

This unholy alliance between CEOs and short-term stock profiteers is encouraged by dealmakers who charge hefty fees for their services, rob long-term shareholders of wealth they would have had if the companies remained smaller and separate, while, at the same time, messing up the lives of the thousands of employees laid off in the post-merger shuffle. "Maybe," writes Rich Karlgaard, publisher of *Forbes* magazine, after reflecting on Carly Fiorina's dismal failure to make Hewlett-Packard's merger with Compaq work, "we need to go deeper and challenge the very premise of these mergers: that large scale is a requirement of success in the global economy. Carly clearly believed this. But maybe the opposite is true—that speed and flexibility now trump scale. The cheap revolution has armed startups and small companies with powerful, cheap technology and access to global labor pools."[82]

## Efficiency Is Not Destiny

The persistence of mergers despite the absence of compelling business advantages is a poignant reminder that executives' decisions often follow their own self-interest. This highlights, again, the importance of enlightened boards and shareholders that demand that executives choose the most efficient and profitable scale of production. As we can see, such decisions do not come about automatically.

Given the gross imperfections of corporate governance today, it may be easier to create new LOIS businesses to seize emerging small-scale business opportunities than to persuade TINA businesses to shrink. And, yet, there are some intriguing examples of the latter. AT&T stunned financial analysts in October 2000 when it announced that it was carving itself up into four, more versatile companies. In May 2001 British Telecom unveiled a plan to spin off its wholesale arm, part of its wireless business, and numerous assets in Asia. As economies of scale shrink, who knows who else will follow?

The trends suggest that place-based production, which already constitutes most of the U.S. economy, is poised to expand, perhaps dramatically. But the speed with which this can happen will depend on the trillions of choices we each make as consumers, as investors, as entrepreneurs, as policymakers, and as community builders.

If we sit around and wait for Adam Smith's invisible hand of the free market, too many communities will disappear, too many ecosystems will be irreparably ruined, and too many people's lives crushed. Despite promising community-scale food businesses, the fact remains that over the past two generations TINA has systematically ripped up local supermarkets, wholesalers, and distributors, just as the U.S. automakers tore out viable trolley systems in U.S. cities in the early part of the twentieth century. Rebuilding local infrastructure requires new business plans, new entrepreneurs, and new investment, all of which could take decades. And the hourglass for too many things we care about is running out.

★★★★★★★★★★★★★★★★★★★★★★★★★★★★★★★★★★★★★★★★★★★★

# PART TWO **THE SMALL-MART PATRIOTS**

★★★★★★★★★★★★★★★★★★★★★★★★★★★★★★★★★★★★★★★★★★★★

It does not require a majority to prevail, but rather an irate,
tireless minority keen to set brush fires in people's minds.

—SAMUEL ADAMS

# four

★★★★★★★★★★★★★★★★★★★★★★★★★★★★★★★★★★★★★★★★★★★

# CONSUMERS

Who stands in the way of the Small-Mart Revolution? Are the biggest opponents the captains of TINA businesses, who will resist cutbacks in public pork? The politicians who receive lavish TINA campaign contributions? Or the economic developers who promote elephant-mouse casserole? As ubiquitous and powerful as these obstacles are, I would nominate a more formidable opponent. If you'd like to meet him or her, please step in front of a mirror.

Okay, as my journey to Wal-Mart suggested, I am no saint, either. In fact, my life is riddled with hypocrisy. On the one hand, I drive a Japanese car, my shoes come from Italy, my drink of choice is single-malt whiskey from Scotland, and my pension sits in the Nasdaq 100 Index Fund. On the other hand, I work at home, drive very little, favor local restaurants over chains, wear clothes twice as long as the fashion police think I should, and give priority to local charities. I'm not perfect. But I *am* trying gradually to localize my own purchasing habits. That's my modest hope for you. The Small-Mart Revolution depends on a reasonable evolution of our consumption patterns. The small steps we take as individuals matter, both because others pay attention to our exemplary behavior and because modest changes by many people can quickly add up to significant shifts in the entire economy.

So how far can you go in localizing yourself? Most of us, dizzy from the millions of fabulous options in the global marketplace, suspect the answer is "not very." How could my own town possibly build its own computers, air conditioners, and jet engines? There are so many thousands of products in our lives, coming from so many places, that localization seems not only impossible but ludicrous. The reality is, however, that most of us spend most of our money locally *already*. The challenge is how much and how fast we can boost that local portion.

Over the next sixty seconds Americans collectively will spend about $23 million. A little less than $16 million will be on personal needs, everything from food to Frisbees, nannies to nightclubs.[1] Every one of these dollars carries enormous power because every purchase is essentially a vote. It's a vote for a retailer, a vote for the local firms that supply the retailer, a vote for the communities where all these businesses operate. Unlike political elections, which are so rare and irrelevant that most eligible voters in this country have stopped participating, economic elections never stop. Everyone is always eligible to participate, even children. Every single day, every hour, every minute we are opening our wallet and casting our ballots.

## Localizing Your Household

Each year the Bureau of Labor Statistics in the U.S. Department of Labor looks systematically at expenditures by the average household in its Consumer Expenditure Survey. In table 1, we can see how much we spend on average in various categories, based on 2002 data. A closer look at these expenditures begins to suggest an exciting range of opportunities to localize.[2]

In the spirit of late-night talk shows, I'd like to suggest the top ten actions you can take to localize your community economy, from smallest to largest. Some may require more careful shopping, and a few might require modest lifestyle changes. None demands that you spend more money. Each item is followed by the target amount of "localization potential," which refers to the amount every American household can inject into the local economy through the prescribed action. As impressive as this list may seem, it barely scratches the surface of what's possible. Just these simple steps can localize half of all household expenditures.

Without any further ado, the tenth best way to localize is . . .

### 10. DRINK LOCAL AND STOP SMOKING
*Localizing Potential: $700 per household per year*

Bathtub gin, anyone? The $376 spent each year on alcohol is being increasingly localized through microbreweries and niche vineyards.

## Table 1
### Annual household expenditures (2002)

| | | |
|---|---|---|
| Housing | $13,283 | 32.66% |
| Transportation | $7,759 | 19.08% |
| Food | $5,375 | 13.21% |
| Pensions and Social Security | $3,493 | 8.59% |
| Health Care | $2,350 | 5.78% |
| Entertainment | $2,079 | 5.11% |
| Apparel and Services | $1,749 | 4.30% |
| Cash Contributions | $1,277 | 3.14% |
| Miscellaneous | $792 | 1.95% |
| Education | $752 | 1.85% |
| Personal Care Products and Services | $526 | 1.29% |
| Insurance | $405 | 1.00% |
| Alcohol | $376 | 0.92% |
| Tobacco | $320 | 0.79% |
| Reading | $139 | 0.34% |
| TOTAL | $40,675 | |

*Source:* U.S. Department of Labor, Bureau of Labor Statistics, "Consumer Expenditures in 2002," Report 974, February 2004, p. 3.

As with other food products, local producers are ideally situated to apprehend local tastes and meet them with just the right products.

As for tobacco ($320), although small amounts can be grown in local greenhouses, maybe even in attics once outfitted by hippies for other mini-crops, tobacco depends intimately on very specific features of climate and soil. Obviously, the better solution is simply to quit. This has a number of secondary localization benefits, such as increasing your productivity at work and reducing the chances you'll need exotic, nonlocal medical equipment to treat lung cancer.

## 9. LOCALIZE CAR SERVICES
*Localizing Potential: $1,000 per household per year*

Care for and feed your cars locally. Every household spends an average of $1,000 a year washing, waxing, repairing, detailing, or renting automobiles. Chances are that there are competitive LOIS establishments in your community that provide these services. Who needs Midas Muffler or the Wal-Mart repair department? Use the local guys, who, incidentally, provide some of the best-paying blue-collar jobs in town.

### 8. GIVE TO LOCAL CHARITY
*Localizing Potential: $1,300 per household per year*

More than 6 percent of the U.S. economy is nonprofit. The largest nonprofits are hospitals, universities, and churches, but they also include hundreds of thousands of do-good and advocacy organizations. Much of their revenue comes from the $1,277 in tax-deductible contributions given by every American household annually.

There's hardly a square inch of the United States over which nonprofits have not proclaimed their mission to improve, save, or restore. Making these contributions local is therefore a cinch. It also improves the quality of charitable giving when check-writers have an opportunity to see, close up, how well their dollars are being spent.

### 7. LOCALIZE HOUSEHOLD ENERGY USE
*Localizing Potential: $1,300 per household per year*

One of the largest items under "Housing" in the Consumer Expenditure Survey (see table 3) is for "Utilities, Fuels, and Public Service." Most of this expenditure is on energy, either through direct burning of fuels like oil and natural gas or through the use of electricity. Today, nearly all our energy dollars fly out of the community, and this leakage will grow exponentially as the prices of oil, natural gas, and other fuels rise. The high potential cost of delaying local energy independence highlights the urgency of acting now.

Some of these strategies were suggested in chapter 3. Conserve energy. Use local fuels such as ethanol, wood, wind power, or biodiesel. And if the opportunity presents itself at the ballot box, create a municipal utility. Amory Lovins, head of the Rocky Mountain Institute and widely recognized guru on energy efficiency, argues that since the first oil shock, efficiency measures overall have saved our economy $300 billion.[3] Undertaking all the cost-effective efficiency opportunities *at 2001 energy prices,* he calculates, would save another $300 billion, which works out to about $3,000 per household.[4] In other words, this step can save you lots of money.

## 6. BUY FRESH FOOD
*Localizing Potential: $1,700 per household per year*

More than half of our at-home food expenditures each year are for relatively unprocessed foods that fall into three broad categories: "meat, poultry, fish, and eggs" ($798 per household per year), "dairy products" ($328), and "fruits and vegetables" ($552). While local suppliers of these items are sometimes difficult to find or expensive, regional suppliers are plentiful and competitive.

Agriculture depends intimately on the environment, which is why it's easier for Mainers to find affordable local lobster and Montanans affordable local beef. But it's also worth noting that every state in the United States has a rich agricultural sector, and technologies like greenhouses and hydroponics are expanding the range of locally grown products everywhere. A cottage industry of local recipe books has sprung up —the *Eating Fresh* series, for example—that lets consumers know how to use more local ingredients each season.[5] Some remaining gaps can be filled with appropriate local substitutes. Rather than import processed white sugar, for example, New Englanders can rely on local maple-syrup sugars. Eating local almost always means eating better, which helps with the next item.

## 5. USE LOCAL HEALTH CARE
*Localizing Potential: $1,850 per household per year*

U.S. households spend and average of $2,350 per year for health care (see table 1). About $1,850 of this goes to doctors, dentists, therapists, hospital staff, and nursing home caretakers, all of whom are local or could be. The rest is for insurance and drugs.

Most insurance plans and health maintenance organizations these days are not local and, by global standards, wildly inefficient. For the forty-six million Americans without health insurance but lucky enough to qualify for Medicare and Medicaid, the dollars they take out of the system may or may not equal the dollars local taxpayers pour into the system. Fixing the national health care crisis, so that every American enjoys at least basic coverage administered as simply as possible, is essential to plug this leak.

Efficient health care systems, in theory, can be regional. The vast majority of diseases, disabilities, and problems can be found in every population pool of a million or so people. Only a few maladies are so specialized that the patient needs to be treated outside a region. Centralizing health care beyond the regional scale inevitably introduces more—and more expensive—layers of bureaucracy that erode the quality of health care itself. The ability of a country like the Netherlands, with a population of sixteen million, to organize an outstanding regional system with dramatically lower administrative costs suggests the possibilities for state reform throughout the United States.[6]

There are two elements of the health care establishment that are decidedly not local—high-tech equipment and prescription medications. The purveyors of medical instruments and drugs are among the largest companies in the world. Some degree of localization is possible if these items are bought through local retailers and if purchases are prioritized from national companies with locally owned suppliers. But the only real way to localize these expenditures is by making a long-overdue shift in U.S. medicine from treatment to prevention.[7] As Americans take better care of themselves through regular exercise, good nutrition, strong families, psychological support systems, and healthy communities—all inherently local activities—they will have less need for nonlocal life-saving instruments and prescriptions.

### 4. FIND LOCAL ENTERTAINMENT
*Localizing Potential: $2,100 per household per year*

The typical household spends $2,079 each year on "Entertainment" (see table 1), a category that includes services that are easily localized and gadgets that are not. Many forms of amusement, such as plays, recreational facilities, and fraternal clubs, are almost always local.[8] Another big item easily localized is health clubs.

"Entertainment," however, also is increasingly under the control of global media conglomerates. It's getting harder to find television, radio, or cable stations that are locally owned, and the equipment needed to enjoy these pastimes almost always comes from global assembly lines. Tapes and DVDs are largely under the control of huge music empires. Local manufacture of toys, playground equipment, electronic games, and video games is rare. The best one can do usually is to purchase these items from locally owned retailers.

The big challenge for every community is how to prevent mass culture from drowning out local culture. The more a community can unglue residents from their television sets and involve them in local music, dancehalls, film festivals, fairs, and street parties, the more likely that community can succeed economically. Recall, again, Richard Florida's argument that homegrown fun is a critical element in maintaining a "creative economy" and in attracting and retaining business talent.[9] For rural communities, expansion of the local entertainment economy may be the best way to convince chronically bored young people to stick around.

### 3. EAT OUT LOCALLY
*Localizing Potential: $2,300 per household per year*

Americans increasingly are eating out, with each household spending an average of $2,276 on restaurant food annually. Much of this goes to fast-food outlets like McDonalds and Wendy's, chains that are successful at addicting young children—mine included—to high doses of fat, salt, and sugar, cheap Chinese toys, and crass commercialism. Finding locally owned alternatives like diners and family-owned eateries is a huge step forward. And the spread of low-cost ethnic restaurants— serving everything from Thai to Salvadoran cuisine—gives parents the opportunity to engage in a little cultural education as well.

As one moves up the eating-out food chain, locally owned restaurants are the norm. Yes, there are a few high-end chains like Mortons and the Chart House. But a special night out usually means finding an eatery where the food is one of a kind.

One important point here is that eating local, unlike other kinds of local purchases, is almost always an option. Exercise it.

### 2. HALVE AUTO USE
*Localizing Potential: $2,450 per household*

Americans spend one out of every five dollars to move about (see table 1). As we can see in table 2, adding the cost of owning an automobile (depreciation plus interest on car loans) to the cost of fuel, we're talking $4,900 per year. Over the next decade or two, we should be able to replace imported oil with locally produced biofuels or hydrogen, and maybe even begin to produce cars regionally. But for the immediate future, how can you cut this expenditure?

### Table 2
### Annual household expenditures on transportation (2002)

| | | |
|---|---|---|
| Vehicle Purchases | $3,665 | 47.23% |
| Gasoline and Motor Oil | $1,235 | 15.91% |
| Other Expenses | $2,471 | 31.84% |
| Public Transportation | $389 | 5.01% |
| TOTAL | $7,760 | |

Source: U.S. Department of Labor, Bureau of Labor Statistics, "Consumer Expenditures in 2002," Report 974, February 2004, p. 3.

Purchasing readily available high-efficiency vehicles can reduce average fuel costs by half or more. So can simply choosing to drive less by walking, biking, skateboarding, jogging, skating, or rolling in your wheelchair. In a country facing epidemic levels of obesity and diabetes, where exercise is often getting up from the plush couch to change the channel without the remote, the use of one's body to get around may be one of the most powerful tools to improve the health of simultaneously one's self, one's family, and one's community.

Minimizing our dependency on automobiles will contribute to community prosperity in other ways as well. We'll decrease the damage to our neighbors' health by reducing air pollution. Largely because of cars, according to a U.S. Environmental Protection Agency report in 1997, 113 million Americans live in counties with unhealthy air quality.[10] We'll also raise property values by not paving over natural landscapes for streets, parking lots, and garages—some estimate that half the surface area of Los Angeles is pavement—all of which also costs us in terms of higher levels of runoff and erosion, greater risks of landslide, massive pollution of the water tables with oil residue and garbage, elimination of the trees that might otherwise absorb some of the carbon dioxide the vehicles are spewing, and greater microclimate temperature swings that require more air conditioning in the summer and more heat in the winter.

Mass transit is another approach. We currently spend a nickel of every transportation dollar on trains, subways, and buses. Expansion of mass transit is limited by the absence of "density" in our society, in turn due in large part to our auto addiction. Our politicians also demand that the users of mass transit systems cover the costs, but they do not place equal demands on the users of the highway systems and do not factor in the multiplier benefits of localizing transportation dollars through community-owned transit systems.

Okay, ready for number one? Drum roll, please . . .

## 1. LOCALIZE YOUR HOME
*Localizing Potential: $7,800 per household per year*

Topping the list of annual household expenditures is housing at $13,283 (see table 1). Looking at the numbers in table 3, we see that roughly 60 percent is for good old shelter. Consumers spend one out of every five disposable dollars to put a roof over their head. The easiest way to localize this expense is to own your residence, free and clear, or to rent from a neighboring landlord. Back in 1979 a study in East Oakland, California, found that one of the biggest annual leaks of dollars outside the community economy—roughly $43 million—was from local tenants to outside landlords, and in many poor communities, where home-ownership rates are low, plugging this leak probably represents the best single opportunity for improving the local economy.[11]

When Americans graduate from being renters to home owners, they usually assume a twenty- to thirty-year mortgage. The shelter category above, however, includes only interest payments, not principal. For most of us, then, shelter is not just about your house but about your mortgage and the banking institution that provides it. So localizing your housing expenses really means moving your mortgage to the local banks and credit unions, which, as we have seen (see chapter 3), typically offer the best deals anyway.

But there is a caveat. Many financial institutions repackage and sell their loans on national secondary markets. Some of these secondary market programs bear the names of familiar government programs like Ginnie Mae, Freddie, Fannie Mae, and Freddie Mac. In one way, these programs benefit communities. The buying up and reselling of a bank's portfolio of mortgages means that it can extend more mortgages and help more families own their own homes. But the outflow of money—in the form of interest payments, principal payments, transaction costs—from the community to bondholders across the nation (and increasingly across the world) also represents a huge loss of eco-

## Table 3
## Annual household expenditures on housing (2002)

| | | |
|---|---:|---:|
| *Shelter* | | |
| Owner Occupied | $5,620 | 42.31% |
| Rental | $1,772 | 13.34% |
| Other | $437 | 3.29% |
| SUBTOTAL | *$7,829* | *58.94%* |
| *Utilities, Fuels, and Public Service* | | |
| Electricity | $853 | 6.42% |
| Gas | $314 | 2.37% |
| Water and Sanitary | $409 | 3.08% |
| Fuel Oil and Coal | $112 | 0.84% |
| Telephone | $996 | 7.50% |
| SUBTOTAL | *$2,684* | *20.21%* |
| *Household Operations* | *$706* | *5.32%* |
| *Household Supplies* | *$545* | *4.10%* |
| *House Furnishings and Equipment* | *$1,518* | *11.43%* |
| TOTAL | $13,282 | |

*Source:* The principal categories come from the Consumer Expenditure Survey. *See* Department of Labor, Bureau of Labor Statistics, "Consumer Expenditures in 2002," Report 974, February 2004, p. 3. The subcategories and associated percentage breakdowns come from the Bureau of Economic Analysis. *See* U.S. Census Bureau, *Statistical Abstract of the United States: 2004–2005*, Table 649, p. 431.

nomic multipliers. One important challenge for the Small-Mart Revolution might be to create *intra*state secondary markets that forge a stronger tie between bondholders and households carrying mortgages. In the meantime a careful mortgage shopper usually can find a local bank that doesn't use secondary market instruments.

## Localization Numbers

*If every American household took the above ten steps, more than half of all consumer expenditures would be localized.* Because nearly all the items on the list are not localized right now (except, perhaps, health care), we're really talking about opportunities for localizing about half of the 42 percent of the economy that is not already place-based.[12] In other words, if consumers took these ten steps and if government and business spenders followed suit, the place-based economy could expand to perhaps 70 or 80 percent of the total U.S. economy.

How difficult would it really be for each of us to take these ten steps? Several items are purely discretionary and shouldn't be difficult at all. There's no good reason not to choose to spend these dollars on alcohol, charity, entertainment, and eating out locally. Other items, like stopping smoking, improving household energy efficiency, or driving less, may require some real effort, but they also can result in significant household savings. Only a few items like localizing the purchase of car services, health care, fresh food, or a home mortgage could cost more if we shop poorly, but affordable local options, as discussed in the previous chapter, are increasingly available everywhere.

Another way to look at the prospects for localizing household expenditures is to take each item of the Consumer Expenditure Survey and evaluate how easy or difficult it is to localize. In Table 4, I do this by placing all of the items in one of three groups: easy to localize, hard to localize, and an in-between category.

Here's what's easy. Households already do a reasonably good job of localizing utility services (at least the nonenergy portions like water provision and trash collection), public transportation, and education. Add the steps outlined above to localize the purchase of fresh food, energy, health care, eating out, entertainment, and charitable giving. All together, these account for more than a third of household expenditures.

Turn next to what's hard. Anything mass produced—cleaning products, household supplies, automobiles, textiles, clothing—is difficult to manufacture competitively in our own backyards. Too many sweatshops around the world are too firmly entrenched to imagine these factories returning to the United States any time soon. But as labor standards rise in places like China and transportation costs increase, the manufacture of these items locally may begin to make sense again. The other items that are difficult to localize, finance and insurance, depend on an ownership revolution in the United States that's conceivable (see the next chapter) but will take years to achieve. In the worst case, then, 27 percent of household expenditures represented in these categories are relatively impervious to localization.

What's left are a bunch of items that are simultaneously easy and hard to localize. Home ownership is easy, household finance less so.

## Table 4
## The localization potential of household expenditures

| | |
|---|---:|
| *Easy to Localize* | |
| Utilities, Fuels, and Public Service | $2,684 |
| Household Operations | $706 |
| Public Transportation | $389 |
| Meats, Poultry, Fish, and Eggs | $798 |
| Dairy Products | $328 |
| Fruits and Vegetables | $552 |
| Food Away from Home | $2,276 |
| Health Care | $2,350 |
| Entertainment | $2,079 |
| Cash Contributions | $1,277 |
| Education | $752 |
| TOTAL | $14,191 |
| *Less Easy to Localize* | |
| Shelter | $7,829 |
| House Furnishings and Equipment | $1,518 |
| Gasoline and Motor Oil | $1,235 |
| Other Vehicle Expenses | $2,471 |
| Cereals and Bakery Products | $450 |
| Miscellaneous Expenses | $792 |
| Personal Care Products and Services | $526 |
| Alcohol | $376 |
| Reading | $139 |
| TOTAL | $15,336 |
| *Hard to Localize* | |
| Household Supplies | $545 |
| Vehicle Purchases | $3,665 |
| Pensions and Social Security | $3,493 |
| Apparel and Services | $1,749 |
| Other Processed Food | 970 |
| Insurance | $405 |
| Tobacco | $320 |
| TOTAL | $11,147 |

*Source:* These data all come from tables 1–3. The allocations to each of the three categories is subjective, based on the discussion in the text.

Home furnishings usually can be made from local wood and fiber, but home appliances cannot. Conversion of cars, trucks, and planes from petroleum to biofuels won't be easy or fast, but a bunch of automobile manufacturers (most of them not American) are already engineering for this transition. Cereals may need to be mass-produced, but bakery goods worthy salivating over are usually local. Newspapers today are easily localized through recycled paper, but books published through media conglomerates are not. In each of these categories, careful work by local proprietors can create competitive goods and services.

*The bottom line is worth repeating: Most American households, simply through small lifestyle changes and careful shopping, can localize roughly three quarters of their spending without major cost—and perhaps even with significant savings.*

## Making Local Shopping Easier

One of the real obstacles to achieving the above goals is to get good information. Where can I find a good local bank? Who will deliver fresh local produce to my door? Which restaurants are locally owned? Only when you have this information at your fingertips can you begin to make smart choices. That's where "buy local" campaigns fit in. If you're lucky enough to live in a community with such a campaign under way—or are inspired to start one yourself—you'll be better equipped to do your part in the Small-Mart Revolution. Consider some of the other tools that have already been developed, and if you're really ambitious, you can replicate or improve upon them.

Several years ago I put together a directory of locally owned businesses in the capital city of Maryland called *Buy Annapolis*. Inside the directory were coupons worth several thousand dollars to induce users to patronize these businesses. The *Chinook Guides* do this for greenish small businesses in Portland, Seattle, and Minneapolis, and participating companies then put official logos on their stores and in their advertising. The state of Massachusetts publishes an annual directory of foodstuffs produced by in-state farmers and food processors. Various community groups have put the names of local businesses on paper cups (listing local coffee shops), bookmarks (local bookstores), placemats (local restaurants), and in advertisements galore (everything from posters to the sides of buses).

Various groups have declared buy-local days, weeks, or months to help cement good relationships between consumers and local businesses. The Austin Independent Business Association holds a one-day event every November called Austin Unchained. The San Francisco Locally Owned Merchants Alliance convinced the city to declare December 5 to December 10, 2005, Shop Local First Week. Responsible Business of Philadelphia put together a buy-local month in May 2005. Besides spreading consciousness and improving local business, organizers have found these initiatives to be terrific for recruitment for associations of local business.[13]

Another tool to help you buy local, which is present in one form or another in several hundred U.S. communities, is local money.[14] "Local currencies" come in several flavors: paper money systems, like Ithaca Hours; computer-based tallies of exchanges of dollar-denominated transactions through Local Exchange Trading Systems (LETS); and computer-based tallies of exchanges of hours through Time Dollars. The one clear virtue of all of these systems is that Wal-Mart will never participate. The willingness of a business to join these systems turns out to be not a bad litmus test of its LOIS status, because only businesses that are well plugged into a community can actually make use of these forms of exchange. If, like Wal-Mart, your corporate bottom line is driven by sucking in dollars to line the pockets of a half-dozen billionaires living in Arkansas, then local money is useless. If, on the other hand, you spend most of your money on local vendors of goods and services, these tokens can be quite valuable.

Particularly popular in the United States are experiments to print, circulate, and use homegrown money. Participants usually pony up a modest initial fee in real dollars, and are given an equivalent amount of local currency, which can only be spent at participating LOIS businesses. The community's equivalent of the Federal Reserve Board might occasionally give currency to certain businesses, providing essentially a Keynesian boost to the local economy.[15] Perhaps the best-known local-money system is Ithaca Hours, which has issued notes totaling $120,000. They have been used over a decade and a half for many millions of dollars of transactions.[16] Its architects knew their moment had arrived when a local restaurant was robbed, and the thief insisted on both cash and Hours.

Outside the United States, particularly in Western Europe, Australia, and Canada, the most popular form of local money has been LETS. Each community-based LETS system encourages members to enter contracts with one another for goods and services in the national currency, and keeps a public tally of the credits and debits. No bills or coins are ever exchanged. Peer pressure is then applied to those with high debits to contribute more to the system, and to those with high credits to contract with more potential input suppliers. Some fifteen hundred LETS systems now operate worldwide.[17]

Time Dollars were pioneered by Edgar Cahn, a law professor and founder of Legal Aid, to facilitate local exchanges of people's time for human services. For example, a student mows the lawn of an elderly neighbor in exchange for the latter tutoring the former. Hundreds of these systems have proliferated nationwide and demonstrated that even economies that are cash poor can be fabulously wealthy in generosity, love, and solidarity. Because the exchanged hours are deemed to be voluntary, the government neither tracks nor taxes Time Dollars. (But transactions done through alternative currency or LETS are, like barter, fully taxable.)

All of these systems are fabulous tools for educating a community about the local economy, but ultimately—and this is the bad news— they are rather tiny experiments. Even Ithaca Hours, the largest such system, is used for far less than even a single percentage point of purchasing in the region. Two other problems also afflict these otherwise noble efforts.

The first is politics. Many local currency groups position themselves to attract people of "alternative" beliefs—lefties, environmentalists, church activists, labor organizers, cooperative loyalists, anthroposophicals, socialists, greens, feminists, anarchists, vegetarians, New Agers, you name it. Counter-culturalists, eager to opt out of the mainstream economy, have seized upon LETS and other local money systems. This is fascinating from a historical perspective, considering that some of the earlier "free money" advocates were anti-gold, fundamentalist populists like Williams Jennings Bryant, who also had argued against evolution in the Tennessee Scopes Trial. The enthusiastic embrace of local money by the right, which continues to this day, and now by the left, frankly deters adoption by mainstream partners.

A second problem is how to make local money systems self-financing. Sure, assemble enough government bureaucrats, mobilize a critical mass of grants, capture the hearts of a half-dozen Bill Gates, and these activities can proceed apace. Now let's get real. Government budgets are being butchered worldwide. If you're a brilliant schmoozer, you can get foundations and philanthropists to contribute seed capital, but never reliable, ongoing support. Only if local currency systems are designed like any successful business, so that costs are covered through ongoing revenue streams, are they likely to be spread to all kinds of communities, especially those with deep antipathy for government activism and with few philanthropic resources.

(Some smart entrepreneurs have begun to come up with some intriguing solutions to these challenges that we'll look at in chapter 6.)

## A Purchasing Ladder

Even if you can find good tools that help you buy locally, you'll still face some vexing decisions. Since few goods and services are perfectly local, how should you weigh various imperfections? Ultimately, the answers will reflect your own tastes, values, and interests. Here's what my hierarchy of choices looks like and why. Yours, of course, may look quite different.

**1. Buy Less.** In an era of increasing environmental problems and deteriorating ecological life-support systems, my overriding objective is to not waste resources. To the extent that you can grow your own food, walk instead of drive, or avoid impulse purchasing, do it. A self-reliant community ultimately must be grounded in more self-reliant individuals, families, and institutions.

**2. Buy Local — The Triple Crown.** If you must buy, try to find (a) a locally owned store, (b) selling locally made goods, and (c) using locally found inputs. Remember that one of the challenges for a buy-local campaign is to help identify which goods and services score highest on all three scales so that consumers don't have to do this voluminous homework by themselves.

**3. Buy Local — Imperfect Choices.** Finding the perfect storm of local-ness in everything you buy will not usually be possible. The next best approach is to find at least one element that's local. For example, I prefer to buy local produce from Giant than nonlocal organics from Whole Foods Market. Neither is locally owned, but at least one offers me a way to support local farmers.

**4. Buy Regional.** If a reasonable local option is not available, perhaps a regional one is. "Region," of course, is a vague term. It usually refers to an area defined more by ecology, geography, and culture than by legal and jurisdictional boundaries—the Palouse region of eastern Washington and northern Idaho, the Northern Forest across the U.S.-Canadian border, the New York–Washington Corridor. The multiplier from buying regionally will be lower than if you had bought locally, but it will not be irrelevant.

**5. Buy Bi-Local.** If you cannot possibly get a local or regional source for something, try to establish a direct relationship with a more distant LOIS producer. To get fresh, wild Pacific salmon, my friends Oran Hesterman and Lucinda Kurtz organized forty families in their neighborhood in Ann Arbor, Michigan, to form a buyers' club. For each weekly shipment, these Michiganders pay about half the per-pound price local supermarket charge for salmon of lesser quality and put four times as much money per pound into the pockets of the partner fishermen.

**6. Buy Fair Trade.** A variation of bi-local is "fair trade," which connects purchasers of basic products like coffee, cocoa, tea, and clothing in the developed world with responsible producers in the developing world. Usually, "responsible" means removing middle-people and improving labor conditions, but local ownership is, at best, an afterthought. Local First needs to collaborate with Fair Trade networks to change this.

**7. Everything Else.** 'Nuf said.

You may have noticed that my list does not include Buy American, a traditional purchasing regime promoted by the U.S. labor movement and present in the fabric of some state and local contracting laws. This policy never bore much relationship to the welfare of specific communities and, frankly, no longer even does much for American workers. In a country as large as the United States, a purchase in one part of the country is unlikely to have any multiplier benefit in another that's not nearby (hence "Buy Regional"). The typical products to which Buy American campaigns have been applied, moreover, such as automobiles or refrigerators or computers, are usually produced by companies headquartered in the United States with multiple plants overseas using largely foreign components and other inputs. Most of these companies have awful labor practices, increasingly are outsourcing production and laying off U.S. workers, and are decidedly not locally owned.

Another problem with Buy American is that it contains a strand of America First-ism, which runs aground of the global engagement ultimately required by the Small-Mart Revolution. Some promoters of Buy American intend to reward Americans at the expense of others in the world. The Small-Mart Revolution, in contrast, is about mobilizing every community, here and abroad, to become as strong as possible through mutual support for the goal of self-reliance. It presumes that the strength of every American community ultimately comes from the strength of every non-American community. This is a theme we'll return to in the last chapter.

## Choose Wisely

In the popular Stephen Spielberg film *Indiana Jones and the Last Crusade*, the beleaguered hero, having overcome snakes, Nazis, fires, propeller blades, rats, machine guns, and flying swords, now must decide which of several dozen cups is the magical one from which Jesus drank. The several-hundred-year-old guardian of the crypt warns, "Choose wisely." Indiana's nemesis grabs the most ornate of the cups and spontaneously combusts. The guardian glibly pronounces, "He chose poorly."

We, too, are choosing poorly. Our purchasing decisions do not reflect real bargains, but the illusion of bargains. Few of us really take the time to do serious comparative shopping. But here's a basic community calculus to remember: The more of us who buy from LOIS businesses, the more existing LOIS businesses will thrive, the more new entrepreneurs will start new LOIS businesses, the more TINA businesses might consider restructuring themselves into LOIS businesses, and the stronger our community economies and our communities will be.

*Whether or not you ultimately buy local, you should at least ask the right questions before each purchase.* The next time you're tempted to buy an appliance at Sears or Best Buy, visit locally owned competition and compare the prices. Think about the dozens of items you spend most of your money on, and pick one for localization each month. Or just try to buy your next round of holiday gifts locally.

We hold the keys to our own future.

## SMALL-MART REVOLUTION CHECKLIST
# Twenty-seven Items for Consumers

### BEST PLACES TO LOCALIZE SPENDING (AND OFTEN **SAVE** MONEY)

\* *All* the items below can be at least cost neutral with careful shopping, but items with an asterisk actually can yield significant household savings.

1. **Localize Your Home.**\*  Rent from a local landlord, take a mortgage from a local bank, or own your home.
2. **Live in Local Style.**  Use local building materials for your house, with local architectural designs. Furnish with locally fabricated tables, chairs, beds, and couches.
3. **Minimize Automobiles.**\*  Ride your vehicle less by walking, biking, carpooling, living in "walkable communities," and using mass transit.
4. **Fuel Up Locally.**  Make your next car very fuel efficient. Use local bio-diesel and ethanol as they become available.
5. **Local Car Services.**  Find a good local mechanic whom you trust and who charges reasonably. Use the local car wash, local auto-parts store, and local insurer.
6. **Eat Out Locally.**  Avoid chain restaurants, especially fast-food joints that addict children to high-fat, high-salt food.
7. **Buy Fresh.**  Link up with local farmers and hydroponics operators for fruits, vegetables, and meats through farmers markets, co-ops, direct delivery services, and community-supported agriculture (CSA) programs. Rediscover local bakers, butchers, cheese makers, chefs, and caterers.
8. **Support Local Retailers.**  Dump Safeway, Albertson, Wal-Mart, and even Wild Oats for local grocers. Be loyal to competitive local pharmacies, bookstores, hardware stores, coffee roasters, photocopy centers, and so forth.
9. **Play Local.**  Minimize your passion for high-end electronics and television. Spend more time at local sports events, health clubs, playgrounds, pools, parks, games, films, plays, puppet shows, dancing, music, and debate leagues. If you must gamble, favor local lotteries, casinos, and horse tracks.
10. **Heal Local.**  Use local doctors, dentists, therapists, acupuncturists, and nursing homes.
11. **Live Healthy.**\*  Emphasize local nutrition, exercise, emotional balance, and spiritual nurturing, all of which minimize the need for nonlocal pharmaceuticals.
12. **Sign a Living Will.**\*  Have the hard conversation with your family about end-of-life decisions to save them and you from expensive, nonlocal life-support systems.

13. **Minimize Household Energy Use.\*** Add insulation, double pane the windows, buy compact fluorescent lights, replace the inefficient furnace and appliances, and do the 101 well-known items that cut purchases of nonlocal electricity, oil, and natural gas. Better still, put photovoltaics or a wind-electric generator on your roof and sell your electricity back to the utility.
14. **Give Local.** Target charitable giving at local causes and nonprofits.
15. **Axe Bad Habits.\*** Minimize consumption of booze (except local microbrews and wines), cigarettes, and naughty Internet sites, all of which are hard to localize.
16. **Educate Locally.** Support local public schools. If they are beyond repair, send your kids to local private schools.
17. **Read Locally.** Buy books from local authors or local publishers, sold at local bookstores. Advertise in the local papers. Become a regular at the local library.
18. **Honor Junk.\*** Pare down your piles of "stuff" by repairing, reusing, and refurbishing. Substitute hand-me-down clothing, especially for young kids who never heard of Nordstroms. Give more gifts from the heart and fewer gift certificates to Best Buy.
19. **Rent More.\*** Rent or lease more big ticket items, like Zip cars. Create neighborhood tool sheds for shared lawnmowers or snow blowers.
20. **Recycle More.** Send your paper, glass, and plastic to the local recycler not only because it's good for the environment but also because it gives local industries affordable local inputs.

### TOOLS TO ASSIST LOCAL PURCHASING

1. **Directories of Local Business.** Create lists for your neighbors in print, online, in newspaper ads, and on coffee cups.
2. **Directories of Local Products.** Highlight, again in print or online, the many locally made goods or locally provided services that are available.
3. **Local Labels.** Develop an insignia of local ownership, so that you know if a store is locally owned or if a product is locally made.
4. **Buy Local Days.** Or weeks, months, or seasons, all of which can provide the basis for a buy-local campaign.
5. **Local Currency.** Mobilize your community to print its own "money" that can only be used by local businesses and consumers.
6. **LETS.** Create computerized trading systems, which are especially popular in Europe, that encourage locals to trade with one another without touching mainstream money.
7. **Time Dollars.** Set up a computerized system for tracking volunteer hours as a way of legitimizing and expanding such contributions for the community.

★★★★★★★★★★★★★★★★★★★★★★★★★★★★★★★★★★★★★★★★★★★

# INVESTORS

Do you bank locally? When I give talks, I usually ask the audience this question and most hands instantly pop up. (This would not be true for the U.S. population generally, but those who come to learn about localization are naturally predisposed to putting their money in local financial institutions.) I then ask how many have pension funds. Almost every adult pays something into Social Security, but most think only about private pensions, so about half the hands appear. Then I ask how many of their fund managers are investing in locally owned business. Usually, only one or two hands are left up, and I must explain to these well-intentioned souls that, most likely, they are mistaken.

Although place-based businesses in the United States account for 58 percent of the economy, very few investment dollars find their way into LOIS businesses. Even those of us who want to invest in the Small-Mart Revolution have no reasonable way to do so. Sure, I could knock on the door of my favorite local entrepreneur and ask if she would be willing to let me put one thousand dollars into her business, and she might be able to figure out some way to restructure her company to accommodate my wishes. But putting our life savings in any one, two, or three LOIS businesses this way requires lots of expensive paperwork by you and the entrepreneur. It's also not very prudent. The risk that any one business will perform poorly or go belly up is simply too great. Most of us do not invest for a living and are looking for simple, cookie-cutter, low-cost, low-risk ways to protect and grow our savings for our kids' college education or for our retirement. We typically accomplish this by putting our money into diversified funds made up of the stocks and bonds from hundreds or even thousands of individual companies.

Millions of Americans now entrust their portfolios to mutual funds. And if you ask them to find you a stock, a bond, or a fund that specializes in local small business, they will look at you as if you've just arrived from Mars.

Beyond the quirky adventurism of a few noble LOIS-friendly angel investors, institutional funds that specialize in LOIS businesses simply do not exist in the United States. A handful of hedge funds and venture funds are beginning to dip their toes into LOIS waters, such as the Mesa Fund in New Mexico, but these are only open to rich people—so-called "accredited investors." A dozen or so community development venture capital funds admirably target low-income entrepreneurs or businesses in low-income communities, but at the end of the day they are looking for an exit through a public offering that will almost always destroy local ownership. If you have a pension fund tied to your workplace, the fund manager will tell you that there are no local investment options, and even if there were, he would be violating his fiduciary duties by investing in such businesses because they are so risky and unprofitable. In addition, even funds bragging about their social responsibility are, in fact, only screening out the worst TINA companies, such as those involved in nuclear weapons, tobacco, or sweatshops; none are screening *in* LOIS businesses. It's fair to say that when it comes to LOIS the entire securities industry is in the Stone Age.

This is what economists might concede is a "misallocation of resources," though I have yet to find one who has actually used the term to acknowledge what is, frankly, a huge pro-TINA bias in our capital markets. If 58 percent of the economy is place-based, then, roughly speaking, 58 percent of investment capital should be going into place-based businesses. But because investors are systematically shut out from more than half the economy, LOIS businesses wind up being underfinanced and TINA businesses overfinanced. When too much money enters public markets, as happened with tech stocks on the NASDAQ Exchange a few years back, a bubble develops, and when it bursts, the assets of many companies and investors evaporate. When too little money enters, as is true for LOIS companies now, fabulous opportunities for strengthening communities and profiting personally are lost.

Like the old Aesop fable about the eagle killed from an arrow made with its own shed feathers, those of us committed to strengthening our local economy are, out of necessity, putting our retirement monies into Fortune 500 companies and starving our favorite homegrown companies. Ending this self-destructive behavior and making sure that LOIS firms get their fair share of the nation's investment dollars are essential requirements for the Small Mart Revolution. But this kind of "ownership society," to borrow the term being used by President George W. Bush, will take years to achieve.

So let's start with the simple things you can do right now.

## Starving the Bankasaurs

Some of your household's biggest expenditures are for shelter, transportation, and college, and these all involve borrowing (see chapter 4). If you are using one of the bankasaurs, your interest payments on home, car, and school loans are almost certainly flying out of your community and taking with them potential multiplier benefits. Banking locally is therefore a critical first step to localizing your own capital.

The news about community banking is mixed. The bad news is that many frenzied years of consolidation have greatly reduced our banking choices. In 2003 the single largest business category of mergers and acquisitions, by total value, was commercial banks and bank holding companies.[1] Between 1990 and 2003 the number of financial institutions in the United States shrank by a third, even as assets more than doubled.[2] Yet, in 2003 many relatively small institutions with assets under $100 million in assets remained—3,911 commercial banks, 479 savings and loans, and 8,248 credit unions—undoubtedly boosted by their superior performance over the bankasaurs (see chapter 3).[3] Almost anywhere a careful shopper can still find at least one bank that is at least regionally owned. Still, the assets of the small banks account for less than 4 percent of the entire banking sector.

Capital-hungry LOIS entrepreneurs should, like consumers, prefer getting business loans from community financial institutions, since the resulting multiplier kick will increase the spending power of consumers to purchase their goods and services. Or they might turn to an expanding number of community loan funds, state business borrowing programs, or local funds enjoying federal designations like a

Community-Development Financial Institution or a New Market Fund. Many rely on local family members or friends. Members of certain ethnic communities, like the Koreans, have developed formidable credit circles. Ted Nace created a reserve fund for his first for-profit, Peachpit Press, by agreeing to pay friends, family, colleagues, and investors 7 percent.[4] They could withdraw their funds at any time, but most lenders liked that they were getting double the interest that banks were paying.

Where options are limited, LOIS entrepreneurs can be forgiven for grabbing capital from whoever will give it to get their business up and running. Some will turn to the bankasaurs, who are legally obligated, under the Community Reinvestment Act (CRA), to invest locally.[5] Others will simply turn to high-interest credit cards.[6]

While lending discrimination persists against the poor and non-whites, the reality is that most entrepreneurs with some kind of decent credit track record and a plausible business plan can get $5,000 to $25,000 in startup capital. For those who can't, there are microlending programs sponsored by nonprofits like Accion, though too many of these programs have surprisingly high interest rates and, unlike their Third World cousins, have become big money losers.[7] More formidable gaps in available loan capital occur when a successful LOIS startup needs $50,000 to $250,000 to expand to the next level of operation. Faced with the prospect of putting her house on the line, the entrepreneur often decides to slow down expansion until she can amass the needed capital through earnings.

There remains much to do to strengthen and spread the community banking industry, yet the big questions have essentially been solved. We know how to create such banks at the right scale, and we know how to operate them profitably to benefit local consumers, students, and entrepreneurs. It's really up to us, as consumers and as entrepreneurs, to choose them—wisely—over the bankasaurs.

The same cannot be said for the rest of the financial universe. Even if all the hard work of community-banking proponents brilliantly succeeds—if *every* bank, thrift, and credit union were localized, and LOIS firms received many trillions of new loan dollars annually—TINA could still win. In 2003 U.S. households had $34 trillion in financial assets, according to data from the Federal Reserve.[8] Only about one in seven dollars are in depository institutions (primarily banks, savings and loans, and credit unions). The rest—that is, about $29 trillion—is in stocks, bonds, mutual funds, and insurance funds, the managers of which operate with no CRA-like obligation to invest locally and have not even begun to conceive of the possibility.

Two exceptions are worth noting. The Philadelphia Reinvestment Fund makes it possible to park retirement monies in funds that are re-lent exclusively to local businesses, commercial real estate, affordable housing, workforce development, and sustainable energy projects in Philadelphia.[9] And Leslie Christian, a successful fund manager in the Pacific Northwest, is now raising capital for a holding company called Upstream 21, to create what she calls the Berkshire Hathaway for small, regional businesses.[10] The fund will buy LOIS businesses, improve them, and ultimately spin them off into higher-performing entities. Even though these efforts constitute important baby steps in the right direction, what's needed are giant leaps.

## Thank God for Mississippi!

This is the mantra New Mexicans recite when they hear that their state has the second worst rate of poverty in the country. Were it not for the rich enclave of Santa Fe, the state would probably be dead last. Over the past three years, I have been studying capital market gaps for LOIS business in the state. Superficially, New Mexico seems like a cornu-copia for cutting-edge Southwestern fashion and culture, high-end chili cooking, an oasis of arts and crafts, and a technological center with Los Alamos, Sandia, and several other national laboratories. And yet the New Mexico economy is remarkably hollow, highly dependent on sales of dwindling resources of gas, coal, and minerals and on fed-eral dollars that pour into military labs and Native American reserva-tions, both of which have poor local multipliers.

New Mexican households hold roughly $165 billion worth of savings, which in principle could be invested in the state's LOIS businesses.[11] About $56 billion of these savings—deposits and equity in non-corporate business—represent assets with a relatively higher degree of local ownership. The other $109 billion goes into institutions with almost no local content—bonds (including Treasury Bills), corporate equities, mutual funds, life insurance funds, pension funds, and trusts (which are obligated to invest in the preceding items). Even though most of the economy of New Mexico is place-based, only about a third of all equity investment is going into place-based business. This means that many investors, rather than placing their funds in the businesses with the best track records and the best shot at improving the New Mexican economy, stick all their money into available TINA options.

The gap is actually much wider. Nationally, non-place-based firms pay 55 percent of payrolls; in New Mexico they pay only 47 percent. That means a greater percentage of the New Mexican economy is made up of small, place-based businesses. And does a third of New Mexican savings stay local? It seems dubious. As is true nationally, New Mexico's banking sector has seen massive takeovers, consolidations, and mergers that make it likely that only a small fraction of these savings stay in state. The gap between promising small-business investment opportunities and equity capital to meet them is therefore huge.

Even if the reluctance of strictly private institutions to take steps to fill this gap is understandable, the unwillingness of public institutions to do so is not. Take, for example, the Public Employees Retirement Association (PERA) of New Mexico, which runs the single largest pension fund in the state.[12] Public pension funds have a long history of injecting "social criteria" in their investments before private funds are prepared to do so. During the 1980s the pension funds from 25 states and 164 localities divested funds from businesses involved in apartheid South Africa, a movement that precipitated one of the most important bloodless revolutions of the twentieth century.[13] Of the $9.4 billion entrusted to PERA in 2004, however, less than two-tenths of 1 percent went to locally owned business in New Mexico.

The situation is little better in another set of public funds run by the State Investment Council (SIC). Historically, New Mexico has been blessed with two unusual income streams: one from "land grants" made by the state to various institutions, which pays leasing and rental fees for use of public land; and the other from severance payments on extractions of oil, gas, coal, metals, and other precious minerals from state-owned lands. All together, these funds total about $13 billion, nearly all of which is placed in traditional stocks, bonds, and treasury notes with little connection to New Mexico.[14]

To its credit, the SIC has reserved a sliver of finance—about $94 million—for "economically targeted investments" in businesses with major contacts in New Mexico. This doesn't mean that New Mexicans own or control these firms, only that a major plant or office sits in the state.[15] A subdivision of the SIC, called the Small Business Investment Corporation, has more conscientiously embraced the idea of supporting small businesses based in New Mexico. But $94 million of a $13 billion fund represents one half of 1 percent. The SIC is placing four times more investments in emerging markets—that is, countries like Malaysia and Singapore—than it's putting in New Mexican business. No wonder the state's economy is in such awful financial shape.

## Revolutionizing Capital Markets

Why do investors and capital markets shun LOIS? There are at least six culprits who bear most of the responsibility.

Part of the problem originates from LOIS entrepreneurs themselves. For understandable reasons, they treasure their independence and structure their businesses as sole-proprietorships, partnerships, or privately held companies so that they can retain control. This impulse toward autonomy, however, deprives the rest of us of LOIS investment opportunities and forces us to put our money into the TINA alternatives. Were there an easy and inexpensive way of doing so, many entrepreneurs actually would gladly give others modest stakes in their company in exchange for new capital. After all, a good many LOIS entrepreneurs are willing to put their houses and life savings on the line just for a line of credit from a commercial bank.[16] But standing in the way is a second problem, a bureaucratic nightmare known as U.S. securities law.

Sure, if a wealthy investor comes knocking on the door with an open wallet, an entrepreneur certainly will find a way to be accommodating. A sole proprietor might convert his or her business into an S-corporation or a limited liability corporation. A partnership always has room for another general or limited partner. A privately held company can issue more stock for a new investor. But if the investor is not wealthy, U.S. securities laws forbid many of these investments unless and until a mountain of paperwork is filed.[17] A firm receiving such an investment must make filings at the federal level and in every state in which it sells securities, and the legal expenses for this can easily exceed fifty to a hundred thousand dollars per state.

The current threshold for an "accredited" investor—that is, sufficiently wealthy for a company to be excused from expensive filings—is that you must be worth $1 million or earn $200,000 per year ($300,000 if you count your spouse's income).[18] That means that fewer than 2 percent of American households are presumed by the government to be smart enough to understand the risks involved in investing in private companies. For everyone else, the government insists on protecting you by effectively banning your being an investor. Since it's unlikely that a bunch of small investors will pony up enough to cover even the legal costs, small businesses logically conclude that going public is simply not worth the hassle.

What is not widely appreciated is that the paperwork and expenses for issuing publicly traded stock shrink considerably when the total amount of capital sought is under $5 million, and even more so if the capital sought is under $1 million. Mark Perlmutter, founder of Micro-Angels, has developed a cottage industry around helping small entrepreneurs create small-business stock issues on the cheap and runs investor clubs that specialize in buying and selling these securities.[19]

Several U.S. communities have taken advantage of these nooks and crannies in securities law to create community-owned alternatives to Wal-Marts called Mercantiles, or Mercs. When the 5,200-resident community of Powell, Wyoming, lost its general merchandise store, Stage, in 1999, and failed to lure a big-box store to take its place, it resolved to create its own store.[20] Its leading businesspeople decided to follow the model of Little Muddy Dry Goods in Plentywood, Montana, which sold twenty shares of $10,000 each to local partners to secure the start-up capital of $200,000. They formed a committee and sold stock in the yet-to-be-formed business for $500 a share. The editor of the local newspaper hawked the stock in his regular column, and ad campaigns contained testimonials for various stock purchasers whose ages ranged from nine to ninety-four. After $325,000 was raised from 328 investors, the store opened in July 2002, selling mostly clothing, shoes, and accessories. The Powell Merc made money "from day one," according to its board chair, Ken Witzeling, a retired pharmacist, and cleared a half million dollars of sales in its first year. It has since become a tourist destination, as well as an inspiration for other communities. The model has since been replicated by Washakie Wear in Worland, Wyoming, Our Store in Torrington, also in Wyoming, and the Garnet Mercantile in Ely, Nevada.

If you wanted to create a small-stock general store in New Mexico, the state has streamlined the process in a law called Public Law 27-J. Put on paper your business plan, fill out a few simple forms, send in $350, and—voila!—you can issue stock.

But even in New Mexico, a third problem looms large: How might a New Mexican small business that created local stock on the cheap actually sell its shares? When a big company goes public, an underwriter usually steps in and, for a flat fee or a percentage, sells the "initial public offering" through a network of broker-dealers. But few broker-dealers or underwriters, not just in New Mexico but everywhere, consider the small potatoes of, say, a one million dollar stock offering worth the transaction costs of performing due diligence on a small company. How, then, can a small business sell its shares directly to the public? No marketplace like eBay or the "bulletin boards" on the national stock exchanges exists for selling LOIS public offerings, and few small business people have the time, energy, or focus to negotiate around all the regulatory barriers to set something like this up from scratch. No dedicated stock market for LOIS business exists either. So, from the standpoint of a New Mexican business, why bother to use 27-J when selling the stock—rather than developing your business—has to become your full-time job?

In fact, none of the critical features of TINA capital markets currently exist for LOIS firms. For example, the absence of the traditional evaluating institutions, like Moody's or Standard & Poors, makes it hard to get objective information about the value of LOIS stock shares. Buyers, of course, face the same problems evaluating thousands of penny stocks that come and go onto the national stock exchanges. Stock exchanges in small countries, like Ljubljanska Exchange in Slovenia, arguably have even less demand than a U.S. state, and their securities get even less scrutiny than what stocks from New Mexico might get. Still, until a combination of capital-market pioneers and visionary state regulators set up the basic institutional features of a virtual state stock exchange, these missing pieces in the LOIS capital markets are likely to scare off investors who will always want to know how, ultimately, they are going to sell their shares to other buyers. Once I buy these shares of Joe's Deli down the street, how can I exit and cash out?

A fourth challenge is the absence of so-called intermediaries to diversify one's LOIS investments. Even if Joe's Deli seems like a gold mine, no LOIS-minded investor should put more than a small fraction of his or her money into it. There's a need for a wide range of new intermediaries to present LOIS investors with choices that fit their own particular tolerance for risk. LOIS venture funds might focus on a small number of high-growth, high-risk businesses, say the possibility that Joe's slurpies would become the rage in China. LOIS hedge funds might combine one set of high-risk LOIS investments with another (hopefully with greater integrity than many of their mainstream cousins). Both venture and hedge funds, however, are legally open only to very wealthy investors.

To make LOIS investments available to the general public, pension and mutual funds must come aboard, which requires overcoming a fifth challenge. The U.S. Employment Retirement Investment Security Act (ERISA) sets out rules of fiduciary responsibility for the managers of pension and mutual funds managing 401(k), 403(b), and other employee savings accounts.[21] The absence of a track record from hedge or venture funds investing in small business means that pension and mutual fund managers believe they risk violating their ERISA-defined fiduciary responsibilities if they put money into small business. Of course, this is a chicken-egg problem: you need a track record to attract institutional investment, but without institutional investment there is no track record. The problem is as much psychological as legal, since almost every state defines "fiduciary responsibility" in broad terms. The largest public pension fund in the country, CalPERS, has already undertaken some modest experiments investing in California-owned low-income housing.[22] The bigger obstacle is the conservative attitude held by most fund managers.

The sixth challenge, therefore, is overcoming the beliefs of many investment specialists—supported more by faith in TINA than by data—that LOIS businesses are poor investments, because they are both too risky and not sufficiently profitable. One reason LOIS firms *seem* so risky is that investors automatically focus, incorrectly, on small-business start-ups, which *are* risky. But the LOIS businesses most likely to be searching for equity investment will be those with many years of profitable experience already under their belts looking for resources for expansion.

Another concern goes to the very heart of local investing: aren't investments in any one place inherently risky because they are vulnerable to the inevitable ups and downs of the local business cycle? Isn't it better to diversify places? Not necessarily. Done well, place-based investments actually can reduce risk. Local investment allows investors to inspect the company in which they are investing, to "reality test" claims made on paper, sample the goods and services, and sniff out WorldCom-style fraud by talking with company insiders. Local investment gives investors the possibility of being the key consumers and allows LOIS businesses to harness their enthusiasm as marketers and promoters. Local investment in small communities or neighborhoods yields significant multiplier benefits for the community, improving the business climate for all local investments. When South Shore Bank decided to extend home-improvement loans to ten thousand adjacent properties in a low-income neighborhood in Chicago, it was able to raise overall property values, enhance the underlying security of the loan, and reduce the portfolio's risk. Finally, localized investments offer the possibility of investing in multiple businesses that buy and sell from one another, perhaps in the component firms of an industrial ecology park (where the waste heat from a smelter can become an input for a greenhouse). Such investments, if carefully structured, can reduce the risk of any one firm failing.

Okay, but what about profitability? In fact, sole proprietorships and partnerships (which tend to be LOIS firms) generate three to seven times more net income for every dollar of business than do corporations (which tend to be TINA firms).[23] The real problem here is investors' expectations. We live in a peculiar moment when memories about the years when various stock markets yielded double-digit gains (1998–2000) are sharper than the years when the same markets yielded double-digit losses (2001–2002). Between 1900 and 2005, in fact, the inflation-adjusted rate of return for the Dow Jones Industries has been about 5.5 percent per year. Investors more averse to risk these days can earn 2 to 5 percent in certificates of deposits, 3 to 4 percent in money market accounts, 5 to 6 percent in high-grade corporate bonds, and 3 to 5 percent in tax-free public bonds. A recent study from Princeton found that the returns on highly touted venture and hedge funds between 1996 and 2003 were, in fact, no better than Standard & Poors' 500 index funds, and many have recently gone belly up.[24] No one really knows the performance of these funds, because they—and their reporting standards—are largely unregulated. The point is that a reasonable expectation for an investor, historically, should be in the range of 3 to 6 percent per year, not 15 to 20 percent. With this more sober standard, what some call a "living rate of return," many LOIS businesses are fabulous bets.

A serious effort by any state, or even a large city, to overcome these six challenges could make enormous progress in bridging the capital gap afflicting LOIS businesses. Enter Maine Securities, an initiative my colleagues at the Training & Development Corporation and I are developing to make it easier for people like you and me to invest in LOIS businesses. (A similar effort is under way in Northern California.) We envision our first major step to be the creation of an underwriting company that helps LOIS businesses, maybe a dozen each year, go public within the state. Only Maine residents will be able to buy the stock, which effectively will keep ownership of participating firms local. We will create a streamlined process for companies to meet the legal and administrative requirements of going public, then help them keep on top of the otherwise burdensome quarterly filing requirements for public companies.

As more and more LOIS businesses go public, other institutions will gradually reshape the face of the capital markets in the state. Specialized venture and hedge funds will form to invest in local stocks. Mutual and pension funds will then invest in these local venture and hedge funds. It's even conceivable that an electronic platform might be created on the Internet to facilitate the trading of these stocks, something like a Maine Stock Exchange. And unlike existing stock exchanges, this one might have the kinds of reforms many experts have been suggesting—without a prayer of success—for the New York Stock Exchange and the NASDAQ. A Tobin Tax—a small fee, between a tenth and a quarter of a percent, placed on all stocks held for less than, perhaps, six months—might be imposed to discourage speculation.[25] No business might be allowed on the exchange unless it paid living wages and met certain sustainability criteria. Any firm guilty of fraud or other felonies might be banned.

Entrepreneurs who still are unsure of the value of "going public" locally might consider two powerful advantages local stock can confer. First, a direct public offerings provides LOIS proprietors nearing retirement with another option for exit and cashing out, but one that does not require selling out to a national chain and destroying the value of the company for a community.

Second, entrepreneurs could see an escalation of value in their companies. A common way the value of a company is estimated these days is as a multiple of its annual earnings. The valuation of all the traded shares of stock for a typical company on the New York Stock Exchange is about fifteen times annual earnings (or, more formally, a "price-to-earnings ratio" of fifteen). But if you were to buy a company through a private, one-on-one negotiation, you probably would pay closer to three times annual earnings.[26] Are publicly traded companies inherently more valuable? Not at all. As an owner of a public company, you are paying a premium for liquidity, the freedom to buy and sell shares at a moment's notice. A privately held company is worth less to you as an investor because the timing and speed with which you can execute a sale of your stock is limited. You may not be able to sell your shares at all for five, ten, or more years. My guess is that the liquidity of state stock markets would probably fall somewhere between national stock exchanges and private deals, maybe with a price-to-earnings rate of seven to one. That extra value, seven times earnings instead of three times, would be pocketed by both the shareholders and the LOIS entrepreneurs. Clever LOIS companies might also be able to issue two types of stock, common shares on the state exchange and preferred shares on a national exchange, which would still keep working control of the company local.

To summarize: Small-Mart revolutionaries need to make it easier and cheaper for LOIS businesses to create shareholder opportunities; we need to create incentives for underwriters and broker-dealers to take on LOIS securities; we need to set up virtual stock exchanges for intrastate selling and exchanging of securities; we need to help hedge, venture, and index funds move into LOIS securities; and we need work with pension and mutual fund managers to rethink their concerns about fiduciary responsibility. Together, these actions could dramatically transform the equity landscape for small business. And there's no reason why further capital contributions to these new intermediaries could not come from banks, insurance companies, and other institutions eager to demonstrate their support for a local economy, creating win-win solutions for everyone.

## A Real Ownership Society

Local stock markets invite unprecedented collaboration between conservatives and progressives. Conservatives will like the focus on small business, market solutions, and state empowerment, as well as on the yet-to-be-defined "ownership society." Progressives will like the focus on community ownership and empowerment. Yet, stunningly, these ideas are totally absent from chambers of commerce, city halls, and the corridors of Congress.

Instead, the nation is currently in the midst of an *Alice in Wonderland* debate on the future of Social Security. Legitimate questions about how to improve the solvency of the system by tinkering with levels of contributions and mandatory retirement ages have been conflated with ideologically driven proposals for privatizing parts of it. From the standpoint of localization, the entire debate offers nothing constructive. The Social Security trust fund is currently being drained as fast as it is filled, with the periodic sale of government bonds providing some financial flexibility. To the extent that these bonds are financing national deficits caused by corporate welfare for TINA and tax breaks for the least deserving, it's hard to embrace the status quo. All the privatization schemes being floated envision some fraction of Social Security monies supporting TINA securities that are already being overbought.

What's really needed is a fundamental realignment of Social Security trust funds with local business. We should give every state responsibility for reinvesting its share of trust-fund collections and allow— even demand—that each state invest in LOIS businesses that are most likely to support the very people who the trust funds were designed to benefit.

But an ownership society should not stop with Social Security. One of the perverse features of federal and state securities laws is that, in the name of protecting the little guy from dishonest dealers, 98 percent of us are essentially locked out of the investment world. We cannot buy private stock issues, and we cannot invest in hedge funds or venture capital funds. Do we feel safer? Or just dissed? There are 1,001 less onerous ways of protecting the little guy. For example, an investor could be limited to invest less than one percent of his previous year's income in any one company. That would make it easy for neighborhood businesses to sell one hundred dollar shares without posing a serious threat to anyone's economic security.

We need a Boston Tea Party in securities law that makes it easier and cheaper for small businesses to issue stock, and easier and cheaper for low- and moderate-income individuals to buy stock, either directly or through intermediaries. Only then, when all household savings are available for local investment, and not just a small percentage of our bank savings, will all cost-effective local business opportunities have the opportunity to flourish.

★★★★★★★★★★★★★★★★★★★★★★★★★★★★★★★★★★★★★★★★★★★

# Fourteen Items for Investors

★★★★★★★★★★★★★★★★★★★★★★★★★★★★★★★★★★★★★★★★★★★

1. **Bank Local.** Favor local financial institutions like credit unions, small thrifts, and small commercial banks, and especially make sure your biggest loans—for your home, car, and college—come from them.

2. **Multiply Local Banks.** If you can't find a good local bank, help start one; credit unions are the easiest and cheapest.

3. **Localize Mainstream Banks.** Use the Community Reinvestment Act to evaluate how well nonlocal banks are recirculating your savings locally and to pressure them to improve their performance.

4. **Cut Up Credit Cards.** Remember that nearly all credit card processing is nonlocal and wastes precious local money on nonlocal high-interest payments.

5. **Expand Small Business Loan Funds.** Mobilize local banks, philanthropists, foundations, and government agencies to expand the assets of revolving loan funds for small business.

6. **Create Micro Funds.** If your community lacks small business funds, set up one in partnership with your bank. Several dozen depositors can pony up money, create a lending pool, and then team up with the bank to administer the loans to whoever *you* think is creditworthy.

7. **Invest Local.** Invest more of your savings in local business as a cooperative member, a program-related investor in a nonprofit, a limited partner, or a shareholder.

8. **Local Venture and Hedge Funds.** If you're a securities industry professional, think about creating a local investment fund that specializes in high-performing local businesses.

9. **Technical Assistance for Small Stock Companies.** Create a company that helps small businesses issue local stock (that is, tradable only intrastate) on the cheap, and then handles the ongoing reporting and due-diligence requirements.

10. **Local Underwriters.** Set up a local investment company that helps successful local firms create local stock issues, and then sells the securities intrastate for a fee.

11. **Local Stock Markets.** Put together an electronic trading platform to help local business investors find and trade with one another.

12. **Local Mutual Funds.** Once a critical mass of local securities are issued, assemble diversified funds of these securities and make them available to local retirement-plan managers.

13. **Local Investment Advisers.** Set up a firm that specializes in helping investors evaluate the performance of local business.

14. **Pension Fund Advocacy.** Pressure your pension fund, whether private or public, to invest in local real estate, local business, local venture and hedge funds, and local mutual funds.

★★★★★★★★★★★★★★★★★★★★★★★★★★★★★★★★★★★★★★★★★★

# six

# ENTREPRENEURS

If I remade the classic film *The Graduate*, the single word of business advice I would offer Dustin Hoffman's character would be not "plastics" but "chicken." Around the country small poultry producers are beating the odds. Eberly Farms, based in Amish country in Pennsylvania, sells a mean organic chicken. So does Nature's Premiere in Michigan, Buddy's Natural Chicken in Texas, Real Chicken in New Mexico, and Petaluma Poultry in California. With the world now on high alert for a deadly avian flu pandemic, it seems likely that Americans are going to become extremely demanding that the poultry meat they put on the table is raised carefully, cleanly, and healthily. That's bad news for a global industry notorious for producing broilers quick, dirty, and cheap, but great news for LOIS entrepreneurs eager to reinvent the poultry industry. Care to become one?

On the surface it might seem that the poultry industry has such a large economy of scale that LOIS competition is all but impossible. Nationally, Tyson controls nearly a quarter of the domestic broiler market, and the top five producers control 60 percent.[1] The ability of these large firms to convert corn and soy into a reasonably tasty protein that costs just over one dollar per pound appears unassailable. But so-called Big Chicken is very vulnerable to defections by consumers once they become aware of its abysmal business practices.

Let's start with the people who raise the chickens for these gigantic firms. The poultry industry engages growers as independent contractors, much as households hire painters or kitchen builders. The big operators, called "integrators" because they have vertically integrated all elements of the business, provide these growers with chicks, feed, and medications (charging them full freight), leave it to the growers to raise the chickens for six or seven weeks, then buy the chickens back at an agreed-upon price. Superficially, this appears to be a very good deal for growers. "Half the hours for twice the pay," many were told. Just do a reasonable job raising the chickens, feel free to go fishing or manage some other lucrative business, and leave it to us to provide the inputs, process the birds, and sell them to the consumers. Moreover, as an independent grower, you can walk away from the business anytime you want, presumably when your bank account is as fat as a Thanksgiving turkey and you're ready to retire.

But there turned out to be a couple of catches. To get started, a grower has to spend $125,000 on a chicken house. If something goes wrong with the flock—an outbreak of avian flu, for example—the grower has to pay for the chicks and feed, even if the chicks provided had poor genetics or weak immune systems. The companies also disavow the manure—proper disposal is the grower's problem. And every contract is only as long as the growing season; renewal is presumed, but not guaranteed.

The economics of this system wind up never looking even remotely like the original promises. An investigative report by the *Baltimore Sun* on the plight of growers on the eastern shore of Maryland found that "a new chicken farmer today can expect an annual net income of only $8,160—about half the poverty level for a family of four—until he has paid off the 15-year loan he took to get into the business, and even that estimate may be overly optimistic. Fewer than half of [the region's] farmers say they're making enough to meet expenses."[2]

If the pay is so lousy, why don't growers just quit? The problem is the mortgages they hold. Unless growers are prepared to abandon their farms, they've got to find some way to pay off the houses. The better answer, many decide, is to build more houses. With two, four, maybe six houses—each with twenty-five thousand chickens at a time—a grower can begin to see a better return. Half-time work becomes triple time.

Quick throughput is the overriding value. Imagine spending your entire life in a crowded subway car without a restroom and with a water spigot and cereal trough to keep you alive. That's essentially what chickens raised by these growers do over their six-week life. They must endure this misery without fresh air or sunlight, while they peck incessantly at one another 24-7. The stench is horrendous and the dust-filled air almost unbreathable.

Once the chickens are fully grown, catchers come onto the scene. They are also independent contractors, with low pay and no benefits, and are trucked in to pack the houses at about midnight, when the winged creatures are less active. Good catchers can grab four clawing chickens in each hand, an essential skill since they are paid by the bird. Having to work in intense clouds of dust and ammonia, all for what turns out to be just above a minimum wage, few catchers last very long in the business. With scarred hands and scorched lungs, they soon seek out other work.

Next the chickens go to a processing plant, where they are slaughtered and put on a line that can move as many as 150 birds per minute. In a split second, line workers must make judgment calls about just where to make appropriate cuts in each carcass, and USDA inspectors must spot which of the birds whizzing by are diseased. These production workers, also paid just above minimum wage, experience one of the highest rates of repetitive stress disorders in the country. Try just touching this page 150 times in a minute, and you'll appreciate the problem.

Once consumers become aware of these problems, they either become vegetarians or, more likely, begin to look for alternative companies that treat their chickens and workers more humanely. Enter the smaller scale competitors. One of the most successful in recent years has been Bell & Evans, based in Pennsylvania. Here's how it markets its product on its website:[3]

*About the company:* "Unlike companies run by conglomerates, where the day-to-day operating decisions are made by managers in remote locations and management strategies are based on the bottom line, we are a family owned and operated company."

*About the chickens:* "We keep our chickens comfortable at all times, in more than 150 spacious and environmentally controlled houses. Unlike other growers, we don't subject our chickens to the stresses of overcrowding or to wide variations in temperature. . . . This precise control of temperature—along with our practice of cleaning out and disinfecting every chicken house before each new flock arrives—prevents many diseases and eliminates the need for antibiotics."

*About their diet:* "At Bell & Evans, our chickens are raised without antibiotics on a proper, 100% natural, all-vegetable diet fortified with vitamins and minerals. Unlike many other chicken growers, we never feed our chicken junk food like rendered meat scraps; bone, feather or fish meal; or animal fats, oils, and grease. You wouldn't eat that stuff and we don't think the chickens should either. . . . Our chickens get their energy from locally grown Extruded Soybeans and Expeller Pressed Soybeans only. . . ."

By highlighting the virtues of the company, its local character, its kinder treatment of its animals, and its dedication to quality, Bell & Evans has become spectacularly successful even though its product costs nearly double what the industry charges for what some call "bionic bird." Its annual sales, including to Whole Foods, Chipotle Grill, and Panera Bread, are now $140 million. When its latest plant expansions are complete, the company will be processing 300,000 chickens per day.

The ways in which Bell & Evans has out-clawed Big Chicken highlights some of the tools LOIS entrepreneurs are using to make themselves more competitive. They are emphasizing quality over price and taking advantage of consumers' growing interest in local and green products. This chapter explores these strategies and many others, and ends with the story of how your humble narrator became smitten with dreams of chicken entrepreneurship.

## The Local Niche

The single most important strategy LOIS businesses use to compete against TINA is to differentiate their goods and services. TINA firms are likely to dominate commodity categories, where shaving down labor costs or employing a new assembly-line technology can have a major effect on the bottom line. But wherever tastes are localized, as noted in chapter 3, LOIS firms have the competitive advantage in producing them in just the right way and at just the right time. Even where tastes are national or global, local companies can capture the hearts and minds of local consumers through good marketing.

Consumers are getting bored with the same old brand names found in chain stores and shopping malls. Commenting on the growing interest of consumers in boutiques, Bob Michaels, president of General Growth Properties, an owner of 240 malls in forty-four states, says, "Retail is about change, and if you don't bring in something unique, you're going to miss the boat."[4]

Sociologist Paul Ray, who pioneered the concept of "cultural creatives," estimates that 36 percent of Americans (45 percent of voters) fall into what he calls the "Wisdom Culture Paradigm." Among its characteristics are: an "anti-materialism . . . that comes partly from movements like voluntary simplicity and ecological sustainability"; an "emerging post-Eighties dimension [that] wants outright prevention of ecological destruction, a slowing of economic growth for saving the environment . . . and an anti-big business, anti-globalization position"; "a mainstream concern for relationships, altruism and idealism"; and an alienation from the "policies, the analysis and positions, and the political processes of both Left and Right."[5] Localness is one characteristic of a product or business that clearly appeals to this group.

Think about the proliferation of signs exhorting "Locally Owned Restaurant," "Local Bank," "We Sell Local Jewelry." Most people would gladly shell out a nickel more for a fresh loaf of bread from the local baker rather than buy its cheaper, tasteless equivalent at Safeway. In fact, one study of residents in Maine, New Hampshire, and Vermont found that 17 to 40 percent of consumers in each state were willing to pay two dollars more to buy a locally produced five-dollar food item.[6] The movement toward community-supported agriculture, farmers markets, and urban farms reflects this growing preference for locally grown fruits and vegetables. With names like "Tennessee Proud" and "Jersey Fresh," some twenty-three states have developed labeling and marketing campaigns around local food.[7]

Across the country, restaurants, grocery stores, and roadside stands are boasting that they are "locally owned" and carry "local food." A recent ten-state survey by the Leopold Center for Sustainable Agriculture found that when given a half-dozen premium features for fresh produce and meats, the number one choice—by 75 percent of consumers and 55 percent of food business proprietors—was "grown locally by family farmers."[8] "Grown locally" ranked significantly higher than "organic" or even "grown locally–organic." There is something visceral about the freshness of local food. Consumers not only taste the difference, but worry about the consequences of ingesting items grown thousands of miles away under standards of unknown reliability.

Local is a niche that goes far beyond food. Homeowners who discover that the electricity they're using is being transmitted from coal and nuclear plants hundreds of miles away may be willing to spend another penny or two per kilowatt-hour for local "green power" alternatives, primarily wind power. At the end of 2004, more than 300,000 residential and commercial consumers were participating in some six hundred such programs in thirty-four states.[9] While this represented only a little more than 1 percent of eligible consumers, the participation rate for some utilities was as high as 4.5 percent, and total green power sales are growing at a rate of 40 to 50 percent per year.

Put another way, it's exceedingly difficult to find a business that brags: "Hey, we're not local—buy from us." Even Wal-Mart now feels duty bound to mention a few community-friendly deeds in its marketing campaigns. One of the largest British banks, HSBC, advertises itself as "The World's Local Bank." In the National Reagan Airport, the McDonald's franchise has a mural under its counter with a newspaper headlined, between the golden arches, "Locally Owned."

## Eco-Thinking

Another emerging niche that LOIS businesses are seizing, also attractive to cultural creatives, is "green." A Gallup poll on Earth Day in 2005 found that, when asked if they "think the U.S. government is doing too much, too little, or about the right amount in terms of protecting the environment," 58 percent of Americans think the government is doing "too little" and only 5 percent "too much."[10]

Consider the many ways eco-thinking stimulates the Small-Mart Revolution. Green-minded entrepreneurs are developing myriad sustainable LOIS industries around local assets. The sustainable management of local land, vegetation, and wildlife promotes local food growing. The sustainable harvesting of wood supports local lumber, furniture, woodworking, and paper industries. The sustainable tapping of wind, water, and solar resources, increasingly sought to prevent

the emission of greenhouse gases into the atmosphere, provides potentially inexhaustible local energy systems. The sustainable management
of nature, as well as the preservation of historic buildings and culture,
can foster a thriving local tourism business.

Eco-thinking means gradually replacing unsustainable TINA industries like "mining" with more sustainable local alternatives. The production of raw materials like paper, wood, glass, and steel once required huge global industries. Copper, for example, came from gigantic
mining companies like Anaconda digging up raw materials in Africa
or Latin America, bringing them back to the United States for processing, and overthrowing a few governments along the way to keep
the wheels of progress spinning. Rising oil prices will make all these
prior arrangements unsustainable. Today, the mining of nonrenewable resources is being replaced with the increasingly competitive mining of our own waste streams in the form of recycling, reuse, and re-
fabrication. As of 2001 the United States had more than fifty-six
thousand recycling and reuse establishments employing 1.1 million
people, paying $37 billion in payroll, and grossing $236 billion in revenue.[11] The collectors of recyclables—the grungy folks who pick up
curbside—turn out to be the smallest part of the industry. On a re-
ceipts basis, most of the action is in reuse and remanufacturing (6
percent), the processing of recyclables (17 percent), and new manufacturing (75 percent). How large are these businesses? The average company in each category has fewer than fourteen employees. Typically,
manufacturing that uses recycled materials, and where the scale of
operations is significantly larger, has only 94 employees per establishment, well within the universe of LOIS businesses.

Growing ecological consciousness combined with rising oil prices
also opens new local business possibilities for replacing the most environmentally damaging human-made products, namely petrochemicals, which are used to synthesize our plastics, fertilizers, paints, inks,
medicines, and synthetic fibers.[12] Petrochemicals are currently being
used to produce 175 million tons of organic chemicals, which get transformed into plastics, solvents, and alcohols, and 20 million tons to
make lubricants and greases. The National Research Council (NRC)
concluded in 1999 that biomaterials could replace more than 90 percent of these petrochemicals. A recent report by the Rocky Mountain

Institute argues that "vigorous industrial activity to exploit today's even better techniques" brings the NRC's prediction within reach.[13] They point out that some of the nation's biggest chemical giants, such as Cargill Dow, Metabolix, and DuPont, are already building major processing plants and bringing down costs. The challenge is whether these giants monopolize this new market before local competitors have a shot. In principle, the biochemical industry could be quite decentralized. Because agricultural and forestry waste is harder to collect and heavier to ship than oil, the most efficient location of processing plants will be close to the farms or forests providing the feedstock.

The proliferation of eco-thinking in consumers, and in entrepreneurs who are scrambling to meet their demands, is really just one example of a larger point. The economy begins in our heads. As advertisers have long appreciated, consumer longings do not descend from the heavens. A clever LOIS entrepreneur will seize inchoate green desires, frame them as eco-enterprises, and advertise their environmentally friendly features until the consumer finally parts with his or her money.

## LOIS Collaboration

Another tool LOIS businesses are wielding to beat TINA competitors is to work together. Judy Wicks, owner of the White Dog Café in Philadelphia, says that after she learned about the wretched lives pigs lead before they are slaughtered, she ordered all the ham, bacon, and pork chops off the menu until she could find a farmer who raised pigs humanely. She ultimately did, but he was one hundred miles away and didn't have a truck to bring his pigs to Philadelphia. Wicks decided to give him a no-interest loan to buy a truck, then convinced other restaurants to switch to his pigs so he could put the truck to its fullest use.

The lesson in what Wicks did goes beyond pigs. Local businesses can and should help other local businesses, *even their competition*. Their livelihoods depend on it. They should offer one another mentorship, technical support, favorable contracts, low-interest loans, whatever LOIS businesses need to defeat TINA. Wicks' help for her competitors in Philadelphia improved the quality of not only her own restaurant but also the entire culinary community in the city. She also helped demonstrate one way city folk can creatively partner with rural folk.

There is a long history of businesses offering one another mutual support in guilds, professional associations, even in barn-raisings. Three quarters of a century ago, local businesses in Switzerland decided to support one another through barter, reciprocal credit circles, technical assistance, and targeted purchasing. The Economic Circle, or Wir, has grown to involve about eighty-five thousand businesses, a fifth of all Swiss firms, and its central bank circulates about $1.2 billion each year.[14]

Every American community has a chamber of commerce that ought to be leading initiatives like these. But most chambers have lost their way, feeling duty bound to serve TINA equally with LOIS in elephant-mouse casserole. Into this breach have stepped two organizations, the Business Alliance for Local Living Economies (BALLE), based in San Francisco, and the American Independent Business Alliance (AMIBA), based in Montana. Over just a few years both have mushroomed into three dozen chapters with several thousand affiliated small businesses. Each promotes local ownership of the economy and pushes for new public policies that remove the tilts in the playing field that currently favor TINA firms. For example, the BALLE chapter in Philadelphia, called the Sustainable Business Network (SBN), was started by Judy Wicks in an upstairs office of the White Dog. It actively encourages members to buy from one another. Several of the bigger members participate in the city's local currency project. SBN nudges its members to place their retirement accounts in the Philadelphia Reinvestment Fund, which, as noted in chapter 5, is one of the very few financial institutions in the country that actually prioritizes LOIS business. Every year, the organization holds a local business fair in which the best examples of competitive LOIS firms are showcased in every category imaginable, including manufacturing. It also has launched an ambitious Local First Campaign with radio spots, ads on the sides of buses, and door-knob hangers.

In some communities, collaborative networks comprise similar kinds of businesses. As was true in Philadelphia, restaurant networks appear to be especially common. Tucson Originals is a group of more than forty restaurants that encourages Arizonans to eat local.[15] It helped create the Arizona Independent Restaurant Alliance, which purchases food and other supplies in bulk and at a discount for its 120 members. Member restaurants in Kansas City Originals have prepared joint advertisements and tabletop signs encouraging patrons to eat at one another's establishments. With a dozen other such groups now operating, a national network of local restaurants has formed: the Council of Independent Restaurants of America.

## Joint LOIS Ventures

Eager to strengthen their competitiveness vis-à-vis the global giants, some LOIS businesses are going beyond collaboration and actually creating joint ventures. A good place to see where this is happening already is in retail.

The percentage of LOIS retailers has been shrinking in recent years, particularly department and grocery stores. The department store universe is dominated by Wal-Mart, Target, and a handful of others. Grocery stores are similarly concentrated with players like Safeway, Albertson's, and Giant. (Actually, the single biggest seller of groceries these days is Wal-Mart, but it's usually counted in the general merchandise category.) LOIS businesses also have seen significant losses in other retail categories over the past decade or two, as noted in the introduction. So how can local business possibly beat the chains? How can they obtain the selection and the bulk discount deals that big chains do?

For one answer, look at hardware. True Value Hardware, Ace, and Do It Best are all networks of locally owned stores that compete effectively against Home Depot. They each have formed producers' cooperatives that bargain, buy, warehouse, and distribute in bulk. More than fifty thousand LOIS businesses participate in these cooperatives—double the number a decade ago.[16] The seven top hardware cooperatives took in $12.5 billion in revenue in 2000 and claim to have saved their members 10 to 20 percent.[17] Similar buying cooperatives or purchasing groups are now serving local pharmacies, groceries, farming, construction supplies, lighting companies, bicycle shops, and music stores.[18] There is no reason why a network of multi-merchandise stores could not do this to compete more effectively against Wal-Mart and Target. In fact, many of the Rocky Mountain Mercs (see chapter 5) undertake joint sourcing and purchasing on a regional scale.

LOIS retailers must, of course, compete on more than price. They must also offer convenience. How can a small retailer in a stand-alone store possibly match the convenience of big chains like Wal-Mart that sell every good imaginable or malls populated by big and little chains? There are two answers, and both require—again—the collaborative efforts of LOIS businesses.

When I was growing up on the South Shore of Long Island, my mom would sometimes take me to the Farmers Market on Hicksville Road, right across the street from the gigantic Grumman Aircraft complex. It wasn't really a farmers market in the sense we understand the term now. Yes, a few farmers occupied booths under the flimsy roof and sold fruits and vegetables, but most of the booths were run by artisans, craftspeople, and retailers who might have had another outlet or were too small to afford their own store. There were three booths I particularly liked: the used magazine and comic-book shop; the magic shop, where a friendly shopkeeper was always amusing us with tricks; and the glassblower, who would transform glass rods into intricate animals and dioramas in front of our dazzled eyes.

Farmers markets like this are common around the world. My personal favorite is the Chatuchak Market in Bangkok, Thailand. An ambitious shopper trying to visit every one of the nine thousand booths would probably wind up walking two or three miles. It's only open on weekends, but it's such an important place for gathering and socializing, along with shopping, that no one wants to miss going there. Many communities have "A Taste of _____" events that allow you to sample the best that local chefs have to offer. These kinds of expositions could be permanently housed by cities in dedicated pavilions where the sights, sounds, and tastes of all the local merchandise can excite the senses and restore loyalty to local merchants. The environment in a Wal-Mart, by comparison, will seem like a morgue.

In small communities, however, even these kinds of markets may not be able to compete easily with a nearby Wal-Mart in two respects: a small customer base necessitates a more modest diversity and inventory of products, and the inconvenience of driving or walking from store to store may outweigh other advantages.

One plausible solution is direct delivery from a regional warehouse maintained by a network of local businesses. Because of the skyrocketing costs of distribution, direct distribution schemes are proliferating. In Vancouver, British Columbia, Small Potatoes Urban Delivery is delivering 650 natural grocery products, most straight from local farms. Let's go one step further with a fantasy I call Local Express, a direct delivery service, running 24-7, that is prepared to rush the products from LOIS merchants right to your door. It's like Peapod, which delivers groceries from Giant and other supermarkets, only it would deliver a broader range of goods from a larger number of stores. I cannot tell you how many times I've made midnight diaper or milk runs wishing such a business existed. Local Express might have a Frequent Buyer program and award discounts to affiliated stores. It might be structured like True Value Hardware, with locally owned delivery services linked through a national producers' cooperative. If goods were not available in your community, they could be brought from one or two towns away the next day.

What about when the economy of scale of production is very large, say for high-tech manufacturing? Again, there is no reason why creative business structures cannot incorporate a web of local businesses. In northern Italy, ever since World War II, small, locally owned firms have come together to work in temporary production teams called "flexible manufacturing networks." They have produced a wide range of complex goods that otherwise would have required a very large economy of sale, including mass-produced foodstuffs, textiles, shoes, paper, wood, chemicals, biomedical equipment, machine tools, even robotic arms. The forces of globalization and consolidation have reduced some of this activity, but by 1996 the Emilia-Romagna region still had almost fifty-three thousand manufacturing firms, and 97.5 percent had fewer than fifty employees.[19] Thanks to flexible manufacturing networks, the region has been transformed from one of the poorest in Western Europe to one of the richest, and the region's per capita income is still the highest in Italy.

U.S. economic developers flocked to northern Italy throughout the 1980s to figure out how these successful models could be transplanted here. Among the factors duly noted were the social ties among the business heads, the supportive industrial policies of regional and local governments, and the traditions of inter-firm collaboration with respect to credit, technology, and talent. The results have been mixed. The cultural predisposition of American entrepreneurs to go it alone and the virtual absence of industrial policies at any level of government have not been particularly helpful. Dozens of major government-funded projects to support flexible manufacturing networks in the United States have been abandoned. And yet in smaller regions, particularly in rural areas, the concept has gained traction in the form of local clusters.

Even though economic developers often use clusters to bolster their policies for TINA attraction or retention, there is no reason why a cluster cannot be made up largely or exclusively of LOIS enterprises. And some of the newest rural clusters demonstrate degrees of interfirm cooperation that are beginning to look like the successes of northern Italy.[20] North Carolina has been building a network of 277 hosiery manufacturers, with the Hosiery Technology Center based at two community colleges providing research, training, and coordination services for the industry. The Appalachian Center for Economic Networks (ACENet) has been creating a cluster of more than 150 food enterprises in southeastern Ohio through a Food Ventures Center, where entrepreneurs can rent kitchen equipment to test ideas. ACENet Ventures also provides long-term, low-interest loans.

When Linda Griefo, a small businessperson who had run a chili stand, assumed the job of revitalizing South Central Los Angeles after the riots of 1992, she abandoned the strategy of her predecessor, Peter Ueberroth, of focusing on TINA businesses. As Alexander von Hoffman reports, she and her colleagues "adopted an unusual strategy to deal with the mom-and-pop entrepreneurs. They worked directly with the small manufacturers to help them organize trade associations, navigate government regulations and upgrade the skill of their workers. In the end, small manufacturers succeeded where large industry failed: they helped rescue the economy of inner-city Los Angeles."[21]

The logic of producer cooperatives, joint stores, flexible manufacturing networks, and clusters all lead to a stunning conclusion: almost *any* type of business can realize a larger economy of scale if enough LOIS businesses work together. Only where TINA businesses enjoy advantages that relate to their geographic dispersal, not to their size— access to cheap labor and unregulated pollution zones, for example—

will LOIS businesses be unable to match or beat TINA's advantage. But remember that it's the very dispersal of such TINA businesses that also makes them vulnerable to rising energy costs and to LOIS campaigns that expose their unethical international behavior.

## LOIS Support Enterprises

Smart LOIS entrepreneurs are beginning to see opportunities for developing special kinds of businesses that support the needs of all LOIS businesses. Consider, for example, businesses to promote local purchasing. As noted in chapter 4, many of the "local currency" experiments have not been put on a sound financial footing. To a number of entrepreneurs, this is an opportunity.

Derrell Ness, for example, is now trying to develop a local gift-card technology for his BALLE network in Portland, Oregon. Go to any supermarket checkout line these days, and one of the purchasing options you'll find—next to the *National Enquirer* and *TV Guide*—are stacks of gift cards. For twenty, fifty, or a hundred dollars you can give someone you love the opportunity to get free booty from Best Buy, Home Depot, Bed Bath & Beyond, and Circuit City. Almost every chain store is plying this gimmick. Small-Mart gift cards could be extremely lucrative. If your card runs short, you can pay the rest in cash. More likely, though, you'll lose the card or pass the fine-print expiration date long before you spend it, giving the card distributor a windfall.

Or imagine a Small-Mart credit card with the standard Visa or MasterCard insignia issued by a local bank. When you present the card to a seller, it operates like any other credit card. But present it to designated locally owned vendors, and you get a 5 percent discount. Until quite recently, Visa and MasterCard would not allow any such discrimination—at a minimum, you'd have to present a second discount coupon—but this policy appears to be changing. It is also permissible to tally special bonus points with locally owned businesses redeemable for bonus gifts or purchases later. The deeper problem with this system is that the industry issuing, processing, and running collections for credit cards is global and that increased revenues brought to local vendors will be reduced by fees to these TINA firms.

Perhaps a better alternative would be a Small-Mart debit card, which would cover each transaction by deducting a payment from your checking account. Like the credit card, this would require an affiliation with a local bank. Unlike credit card systems, debit cards carry smaller fees per transaction and are more amenable to control and processing by in-state banks. But for the moment, the nonlocal Visa International processes most debit transactions.

One problem with gift, credit, and debit card systems is the significant start-up cost—depending on your ambition, anything from $100,000 to millions of dollars. Many LOIS businesses have only crude credit/debit card processing equipment and will require upgrades. Software needs to be written. New electronic networks, or new kinds of relationships with existing network providers, need to be established.

A potentially promising answer to these challenges is Interra.[22] The founder of Odwalla Juices, Greg Steltenpohl, is developing one card, a single electronic vehicle that will integrate local gift cards, local credit cards, and local debit cards. A nonprofit, Interra will also provide a link between existing debit and credit cards and local business loyalty programs in any given community, all to promote "regenerative commerce." Participating businesses contribute a small percentage of every purchase to the system, which in turn is split among the system administrators, community partners, and do-good organizations. In return Interra provides these businesses with low-cost card processing and marketing programs, including a "meta directory" of information that encourages participating consumers to buy from local business. Interra aims to become the community-friendly alternative to Visa, an ambition that is bolstered by the close involvement of Dee Hock, one of the architects of Visa. Nearly a million dollars have already been invested in the venture, and prototypes are moving forward in several U.S. cities. If the project can attract five million members over five years, Steltenpohl estimates it will generate half a billion dollars of nonprofit donations, $44 billion in new revenue to local economies, and ninety thousand new jobs.

Another buy-local innovation that LOIS entrepreneurs could replicate across the country is the Oregon Marketplace, which was founded in the early 1980s to pump up the state's economy by convincing in-state businesses to buy from other in-state businesses.[23] Focusing on the presence of the businesses in Oregon, rather than on in-state ownership, the scheme is only a rough draft of what should be done. It also was an imperfect business model, relying on annual infusions of money from the state lottery. But at the peak of its operation in the early 1990s, the Marketplace was transacting $34 million of input-replacing contracts per year. By charging finders' fees on the new in-state contract recipients, the Marketplace was able to pay some of its way. Unfortunately, the state legislature withdrew funding in the mid-1990s. Sooner or later, a smart LOIS entrepreneur will revive this model, improve it, make it profitable, and organize marketplaces like it across the United States.

Business-to-government (B2G) procurement also offers some intriguing LOIS business opportunities. Few LOIS businesses today bother with government contracts. As is true for participation in most government programs, the paperwork required for bidding, tracking, and accounting is intimidating and certainly beyond the capacity of many small businesses. Proper insurance and bonding is sometimes difficult and expensive to obtain, even though the SBA has programs that can help. And many government contracts require far larger supplies than a local provider can manage. Unless a small business sees government contracting as a major part of its business, it won't bother.

There is no good reason why commercial entities could not arise in every major metropolitan area to mobilize small businesses for all kinds of government contracts. Such enterprises have already gotten started to provide local foodstuffs to public schools. These so-called "farm-to-school" programs develop expertise in the contracting niche, recruit individual farmers who would never consider bidding on their own, handle the paperwork, and aggregate their fruits and vegetables into bigger, more compelling bids. Some of these programs are voluntary or grant funded, while others use existing food cooperatives, farmers markets, wholesalers, or food service companies.[24]

Another area ripe for a LOIS business model is entrepreneurship training. My colleagues and I in Maine have blueprinted an entity we call VenturePower. It would work with business incubators in the state, and attempt to supercharge them to promote LOIS entrepreneurship. Incubators are essentially business support systems based in dedicated buildings. In 1980 there were about ten incubators in the United

States. Today there are eight hundred throughout North America. During this period North American incubators are estimated to have created nineteen thousand companies and more than 245,000 jobs. Even though half of all small business startups fail within four years, nine out of ten start-ups that begin within incubators succeed.

Within Maine today there are nearly a dozen incubators either operating or in the planning stage. Best we can tell, these incubators are disconnected from the needs of LOIS entrepreneurs. Most are focused on high-tech, high growth TINA enterprises. They provide space and technical support, but not what LOIS entrepreneurs really need: salary and working capital. And most are structured as public works programs. Whenever government agencies need to trim their budgets, the incubators are among the first programs to take a hit.

VenturePower Maine aims to address these problems. The basic idea is to use existing incubators to develop new, small-scale industries that can provide goods and services that meet the kinds of demands found in every community. One example is hydroponics—the use of small greenhouses to grow food intensively. With small, well-designed hydroponics companies, almost every community in Maine could have fresh, affordable, locally grown produce. VenturePower might work with half-a-dozen incubators to start hydroponics firms in each. It might then organize a "Learning Community" with six entrepreneurs who would meet two or three times a year, speak on conference calls weekly, and communicate regularly through email. They would be supported by the expertise of established hydroponics operators. This network would share business plans and form a purchasing group that could get discounts on key inputs.

Each quarter, VenturePower would move into a new enterprise. It might build local, general merchandise stores downtown, like the Rocky Mountain Mercs. Over time, this rollout plan will enable VenturePower to develop expertise in an expanding universe of viable local enterprises that it can share nationally.

The current design is for VenturePower to finance itself like a venture capital firm. Its statewide experts would provide participating entrepreneurs with business plans, market analysis, statewide marketing, human resources and accounting services, and introductions to Maine investors. It would give each entrepreneur a salary and working capital for a year or two. "Graduation" would occur, typically, at the end of the second year of incubation. VenturePower would then relinquish control to the entrepreneur and earn back its investment. A participating company is expected to buy back working control from Venture-Power each quarter, taking up to twenty quarters, or five years, to acquire a majority stake in the company. At that point, VenturePower would hold 49 percent of the company and begin looking to sell its shares to other members of the community, such as the company managers, the employees, or simply local investors. In all cases, ownership stays local.

## TINA Collaboration

This is a good place to reiterate that demonizing TINA is not the smartest way to promote the Small-Mart Revolution. The struggle against TINA needs to be won with competitive LOIS goods and services, not spitballs. To be sure, whenever TINA businesses maintain sweatshops, pay sub-standard wages, clear-cut forests, or wipe out endangered wildlife, LOIS competitors can and should expose these nefarious practices and use their superior standards to strengthen their competitive niche for ethical customers and grab market share. As for the many TINA firms that are trying to act more responsibly, I say let's compete without malice. Let's even cooperate.

LOIS retailers frankly have more to learn from the TINA chains than the other way around. By studying the competition, local store owners can acquire the skills to better choose, organize, present, and market their merchandise, and they might pick up some ideas about hours, location, and service that can improve consumer convenience. Learning requires a good relationship, breaking bread with fellow TINA entrepreneurs, even kibitzing with them at the chamber of commerce breakfasts and Rotary luncheons.

The possibilities for rewarding TINA partnerships are everywhere. Because TINA banks get higher ratings under the Community Reinvestment Act (CRA) if they support local business, they should be considered possible sources for LOIS finance if local sources are unavailable. TINA contractors competing for government business score better when they subcontract with local firms, so LOIS businesses should be willing to help them out. TINA charities that brag about helping communities might be asked for grants to support LOIS business development. Let's recruit TINA executives to mentor aspiring LOIS entrepreneurs. And TINA bookstores are welcome, thank you, to sell this book.

Think twice about collaborating, however, if your TINA partnership threatens fellow LOIS businesses. Suppose, for example, a big, new shopping mall is seeking some of the variety offered by local businesses and wants your store, currently located downtown. Malachy Kavanagh, with the International Council of Shopping Centers, says, "Malls can't just rely on big chains anymore if they want to stay competitive."[25] The problem is that the proposed mall could harm all downtown businesses. Most studies suggest that retail purchases in a given area are fixed, which means that every new store is drawing customers away from an existing one.[26] The more responsible stance—and in the long term the more profitable one for a local business—is to stay in solidarity with the other LOIS businesses and keep downtown commercially viable.

But I also can imagine exceptions. Suppose the same mall is being built by a local developer and involves primarily local businesses. Or there also may be instances when a new Starbucks may actually improve a coffee house business across the street by creating a new destination, a new hot spot.[27] Of course, if Starbucks actually tries to buy out a lease from a local coffee shop, the action should be exposed, condemned, and stopped, if possible. Nor does it mean that a penny of public money should go to such TINA businesses—*ever*. But when TINA companies play fair and without government handouts, they can be valuable colleagues.

## The Green Bay Chickens

Three of my four grandparents were peasants from regions of Russia, Lithuania, and the Ukraine, and I suspect that like other peasants their forebears raised and slaughtered their own chickens. Perhaps it's this genetic programming that has drawn me to stick my own toe into entrepreneurial waters with a small-scale chicken company called Bay Friendly Chicken (BFC). So far, the company exists only on paper, in the form of a business plan and a stock offering. But the struggle to define a path toward profitability has given me a real-world appreciation of how LOIS businesses can compete more effectively against TINA using the tools discussed in this chapter.

About one in ten chickens eaten in the United States comes from the Delmarva Peninsula, so called because it cuts across three states: Delaware, Maryland, and Virginia. The regional industry—primarily made up of Perdue, Tyson, Mountaire, and Allens—currently employs 14,052 people and generates $1.7 billion in annual revenue.[28] Delmarva used to be the nation's principal poultry producer, but over time, major companies have drifted to or sprung up in other states such as Georgia, Alabama, and Arkansas.

Poultry is arguably the second dirtiest business in the Washington, DC, region. Almost everything producers could do shoddily, the big poultry companies have done in spades.[29] Investigative reports in recent years on 6o Minutes and in the New York Times, the Washington Post, and the Baltimore Sun have highlighted industry practices, some described in the beginning of this chapter, that are tremendously harmful to its workers, consumers, and the surrounding ecosystems.

One particularly pernicious impact in our region is the environmental consequence of every grower using a limited area of land for intensive chicken growing. Modest amounts of chicken manure make a terrific fertilizer. But huge mountains of poop are harder to get rid of; most farmers, having been generously awarded title to these piles by the integrator, just hope they disappear. Not surprising, the unmanaged pileup of 1.5 billion pounds of manure each year has exacted a steady toll on the Chesapeake Bay, the largest estuary in North America, and imperiled drinking water supplies.

Want to change the system? Better not complain. The companies can occasionally operate a little like the Sopranos, meeting for private chats and discussing ways of squelching dissent. Some growers have been blacklisted and driven out of the business. When we held an early planning meeting for BFC in a Catholic Church in Salisbury, one Perdue executive on the church board pressured the priest to rescind our gathering privileges.

Any legislative talk about improving labor or environmental standards is usually met by Tyson and Purdue whining about the high costs of staying in the region and dropping hints about more attractive deals in Arkansas or Mississippi. For all intents and purposes, regulation is off the table. When Governor Parris Glendening of Maryland signed a scheme whereby growers and integrators were to share the costs of manure disposal, the industry went ballistic, as did cash-strapped growers, and they convinced a court to strike down the measure as unconstitutional.

The experience highlighted the futility of trying to regulate TINA into better performance. It's a political dead end. A better reform strategy, perhaps the only reform strategy, is to rebuild the industry from the ground up through hundreds of LOIS poultry companies around the country, each serving a small region, each locally owned, each acting as a positive example about how to better treat birds, workers, and ecosystems while producing a higher-quality chicken. Viable LOIS alternatives could then draw consumers away from the integrators, forcing the latter to improve their behavior or lose market share. It was out of this vision that BFC was born.

BFC was founded by a team of growers, workers, environmentalists, religious leaders, businesspeople, and policy analysts. Starting in 1998, under the auspices of the Chesapeake Bay Foundation and the Delmarva Poultry Justice Alliance, we met regularly to define cost-effective innovations to the problems described above.

I got my first lesson about scale while designing our plant. The initial business plan was based on designs perfected by our large-scale competitors. It envisioned automated production lines, high-tech machinery, standardized divisions of labor, and sales through existing distribution and retail networks. The model was plausible but expensive, and each tweak to improve standards increased costs significantly. To reduce the rate of carpal tunnel syndrome injuries, for example, we would have had to slow down the production line, which lowered the cost effectiveness of the equipment.

Only when I tossed away the large-scale framework altogether did the costs really come down and did the plan begin to make sense. Low-tech machinery turned out to be much cheaper, and the small labor force didn't justify any high-tech investment. Besides, the low-tech designs offered other kinds of savings as well, in that their slower speed facilitated greater care in cutting the chickens, spotting diseased carcasses, and preventing contamination. Most poultry engineers would look at my choices as strange and irrational, but it's only because they spent their entire professional lives working on a large scale. I also realized that if I could help start similar poultry businesses in many other regions around the country—which some would see shortsightedly as helping the competition—manufacturers of small-scale equipment would themselves be able to move into mass production, which would lower our costs further.

It was clear early on that our product would still be more expensive than that available from most integrators, but the price could be in the competitive neighborhood of what Bell and Evans charges. Following the LOIS playbook, our plans now are to carve out a distinct niche, different from bionic bird, by highlighting the quality of our product and the quality of our production. Both, we believe, can be compelling selling points.

Regarding niche, there's really no such thing as plain-old chicken these days. Some poultry sellers differentiate their products by calling them "natural," by which they mean—though the term has no legally binding definition—that the chickens have not been given antibiotics or hormones to promote growth. A smaller number of producers try to qualify for the USDA certification as "organic," which means that the chickens, besides being antibiotic free, were grown under certain standards and fed certified-organic grains. A few producers go further, saying their chickens are "free range," which can mean anything from chickens roaming a barnyard to those living in a small group cage moved around a grassy field. There are also different rituals and methods of slaughtering that can make a chicken acceptable to kosher, Islamic, or Chinese consumers.

All these points of differentiation apply to whole birds. There are also cut-up chickens; tray packs of wings or thighs or breasts; fresh or frozen; with giblets or without; precooked or raw; fried, BBQ, Cajun, Thai-spiced, peppered; in prepared pot pies, casseroles, stir fries, nuggets, tenders, patties, frozen dinners. The industry claims to have several hundred discrete chicken products.

BFC decided that its main points of product differentiation would be two-fold: natural and air-chilled. While antibiotic-free chicken can be found in most markets, it is still largely shunned by the major integrators. But there is growing public concern that the heavy use of antibiotics as a growth promoter in the poultry industry has increased the risks of antibiotic-resistant bacteria infecting consumers. The Center for Veterinary Medicine of the U.S. Food and Drug Administration estimates that between two and eight thousand Americans are infected with *campylobacter*, which results in several days of diarrhea and flu-like symptoms, and can no longer be treated with one antibiotic, fluoroquinolone. One alternative, proven successful in Europe and by a few U.S. companies, is to grow chickens in more sanitary conditions without any growth-promoting antibiotics whatsoever. BFC also wants to be responsive to consumers' concerns about the use of chlorinated water baths that can spread bacteria from one bird to the others. A better approach, widely practiced throughout Europe and Canada, is to chill the carcasses with a stream of cold air that prevents bacterial cross-contamination. Done properly, air chill also facilitates aging of the meat and tastiness. Only two companies in the United States right now, MBA Partners in Nebraska and Bell & Evans, are using this technology.

At various times, we have considered other kinds of product differentiation. Kosher seemed interesting, but the market was too narrow. Organic would be terrific, except that organic grains are very expensive and, again, the market willing to cover the large price increase for this feature is small. Free range seemed risky (even if it at least superficially offers better animal welfare),[30] given how many chicken germs from bionic bird waft through the air of Delmarva Peninsula and the looming global challenge of avian flu. Over time, we may revisit these ideas, but for now, our product will simply be natural and air-chilled.

Because Bell & Evans does both of these and has a strong presence in our market, we need to differentiate ourselves further still. This is where our commitment to strong labor, environmental, and community standards comes into play. Our company slogan is "Better Bird, Better Taste, Better Bay." Unlike all our competitors, including Bell & Evans, BFC will pay living wages, give growers ownership stakes in the company, and be a locally controlled stock company (Bell & Evans is owned by a family in Pennsylvania). Our bet is that, all other things being equal, discriminating consumers in our bioregion will want to buy local.

We puzzled over various models for capitalizing BFC. Our first business plan estimated we would need $2.7 million in equity. Once we let go of TINA-style mechanization, the equity requirement dropped to about $1.5 million. Our latest plan squeezes the capital requirements to under $1 million. Even this requirement, however, is not exactly small. We were open to a few deep-pocket local investors, but our first efforts at pitching investors—shortly after the NASDAQ Exchange lost 80 percent of its values between 2000 and 2002—were disappointing. Venture capital, which typically extinguishes local ownership, was not an option. A cooperative might have been sensible, except that Maryland has a particularly Neanderthal statute governing co-ops. So what was the solution?

Cheeseheads! Turning back to the Green Bay Packer Model (see chapter 2),we decided to create a local stock issue. We are now in the midst of selling several thousand shares of one-hundred-dollar stock. Not to just anyone, of course, but to residents of the Chesapeake Bay Bioregion. Ideally, we would have issued shares of common stock, which means that holders have the right to vote for members of the board. But a condition of a USDA grant we received was to vest voting control in the growers. We created, therefore, two tiers of stock. The growers hold common stock and residents hold preferred shares, which are nonvoting but carry other benefits (in bankruptcy, for example, preferred shareholders get paid first).

Local stock offers BFC more than just a new way to raise capital. It allows BFC to market itself and get into the consumer's consciousness before producing a single chicken. One idea is to have a picture of my dad's Russian mom, with the caption: "Grandma Anne says chicken stock is good for you!" Who will be our first and best customers? Probably the stockholders. Local stock seems a great way to deploy a huge volunteer marketing force.

BFC is also planning to work with other regional producers to create a nationally recognized brand that certifies all the claims we're making about the quality of the chickens, the responsible character of the production, and the localness of ownership. In France family farmers helped put together a similar La Belle Rouge ("Red Label") system, which today accounts for about a third of the French poultry market and commands the highest prices from quality-minded consumers.[31] While we would ideally like to buy chicks, grain, and other inputs from local providers, monopolization of these products by the integrators in our region makes this impossible; for the moment, we may have to form partnerships with nonlocal suppliers.

There's one other economy of small scale we'd like to realize. It dawned on us that the distribution costs for foodstuffs had gotten so huge that it would be cheaper to deliver our chickens directly to the doorsteps of our customers than to sell them through the stores. The typical store charges a markup of 40 percent, which takes away eighty cents for every pound. For less than those eighty cents, we can take orders online, create a chicken-delivery battalion, and get fresher birds to our customers faster. It helps that we're a regional company and that no chicken will travel farther than one or two hundred miles from the processing plant to the kitchen. And to the extent we can join forces with existing companies that home-deliver groceries, like Peapod or Schwan's, the costs of the regional distribution system can be brought down further.

Direct distribution brings lots of other advantages. We can establish a direct relationship with our consumers. We can recruit stay-at-home parents to run part-time distribution centers for their blocks. We can raise eyebrows and maximize our marketing dollar when the chicken-man or chicken-woman comes to deliver, in special cooler packs, your Bay Friendly Chicken for the week.

I should reiterate that BFC is not yet operating. Its real story, whatever it turns out to be, will have to be told in my next book. But I share the details of our business planning here because they illustrate the strategic thinking being undertaken by thousands of LOIS businesses—or inchoate LOIS businesses—across the nation. And this thinking is that tens of thousands of local entrepreneurs are ready to change, learn, grow, improve, mobilize, collaborate—to do whatever it takes to beat TINA.

1. **Local Niche.** Make local ownership a key part of marketing your business to consumers and to investors.
2. **Go Green.** Make your business an outstanding local environmental citizen by using local renewable resources and reusing nonrenewable resources (through recycling and reuse), and be sure to brag to your customers about your practices.
3. **BALLE Chapter.** Create a local business alliance so that you're not alone. Use the alliance to promote local purchasing, fight chains, solve problems, secure credit, and learn new skills.
4. **Producers Cooperatives.** Join existing producers cooperatives or other kinds of industry-specific affinity groups that collectively purchase, advertise, and lobby for local members. Or start one.
5. **Bazaars.** Help set up and participate in local business mini-malls, whether they are weekend farmers' markets or dedicated shopping destinations.
6. **Direct Delivery.** Create or join a direct delivery service affiliated exclusively or primarily with local businesses.
7. **Flexible Manufacturing.** Form a network of local businesses that is ready and willing to seize manufacturing opportunities as they arise.
8. **Buyers' Cards.** Team up with other local businesses to create instruments that promote local purchasing, such as local credit cards, debit cards, loyalty cards, and gift cards.
9. **B2B Marketplace.** Set up a business that links local businesses to one another and takes a commission on each local "input" substitution.
10. **B2G Midwife.** Create a business that aggregates small businesses into compelling bids for government contracts and handles the mountain of paperwork in exchange for a fee.
11. **Super-Incubators.** Take existing small-business incubators (or start a new one) and rededicate them exclusively to local business. Restructure them to operate on a self-financing, venture-capital model.
12. **TINA Collaboration.** Break bread with nonlocal businesses to learn and work together (at least wherever it does not weaken the local business community).

# seven

★★★★★★★★★★★★★★★★★★★★★★★★★★★★★★★★★★★★★★★★★★★★

# POLICYMAKERS

We would all love to keep politics out of the Small-Mart Revolution. Public policy and public money certainly can spread LOIS business, but just as often "official" assistance can be co-opting, limiting, wasteful, and corrupt. Even the best-intended pro-LOIS programs can move at turtle speed, get ensnarled in bureaucracy, and become so politicized that half the public could wind up hating small business. Nearly all the efforts described so far—local purchasing, local investing, local business building—can be done by the private sector or by nonprofits. Yet, it's hard to continue ignoring the $113 billion advantage that the public sector is conferring on TINA. Indeed, because global corporations have insinuated TINA logic, bias, and money into all kinds of political decisions at all levels—local, state, national, and global—LOIS supporters must rise up to challenge TINA's political monopoly. Policymakers sympathetic with LOIS, inside and outside government, have an important role to play in the Small-Mart Revolution—in their research in local initiatives, in their spending and regulatory practices, and in their national lobbying.

## Studying the Economic Plumbing

One reason TINA has gotten so far over the past generation is that economic developers on government payrolls have cleverly cranked out, publicized, and manipulated pro-TINA studies. The numbers they manipulate wow politicians, shock and awe journalists, and trump commonsense questions the rest of us have. Recall from chapter 1 how BMW paid local economists to assure skeptics that the $130 million subsidy was a good investment? These same tools now must be deployed on behalf of LOIS. And the single most important piece of data a community can demand is how many dollars are leaking out of the economy because of unnecessary imports.

"Leakage" analysis is powerful because it measures how much income, wealth, and jobs a community is losing from its failure to localize; or, put positively, how much income, wealth, and jobs can be gained from the Small-Mart Revolution. The studies undertaken by Civic Economics in Austin (Texas) and Andersonville (Illinois) (see chapter 2) fundamentally shifted the burden of proof from TINA advocates to opponents. The Austin study buried municipal plans to subsidize bringing a Borders bookstore to town.

A nonprofit in Oakland, Calfornia, Community Economics, carried out one of the earliest leakage analysis in 1979.[1] It found three types of leakage from the East Oakland economy that helped explain the persistence of poverty there: $43 million per year flowing to absentee landlords in rent payments; $40 to $45 million going to outside banks for interest payments on mortgages; and $150 million in consumer expenditures being made at stores outside city limits. Oakland residents learned something important. To get the most bang out of any economic-development bucks, they need to expand home ownership, move mortgages to locally owned banks, and create locally owned retail outlets. Unfortunately, the results of the study were quickly forgotten.

In 1977 a small town in Pennsylvania, Chester, looked at its own possibilities for import substitution. With assistance from the Rodale Institute and the Presbyterian Church, the community produced a four-volume study documenting the tiny percentage of purchases of energy, food, and banking services being made inside the community, and how these leaks were robbing residents of the potential multiplier benefits. Overall, only sixteen cents of each dollar earned by a resident of Chester came from local business, and a remarkable eighty-seven cents of every dollar spent went to proprietors outside the community. The Community Renewal Program of the Rocky Mountain Institute, using their *Economic Renewal Guide*, has performed similar studies for dozens of communities around the country, focusing primarily on energy and natural resource leakages.[2]

In the year 2000 Doug Hoffer, an economist, was contracted by Vermont's Living Wage Campaign to analyze leakages in the state economy.[3] Using new databases from the U.S. Department of Transportation on interstate shipments of goods, he was able to improve over earlier methodologies. His findings were stunning. This largely agrarian state was importing annually about $2 billion worth of foodstuffs. Despite a rich array of potential local energy sources like biomass, hydropower, and wind power, the state was importing $1 billion in energy. As in most states, Vermont's financial sector exports investment dollars. More than $1.5 billion in insurance investments are made out of state each year, and mortgage interest payments out of state amount to a half billion dollars. The smallest leakage was perhaps the most striking. The state was losing $250 million per year just from interest payments on credit cards being issued by out-of-state banks. Think about it. If Vermont were to create its own credit card industry and keep that interest, the state could enjoy $250 million more in economic activity, *plus* the multiplier benefits stimulated by it.

These studies highlight the most promising priorities for business development. A smart economic development department will measure leakages and then assess, systematically, the feasibility of plugging them with local entrepreneurs. Vermont would start with the biggest leaks, like food and energy, and then work its way down to the smaller items. Leakage studies help a community identify points of weakness that can be transformed into new points of strength.

Most economic developers today do exactly the opposite. They try to identify only export strengths and build on them. If you're South Carolina and you've decided that your global niche is BMW automobiles, the current practice is to build on the local cluster of automobile businesses—and neglect the rest. Unfortunately, this usually translates into recommendations about how to structure incentives to keep existing producers sited locally and attract other automobile producers from elsewhere on the planet. Once again TINA prevails and the region loses.

This kind of mainstream analysis can be useful, but only if coupled with leakage analysis and LOIS-style thinking. Yes, clusters are critical sources of economic dynamism and synergy. When clusters rooted in locally owned businesses are given priority, the community is nurturing a dependable source of wealth for many years, rather than new excuses for escalating corporate welfare demands. The best use of an existing cluster is not to attract complementary business but to tap the skills, wealth, and entrepreneurial energy generated by it to plug leaks. Economic developers in Silicon Valley might analyze all the goods and services being imported by its computer cluster. If they found that the industry were consuming outside electricity, they might prioritize creating new, local supplies of solar or tidal energy.

What's shocking about the entire field of economic development is how little leakage analysis is used. The United States has some thirty-six thousand municipalities, yet the number of them that have done anything approaching a comprehensive leakage study can be counted on two hands. This means that almost every community is flying blind. Without a leakage analysis economic developers cannot possibly know what the best investment of scarce public resources might be.

A local elected official should ask some tough questions of the economic developers at the next council meeting: Have you studied leakages in the economy? Why not? How do you know which of your efforts will have the greatest multiplier impact? Would you consider doing such an analysis? Well, would you at least help a community group that does? Excuse me, sir, but when does your contract expire?

Studies comparing nonlocal to local stores, as the Civic Economics studies in Austin and Andersonville did, represent a variation on this theme. Rather than look at the leaks in the overall economy, they compare leaks in specific sectors or associated with specific stores or projects.

Leakage analysis can also be used to evaluate proposed public works projects. These projects are currently analyzed following the logic of TINA: calculate how much money is going to be dumped on the project for construction and how many jobs will be created, plug in the numbers from your favorite multiplier database and—poof!—instant job creation. A better approach would be to ask whether this project would plug leaks and then calculate the economic benefits that would flow from import substitution. And better still, compare various projects this way, including the option of leaving money in taxpayers' pockets.

Over the past two years I've been analyzing a proposal in the city of Santa Fe to replace natural gas heating with a biomass-fueled district heating system. District heating systems are very popular in Europe but also can be found in this country in universities, industrial parks, and other planned communities. Rather then leaving it to every building to have its own heating system, they take advantage of the efficiencies that result from larger boilers, pumps, and pipes. Some use the waste heat from the boiler as an input to industries requiring high-temperate heat, or they harness the heat for electricity. The proposed system in Santa Fe would cover only a few square blocks but would help prove a concept that, if viable, could then be deployed citywide.

The reason Santa Fe is considering these alternatives is that, like many U.S. communities, it has become very dependent on natural gas to heat buildings. Historically, natural gas has been clean and cheap, especially compared to burning oil or coal in buildings or running electric resistance heaters that inefficiently convert electricity from distant coal, oil, or nuclear plants into low-temperature heat for end users. But the price rise of natural gas since 1999 has been steady and steep, and over the next generation or two, the price could rise dramatically. Fortunately, the city has a fuel alternative right in its own backyard. Dead wood and scrub brush from nearby forests have become increasing fire hazards, and until now, state and local authorities had planned to get rid of this "waste" wood through controlled burns. The district heating project would actually make good use of this waste by gathering the wood, chipping it, and burning it. Rather than import natural gas from outside the county, Santa Fe could use its own fuel.

The study found that current prices of natural gas made the project uneconomic, but even the smallest price-rise scenario generated a net benefit stream for the region of $27 million.[4] One reason was the multiplier impacts. In the current system natural gas is imported from elsewhere in the state, and every dollar spent with the local utility, Public Service Company of New Mexico, leads to a leakage of 85.5 cents. The proposed system, were it financed locally, would bring down the leakage to 49 cents for every dollar spent.

Once the multiplier impacts are taken into account, a whole range of otherwise "unaffordable" private and public initiatives to localize the economy suddenly become plausible Conversely, many other pet projects without local content are exposed as trivial and even negative for a community. A stadium and sports team built by outside contractors using outside building materials, or owned and operated by an outsider, can be shown to produce little benefit for a community and may even incur huge losses once the opportunity costs of the land, labor, and finance are fully evaluated.

As TINA advocates have long understood, these studies cut across party and ideological lines. Everyone wants to know that public money is being well spent. LOIS advocates must now rise to this level of sophistication. But simply cranking out numbers is not enough.

## Defunding TINA

If LOIS is to realize its full potential, the $113 billion of TINA bias that riddles local, state, and national economic development programs must be exorcised. A total overhaul is necessary. As Sharon Pratt Kelly used to say in her mayoral campaign in Washington, DC, against the incumbent, Marion Barry, shortly after he was arrested for buying and snorting cocaine, "Clean house with a shovel, not a broom." This agenda, which embodies the principles of good government and saves scarce public money, can win support across the political spectrum. To paraphrase President Bill Clinton's aphorism about welfare, government assistance to business should be a second chance, not a way of life.

The first step toward removing TINA from the life-support systems of subsidies is disclosure. The public is largely unaware of the elephant-mouse casserole being cooked up in the economic development kitchen. A comprehensive inventory of business subsidies would shine like a prison spotlight on current abuses, though I have yet to see *any* state, county, or municipality publish one. The several times I've tried to perform this analysis myself, often with the support of one or more key local legislators, I've come up against more stonewalling and excuses and delay than I could overcome on a shoestring budget. But it *can* be done. You'll just have to prepare for a long haul, and make sure you've got plenty of allies inside government to help you dig out the financial skeletons.

The impact of uncovering even one pork-barrel program can be remarkable. Perhaps the best practitioner in the field is Greg LeRoy, founder and executive director of Good Jobs First. His groundbreaking

study, *No More Candy Store*, was one of the first serious efforts to identify the gargantuan size of these subsidies, the self-destructive competition among jurisdictions to attract TINA businesses, and the various
laws and policies that perpetuate this game.[5] Most of the data on subsidies cited earlier (see chapter 1) came from the studies and alerts of
Good Jobs First, and his recent book, *The Great American Job Scam*, is
a compelling summary of nearly twenty years of research.[6]

A good analysis of business incentives would examine all types of
pork, including grants, loans, loan guarantees, capital investments,
bond issuances, tax breaks, export support programs, and mayor's junkets overseas. As you drill into the data, be prepared to find outrageous
examples of pro-TINA programs. In New Mexico, for example, you
would find a statewide industrial revenue bond program, which gives
government guarantees on all kinds of gigantic TINA corporations,
from Intel's microprocessors to Louisiana Energy Services' uranium
enrichment. In Maine steep tax breaks are awarded to investors in
export-oriented manufacturers and outsider-run banks.

I must admit that I'm torn between the libertarian argument to
eliminate all business subsidies, and the progressive argument to refocus subsidies on LOIS business. In one sense it doesn't matter because
either will serve the Small-Mart Revolution. The choice clearly depends
on your community's sensibilities. If you distrust any government
interventions in the market, by all means wipe the subsidies away. But
I see merits in the argument that says, look, it's our tax money, and we
should be able spend it any way we wish. If we know that LOIS businesses confer much more benefit on the community, why not focus
our subsidies exclusively on such businesses?

Maybe you can satisfy both libertarians and progressives by gradually replacing government handouts with government investments. A
local government might create a community investment fund that
transforms every public dollar of assistance into a dollar of stock. This
way, successful "economic development" would build an asset base
that could be reinvested down the road in more development, all while
carefully keeping ownership of the beneficiary businesses local. Residents too might be allowed to add capital to the fund in exchange for
ownership shares.

But don't stop with overt subsidies. The entire economic development establishment, whose ranks include not only development professionals but also politicians running communities and the city managers and civil servants they oversee, needs to be revamped. It's one thing for a community to put out the welcome mat for a TINA business that comes knocking. I'm queasy about legislation that keeps these businesses out, especially in poor communities, where any jobs are essential to relieve suffering. It's quite another to *subsidize any TINA business, even indirectly through the expenditures of official time.* Government personnel should be studiously neutral about TINA.

The economic development establishment attempts to serve all people, all the time. That's laudable when it comes to residents. But there's an enormous difference between serving businesses owned by residents and serving those owned by outsiders. True, both create jobs, pay taxes, and generate multipliers, but we know that the LOIS businesses are much better at doing all these things. To pretend that all businesses are equal is just dumb public policy. The economic development establishment has limited resources, and every dime, every minute, every scrap of paper wasted on TINA is a precious resource not available for LOIS. Moreover, the real-world consequence of serving all businesses equally is to continue dishing out elephant-mouse casserole. My advice: welcome TINA, but serve only LOIS.

The new priority of politicians and economics developers should be to expand existing local businesses and grow new ones. Think of it as the "49ers Theory of Economic Development." Rather than throw risky long bombs, quarterback Joe Montana used to lead the San Francisco 49ers down the field through a steady stream of two to three yard passes and short runs, getting first down after first down, until the team inexorably crossed the exasperated opponent's goal line. That's the key to winning the economic Superbowl.

## A New Public Policy Agenda

TINA biases have insinuated themselves into an enormous range of laws, regulations, and policies. Every existing business support program needs to be reviewed and recast in community-friendly terms. Here are some goals policymakers might keep in mind: Make publicly supported incubators and one-stop small business shops off-limits to TINA. Use public money for educating entrepreneurs, whether through adult-ed classes or full-blown MBA programs, to emphasize LOIS and restrict scholarships to committed LOIS entrepreneurs. Fund studies that focus on the needs of LOIS businesses—on indicators, assets, leakages, entrepreneurship, finance, policy reform—and take advantage of a whole new generation of economists eager to do this kind of research. Send the economic developers to LOIS reeducation camps (well, how about some nice seminars with four-star meals) to help undo their many years of misguided economic thinking—after all, they are important local assets, too.

Every department in City Hall exerts influence on economic development. Take infrastructure. Sure, every business in the community can benefit from better water treatment and high-speed Internet lines. But huge airports and high-speed highways often serve nonlocal businesses coming into town for sales, labor, or resources more than local businesses reaching out. The imperatives for policymakers, again, are clear: Prioritize public investments that support primarily existing LOIS entrepreneurs. Wherever infrastructure expenditures are made to serve one particular business or one cluster of businesses (perhaps an industrial park or a shopping mall), charge the beneficiaries full freight or at least insist on getting an equivalent piece of equity.

Or take zoning. The smart-growth movement has pointed out that it's time to scrap obsolete zoning laws that fragment and separate community functions. The ideal neighborhood should have some residences, some retail outlets, even some small-scale farming and light industrial activity. Many LOIS businesses can thrive in a community that permits a variety of uses. As gasoline prices rise, zoning reform will allow us to reduce our self-destructive dependence on automobiles, the archenemy of localization. It's up to community planners who are mindful of regional patterns to provide the right incentives that will lead developers and investors to redesign and rebuild communities friendlier to pedestrians, bikers, and mass transit.

Zoning reform would eschew new industrial parks, which usually grind up fresh wilderness for new parking lots and are then seized upon by large TINA firms looking for just another subsidy. Instead, we need to emphasize the commercial potential of existing buildings, even our homes. The more efficiently we use already built space, the better we can protect open spaces from the onslaught of new growth. In my neighborhood in northwest Washington, DC, the city forbids me from hiring more than one person to work in my basement and kindly awards my home-based employees with a twenty-five dollar parking ticket every day. Neighborhoods should be revamped into multiuse communities where adults can walk to the grocery store and to work, and where kids can walk to school

Speaking of schools, don't forget that they, too. are important generators of wealth. Around the country, school officials have unwisely decided to bulldoze smaller schools, many of which had provided the demand—through teacher, student, and school purchases—that drove neighboring LOIS businesses. In their place new mega-schools, built on the edge of town, have become the new breeding ground for fast-food restaurants, truancy, and unregulated growth.[7] These decisions, often made in the name of efficiency, have had many adverse consequences. Kids who are already staving off diabetes and obesity from too much junk food and too little exercise now must drive or take the bus instead of walk or bicycle. Poorer students without cars, dependent on the bus, can no longer stay for after-school programs. Each mega-school needs a proportionately larger parking lot to accommodate all these vehicles, which promotes sprawl and spoils the environment. Because schools have parallel but separate jurisdiction from city councils, even communities with strong smart-growth policies are finding that these policies can be eviscerated by misguided boards of education. In short, maintaining older schools turns out to be an important pro-LOIS strategy.

When local government participates in the marketplace like a business, it should give LOIS businesses an equal shot at its contracts or investments. For procurement, local officials might form intermediaries that can aggregate and strengthen LOIS bids. For investments, they might move their banking activities to local banks and team up with the local investment community to set up cutting-edge hedge, venture, and pension funds that specialize in LOIS businesses. The economic development department might help LOIS businesses prepare and sell local stock issues. They might even sponsor the kind of electronic community stock exchange discussed in chapter 5.

State and local governments spend about $1.9 trillion per year.[8]

Redirecting even a small fraction of this business into the hands of LOIS firms could result in a huge boost to the state and local economies. Such preferences are hardly unprecedented. Building on long-standing laws that award bidding preferences to firms that recycle, embrace energy efficiency, use alternative fuels, or are owned by women and minorities, several states give modest advantages to local bidders. Georgia, for example, provides a bidding boost for local forest products, Louisiana for in-state milk, and six states—Alaska, Montana, New Mexico, West Virginia, Wyoming, and California—to all in-state businesses.[9] More than 120 cities have passed a living wage ordinance that denies contracts with companies that pay poverty wages (usually below about ten dollars per hour).[10] With these precedents two dozen cities, including Washington, DC, have enacted purchasing preferences for local businesses.[11]

Government preferences like these invite lawsuits by spurned bidders and may someday be found by courts to violate U.S. trade obligations (see below). Even if these ordinances do pass legal scrutiny, my free-market principles are not entirely comfortable with government tilting the playing field toward LOIS. Still, I believe that it is possible to reconcile market principles with a modest, across-the-board bidding advantage to LOIS businesses. Why shouldn't a municipal authority make the same calculations that businesses and consumers make about the benefits of buying local? If a city can foresee that a local bidder will deliver two or three times the local jobs and tax revenue as a nonlocal bidder, why shouldn't it take this into account in its contracts?[12] A sophisticated public bidding system might ask vendors not only to present the prices and quality of various procurement items but also to calculate the different local multipliers that will flow from the deal and the resulting tax revenues. Properly framed, these rules would probably survive any trade-treaty challenge since, on their face, they would treat local and nonlocal vendors equally.

Some local governments may find themselves limited by state law, in which case they must be prepared to lobby state lawmakers. For example, if state procurement laws prevent bidding preferences to LOIS companies, they will need to be amended.

Minor tweaks in other state laws can yield enormous jackpots for small business. Nebraska recently added a charitable tax credit that it

hopes will lead to residents placing $94 billion in community founda-
tions over the next fifty years, which in turn could finance a wide range
of community and economic development projects.[13] Were Maine to
amend its tax credits so that they were awarded not only to investors in
nonlocal manufacturers and nonlocal banks, as under the current law,
but also to investors in local business (each dollar invested in a LOIS
business, for example, could take forty cents off your state tax bill), it
would set in motion an entire revolution in retirement and pension
funds in the state. That's what happened in Canada, once similar tax
credits were put in place.

A comprehensive overhaul of state and local taxes also could provide
an enormous boost for the Small-Mart Revolution. Many good ideas
are floating around, but two deserve special attention because they are
so obvious and together make such a politically attractive package. That
is, couple what some have called "green taxes" with an abolition of all
business taxes.

First, shift taxes from things we want to augment (income, wealth,
sales, property) to things we want to reduce (pollution, waste, nonrenewable resource use). I don't mean to underestimate the complexities
of such a tax shift. As energy gets more expensive, for example, we naturally will use less and the tax collections could flatten or even shrink.
There would have to be a gradual phasing in of the green taxes and a
phasing out of the old taxes, with annual adjustments to account for
what economists call "price elasticities of demand."[14] There are administrative questions, like where the tax gets assessed—at the oil well or
at the gas pump, for example. And if one bold community or a small
state moves ahead, energy-intensive businesses might move out. This
highlights, again, the need for a LOIS-based economy where most
businesses will adapt rather than flee. Only after these green-tax
options have been exhausted should a community consider reinstitut-
ing other forms of taxes.[15]

To consider how big these new kinds of taxes would need to be,
here's a thought experiment. All levels of government in the United
States—federal, state, and local—currently collect about $3 trillion
dollars in taxes annually. The country burns up about 100 quadrillion
BTUs of energy each year. To cover all these revenues, the tax on a gal-
lon of gasoline (and all its equivalents in utilities and in other energy

products) would need to be about $3.35 per gallon. Given what gasoline currently costs, that would raise its price to five to six dollars per gallon, still well below what many Europeans currently pay.[16]

Americans' romance with their gas guzzlers probably stands in the way of any major federal overhaul of the tax structure. But over the past generation, state and local success stories have begun to lay the foundation for a major tax shift. California assesses one dollar per pack of cigarettes and uses the proceeds to educate the public on the dangers of smoking. Iowa places special taxes on sales of fertilizers and pesticides, and reinvests them in the Leopold Center, one of the nation's leading think tanks supporting sustainable agriculture. A dozen states charge consumers extra for their "rentals" of glass, plastic, or metallic containers, and then rebate the charges when they are presented for recycling.

The other reform, which might even serve as a magnet for TINA businesses (but not to the disadvantage of LOIS), would be to eliminate business taxes altogether.[17] As green taxes are phased in, these would be the first to be phased out. Business taxes currently account for just over 2 percent of all state and local revenues in the United States.[18] Who pays these? For the most part, LOIS entrepreneurs who cannot afford, as TINA firms can, an army of accountants and attorneys to circumvent taxes. Eliminating business taxation is a nice way to stimulate the economy by putting out to pasture the profession that contributes the least to community well-being—namely TINA's lawyers.

A final policy opportunity lies completely outside economics. As communities get savvier in their campaigns to eliminate the most egregious practices of nonlocal business, their opponents will get more aggressive in winning political support the old-fashioned way—through bribes, graft, and political donations. Smart communities need to undertake preemptive campaign finance reform and impose strict limits on what outsiders, especially nonlocal businesses, can contribute to city council, school board, or referenda campaigns.[19]

## Anti-TINA Ordinances

Some jurisdictions are going one step further and fighting TINA businesses directly. Nine Midwest states, which are responsible for a third of the nation's agricultural output, either ban or put significant restrictions on corporate farming.[20] Thomas Linzey, founder of the Community Environmental Legal Defense Fund (CELDF), has been organizing rural communities in Pennsylvania to do likewise. Deploying an ordinance adopted first by the Southampton Township, ten local governments in the state now ban corporate ownership of farmland or corporate participation in farming. Still permitted are family owners, partnerships with real people, nonprofits, and cooperatives, exemptions that essentially keep farm ownership local. Another CELDF-drafted ordinance, passed by Wayne township and two other local governments, gives communities the right to ban any corporation from doing business locally if it has a history of violating laws. Linzey is developing a Pentagon-sized arsenal of these measures that prohibit corporate involvement in mining or forestry, impose fees on imported sludge being used as fertilizer, ban genetically modified seeds and crops, demand various corporate disclosures before awarding permits to businesses, and mandate recycling and solar retrofits of buildings. In a powerful stump speech he gives around the country, tinged with his native Alabama accent, Linzey seems proudest of his new ordinance that will strip corporations of "legal personhood" at the municipal level, denying them rights of free speech, due process, and equal protection that federal laws have increasingly given to corporations over the last one hundred years. He hopes to create a test case that might get the U.S. Supreme Court to review its rulings on corporate rights.

Localities have passed similarly bold initiatives against chain stores. Stacy Mitchell, of the Institute for Local Self-Reliance, has become the unofficial beat reporter for this movement. Peruse her website—www.newrules.org—and you'll find literally dozens of these kinds of laws.[21] For example:

- Kent County, Maryland, and Corvallis, Oregon, have revised their comprehensive plans to limit chain store development and support LOIS business.
- Belfast, Maryland, adopted a six-month moratorium on all box stores larger than twenty-five thousand square feet, and ultimately banned stores greater than seventy-five thousand square feet (most Wal-Marts are double that size). Similar size limits can now be found in Alaska, Arkansas, Maryland, and Oregon.

- Greenfield, Massachusetts, demands that all stores larger than twenty thousand square feet undergo a comprehensive review, and only receive a permit to proceed when outstanding questions about traffic, net tax revenue, public infrastructure, and environmental quality are resolved. A similar ordinance in Stoughton, Wisconsin, also evaluates whether the proposed store would hurt existing local businesses.

- About a dozen communities, including Bristol, Rhode Island; Bainbridge, Washington; and Coronado and San Francisco, California, prohibit or limit the entry of "formula businesses," as judged by their signs, logos, architecture, services, uniforms, and product lines.

- Palm Beach, Florida, allows only businesses where at least half the anticipated customers are local residents.

- Brunswick, Maine, demands that new retailers have facades and store windows that reinforce the pedestrian-friendly downtown.

Some economists would accuse these measures of being "protectionist," and in one sense they are right. Like almost all local laws, these aim to protect the well-being of the community. But it's hard to see this as the same kind of protectionism economists condemn when, as is true almost everywhere today, the market power between players has become so unequal. Chain stores often come into a community, deploy huge national marketing budgets, temporarily undercut local prices, and then jack them back up when the local competition is decimated. The antitrust laws communities once relied on to prevent these market abuses have been all but gutted since the 1980s. For beleaguered communities that have long been on the receiving end of TINA's snowballing power—those struggling to maintain their businesses, their downtowns, their ways of life—these tools finally begin to level the playing field. And if you believe, as I do, that every community should have the right to shape its own economy, these initiatives are wholly reasonable exercises of "home rule" power, the power of self-governance most states grant to local jurisdictions. But I offer several cautions.

Anti-TINA initiatives (unlike pro-LOIS ones) invite lawsuits. Any significant limitation on the ability of businesses to move in and out of communities, particularly if the limitation favors locals to the detriment of nonlocals, may be found by a court to be an unconstitutional infringement on interstate commerce, as well as a violation of our trade treaty commitments. Delicate questions of legal power are implicated, and adversely affected TINA companies will try to claim that existing state and federal laws preempt the local government from acting. Sometimes, the legal challenges get personal.

A couple of Thomas Linzey's opponents have gone after the local officials passing his ordinances, threatening to bankrupt them personally. As Linzey was helping the small township of St. Thomas to oppose a planned quarry, Frank Stern decided to make his first run for public office as a write-in candidate to stop the project. After Stern, a Republican, won, he was stunned to receive a letter from the quarry's attorneys warning him of dire economic consequences, to the township *and to himself,* should he not recuse himself from any town decision-making about the project. Linzey was outraged: "There's something wrong here when a corporation can nullify an election. . . . [T]hree individuals who run the company, coming in and telling 5,800 people in this township that they can't get what they want. It's a fundamental breach. And it's incompatible with the basic founding values of this country."[22]

Linzey is drilling along a brittle fault line in the American legal system that has long sought to balance public and private rights. On one side are property rights advocates, who believe that individuals should have an unfettered right to develop their own land, build factories, operate businesses, and make a living with as little state interference as possible.[23] On the other side are public interest advocates like CELDF, convinced that corporate rights have gone too far and that one of the responsibilities of local government is to step in and protect small business, public health, and endangered wildlife. Both sides are eager to do battle.

Even if the Supreme Court ultimately rejects his view, Linzey believes the fight is worth it because it might ignite a popular backlash against corporate power. And clearly, there are instances where undertaking bold initiatives is appropriate and effective. But the practical questions should not be lightly dismissed: defending against lawsuits is not cheap, and courts these days are not exactly populated by visionary judges.

Sometimes legal action can devolve into a long, expensive cat-and-mouse game. After Calvert County, Maryland, passed a limitation on how much space any one retail store could occupy, Wal-Mart creatively decided to divide its planned stores into two smaller ones, side by side.[24] In fact, it's easy to imagine how clever chain store operators will find ways of tiptoeing around most of these regulations. No formulas allowed? Fine, we'll allow each of our store owners to modify the décor and designs. One new urbanist writer recently reported breathlessly that there are "genuine, if small, signs that a number of [national] retailers are now thinking outside the big box. Retail grocers such as Whole Foods Market and Trader Joe's Inc. are building more aesthetically pleasing stores by incorporating mixed-use and pedestrian-friendly designs into their stores."[25] No chains? Well, okay, we'll just create a bunch of subsidiary companies, one store per company. Thus far, these fears have not been realized. San Francisco, for example, has implemented an ordinance against formula retailers without much problem. But I worry what rabbits Wal-Mart, Target, and Costco will pull out of their legal hats down the road. They have all the money in the world to invent creative new circumventions around local laws—and we don't.

I agonized over these questions when the chamber of commerce and the development corporation of Andersonville, a Swedish-American neighborhood in Chicago filled with fabulous local businesses, asked me to participate in a blue-ribbon panel of experts sponsored by the Urban Land Institute on the future of economic development in the neighborhood. Just before we began our deliberations, Alderman Mary Ann Smith, in whose ward Andersonville sits, told us that she was very interested in passing an ordinance, sponsored by Alderman Patrick O'Connor in the Chicago City Council, forbidding formula retail stores in the neighborhood. Every one of the dozen or so other panel members was either a private developer or a smart-growth expert with sympathy for private developers, and it's fair to say that their views on the ordinance ranged from politely hostile to bitterly opposed. I ultimately told them that I would not endorse the ordinance either, *but only* if they would agree to a strong statement of support for aggressively promoting local business, which they did (some reluctantly).

I'm still reflecting on my experience in Chicago. Ellen Shepard, the

head of the Andersonville Chamber of Commerce, argues that one reason she favors the formula-retail ordinance is that she saw how useful
another city ordinance banning the clustering of nonlocal banks had
been. That ordinance prohibits one bank branch from locating within
a city block of another. Perhaps because this ordinance still allows
some branch banks, but *balances* their commercial interests with a
community's desire to promote local banks and credit unions, I find it
more appetizing. Perhaps similar ordinances that prevent the clustering of chain stores, as opposed to prohibiting them outright, might
offer more market-friendly ways for a community to support local
business.

One difference I have with some proponents of anti-TINA legislation is over our degree of confidence that LOIS can prevail. A few
activists believe that the onslaught of chain stores is *unstoppable*
because they always will be selling cheaper goods. If they turn out to be
right, I may need to rethink my position. But my belief, and the argument of this book, is that with careful shopping, consumers can localize most of their expenditures without compromising quality, price, or
convenience.

## High-Road Business Communities

The domestic rules surrounding the relationship between local laws
and interstate commerce seem quite reasonable: states and localities
are free to enact laws protecting local health, safety, beauty, and welfare, provided that the laws equally burden all businesses, especially
local vis-à-vis nonlocal businesses. Consistent with this principle, I
believe that there is another, legally bulletproof approach communities
can take to keep chain stores away: pass a living wage ordinance.

Despite a few remaining philosophical, economic, and political
quibbles about minimum wages, the public broadly accepts the idea
that no business should be allowed to pay employees beneath a certain
level. The only real argument is what exactly that level should be. In
recent years minimum wages have not kept pace with inflation. The
minimum wage of $5.15 per hour in 2005 buys, once inflation is fac-
tored out, about 68 percent what it did in 1968.[26] Seventeen states and
the District of Columbia—representing 45 percent of the American

people—have found this situation sufficiently disturbing to raise their minimum wages above the national floor.

Even many of these higher minimums, of course, leave a full-time worker in poverty. A growing number of communities find this situation deplorable. One hundred and twenty-three cities and counties have enacted living wage ordinances that raise minimum wages above the local poverty line.[27] Nearly all these ordinances, as noted, simply put restrictions on companies bidding for municipal contracts, but the measure enacted by the city of Santa Fe actually sets a universal minimum (exempting only some very small businesses).

In most of these living wage debates, small businesses—perhaps following the outdated scripts of the National Federation of Independent Business (NFIB)—have been on the wrong side of the argument, both morally and strategically. A few are justifiably worried about the effect on their bottom line, but the vast majority, I believe, really are more concerned about the slippery slope (what might the wage level be raised to next year?) and the effect on the local business climate. What small businesses have overlooked is the relative effect on chain stores. The living wage is to Wal-Mart what kryptonite was to Superman. Most chain stores have business models that depend on paying bottom dollar, and any city that passes a living wage will begin to see the chains pack up and leave.

## Global Trade Politics

LOIS-minded communities need to get more seriously involved in the ongoing debate over the shape of global rules governing free trade. The most critical rules affecting U.S. communities are those articulated by the World Trade Organization (WTO), reinforced regionally through the European Union (EU) and the North American Free Trade Agreement (NAFTA) and ultimately through proposed agreements like the Central American Free Trade Agreement (CAFTA) and the Free Trade in the Americas Agreement (FTAA). While the details of these agreements differ, their impact on LOIS is uniformly pernicious.

Truly free trade is undeniably beneficial to communities. According to the theory of comparative advantage underlying trade agreements, specialization by communities allows each to purchase a global "basket" of goods and services at a lower price. Tariffs and other barriers, the theory suggests, usually boomerang on the country imposing them by denying those communities access to the best and cheapest goods, technologies, and ideas. What WTO advocates don't consider is that a healthy trading system must not choke the beneficial local multipliers that flow from a high degree of self-reliance. A successful trading system, whether local or global, also requires rules over contracts, insurance, torts, consumer safety, environmental performance, labor standards, and monopolistic behavior, and these must be written so that they harness the powers of comparative advantage and the local multiplier simultaneously.

Anyone doubting that this is possible should look at the trade system within the United States over the past two hundred years, largely governed by "commerce clause" jurisprudence in constitutional law and by various statutes passed by Congress. Consider six central principles of our current intrastate trading system:

- **Universal Coverage.** Today's trade rules essentially govern all American players equally, including consumers, businesses, nonprofits, cooperatives, and government entities. For example, when the United States forbids discrimination in hiring, it applies the rules to everyone, including itself. To enact rules that impose limits on, say, just nonprofits and cooperatives, would give other types of business an unfair advantage.

- **Floors, Not Ceilings.** The U.S. trading system encourages legislative experimentation at the state and local level. If a city wishes to impose tougher regulations on business, it should be free to do so, provided that the regulations are nondiscriminatory. Federal standards also should be floors, below which no community can fall. Thus, Santa Fe could enact a living wage ordinance but not a local law permitting wages below the national minimum.

- **Tolerate Subsidies.** The current rules allow state and local governments to subsidize TINA heavily. Irrational as these subsidies are, permitting them is nevertheless important because a top-down ban on subsidies could chill many reasonable government initiatives promoting entrepreneurship, microenterprise, and local purchasing. Courts nowadays tend to step in only in cases where government behavior amounts to predatory behavior (essentially an antitrust standard).

- **Market Participant Rights.** The U.S. Supreme Court treats government agencies as private companies when they act as contractors or investors. Basically, you can invest in or contract with whomever you wish, without worrying about being charged with discrimination (though there are usually local standards about fiduciary responsibilities and competitive bidding). You can also refuse to invest in or contract with certain firms—tobacco companies or firms using sweatshops, for example—without fear. It's only fair that, as "market participants," governmental actors should be held to standards no better or worse than those facing private business contractors or investors.

- **Localist Values.** The current trade rules allow state and local governments broad leeway to legislate in many areas that might touch on trade, such as local safety, health, labor rights, aesthetics, environment, and economic development. Smart growth, local business incubators, and buy-local campaigns all fall within these categories.

- **Universal Enforcement.** The judicial system in the United States is very complex, with overlapping jurisdictions of federal, state, and local courts. But it's fair to say that anyone who feels aggrieved under the nation's trade rules, whether individuals, businesses, localities, or national governments, can find some court to march into and demand that the rules are enforced consistently and fairly.

Can anyone claim with a straight face that these principles have diminished the economic performance of the United States for more than two hundred years? Yet, incredibly, *none* of these principles are being followed or even remotely respected by today's free-trade regimes.

The current trade agreements regulate governments, not corporations. They unfairly give TINA CEOs more power over a community's life than its own public policymakers. In 2003, concerned that open-pit mining would disturb desert lands that native Quechan tribespeople call "The Trail of Dream," California passed a law requiring miners to undertake environmental restoration when they were done with their extraction. Glamis Gold Ltd., a Canadian corporation, is now suing the U.S. government—and effectively California—for $50 million for "indirect expropriation" of the company's property under NAFTA. Trade agreements impose no burdens on mining companies, only on government regulating their activities. As California Attorney General Bill Lockyer says, "California has been a leader in environmental and public health law, and to give foreign investors the authority to effectively nullify these laws under the banner of free trade makes no sense."[28]

TINA-controlled regulatory bodies are setting "scientific" standards that impose regulatory ceilings prohibiting local experimentation. Making a similar argument as Glamis Gold before a NAFTA tribunal, another Canadian company, Methanex Corporation, claimed that California had taken away its "expected future profits" by requiring a phase-out of the additive MTBE in gasoline. California won the case, but not because MBTE was a toxic hazard to human and environmental health that the state was legitimately regulating, but because Methanex only made the "M" (methyl) part of the chemical and therefore lacked standing to proceed with its $970 million claim.[29] A U.S. company making a similar claim against Canadian laws prohibiting a similar fuel additive, MMT, won, leading to a repeal of the law.

As the author of the California law, Representative Liz Figueroa, wrote with Jesse Colorado Swanhuyser: "In this country, our elected official have sworn an oath to serve the public interest and our courts have similar duties to uphold state and national constitutions. Our entire structure of representative government abides by the rules of careful checks and balances. NAFTA's trade tribunals are contrary to that system. With no public forum for oversight or accountability, three individuals decide the fate of the nation."[30]

Subsidies are presumed guilty, while privatization is presumed innocent. A WTO tribunal recently agreed with Brazil's challenge to U.S. subsidies to cotton farmers.[31] The United States is going after European Union subsidies to Airbus, and the Europeans are countering in complaints against U.S. state and local subsidies to Boeing.[32] Every year the EU publishes a list of hundreds of offensive state and local subsidy programs, and the challenges are sure to come harder and faster. Again, the resulting loss of these subsidies may be desirable, but not at the expense of local democracy.

Private investors and contractors are free to do anything, while government investors and contractors must follow rigid rules that give TINA businesses a clear edge. As it became clear that the proposed CAFTA agreement would prohibit local governments from continuing to give preferences to local contractors, a third of the twenty-two governors who had endorsed the U.S. Trade Representatives negotiations withdrew their support by early 2005. Iowa Governor Thomas J. Vilsack proclaimed these limitations "unacceptable."[33]

The prohibitions could go far beyond state and local procurement. Any government measures that promote local purchasing, whether "Made in Maine" labels or an Oregon Marketplace, might be outlawed as well.

And perhaps most alarmingly, these agreements leave local governments and consumers with virtually no role in challenging or defending the rules. Instead, they must rely on their national trade representatives, and the cases are usually argued secretly before three-person "dispute panels" made up of trade lawyers and businesspeople who have very little sympathy for community rights. "Never before in the history of the United States," write Figueroa and Swanhuyser, "has such absolute authority been granted to any one body."[34]

As this book goes to press, a seismic political shift is occurring. A number of players, once uncritically supportive of all trade agreements—the National League of Cities, the National Governors Association, the National Conference of State Legislatures, and the U.S. Business and Industry Council—are now openly expressing doubts and holding back their endorsements for further agreements. For those agreements still under negotiation, there's an urgent need to build on this momentum, to lobby to remove the provisions offensive to communities and, should they remain, to make sure that the U.S. Congress never ratifies them. For those agreements already in place, like the WTO and NAFTA, communities should keep in mind that these rules are largely untested. The more LOIS initiatives that set contrary precedents, the harder it will be for a tribunal to overturn them, and the more likely that any act of global preemption will unleash a much-deserved domestic backlash against these agreements that could bury them once and for all.

That today's trade agreements only regulate government action also turns out to be a gigantic loophole. Consumers and businesses are free to launch any LOIS initiatives they please. For FDR liberals, social-democrat Sweden lovers, and unrepentant socialists, this reason alone should raise doubts about relying on any government body to implement LOIS and highlight the importance of implementing the Small-Mart Revolution primarily through the private and civic sectors.

## A Declaration for Independents

To enact these policy reforms, local government must take itself very seriously. Unlike their counterparts elsewhere in the world, U.S. communities turn out to have a remarkable amount of power. The Tenth Amendment reserves all powers not expressly allocated to the federal government to the states, and most states grant their localities broad home-rule powers. Very few jurisdictions lack the legal authority to implement the agenda above, just the political will to do so.

Local governments sometimes get distracted looking for regional solutions. Sure, there are some large-scale issues like school finance, mass transit systems, and sprawl prevention that would benefit from regional planning. But it is wise to recall what Gandhi said when he visited Great Britain and was asked what he thought of Western Civilization. "It would be a very good idea," he replied. That's about the best that can be said about proposals that our local political authorities should merge and reorganize into something other than what they are now. It's telling that people often speak about regional *governance*, rather than government, to concede the point that, well, actual elected bodies outside the Portland, Oregon, metropolitan area do not really exist.[35]

There is nothing magical about regional scale. To the contrary, regional decision-making often means moving thorny political questions into unelected commissions and backroom committees, where TINA interest groups with the most money get wonderful new opportunities to call the shots. The history of regional initiatives in the United States hardly inspires confidence about their local sensitivity. The Bonneville Power Administration (BPA) and the Tennessee Valley Authority (TVA) brought electricity and water to remote regions, but at enormous environmental and social cost. Bonneville's knuckleheaded infatuation with creating a regional electricity system anchored by five giant nuclear power plants almost bankrupted the entire Pacific Northwest.

Regional planners assert time and again that there is no such thing as a local economy anymore, and that it's pointless for a locality to pretend otherwise.[36] Yet if small businesses are thriving in almost every sector of the economy, if entrepreneurs can use the Internet to work across space and time, if the demand for local services is growing, and all the other trends of deglobalization discussed earlier play out, what's the empirical case for this? Scott Campbell, a professor of urban and regional studies at the University of Michigan, says his profession's increasing obsession with regionalism is a symptom of what he calls Goldilocks Syndrome: the national level is too big to get anything done and the local level is too small, so the in-between level of the region must be "just right."[37]

Most worrisome, regionalism has become an ideological whip for communities to consolidate and unify their bids for globetrotting corporations.[38] But if recruitment is deemed counterproductive, the flimsy rationale for this kind of cooperation vanishes. For regionalism to work effectively on the few issues that localities truly cannot handle on their own, the principle of subsidiary must be respected and local power should be employed as often as possible. Public policy must proceed first and foremost at the city, community, neighborhood, and block levels.

## Taking Back City Hall

The public policy agenda outlined above may not happen without a huge political fight. Even politicians sympathetic to LOIS are afraid to challenge powerful TINA interests. Only when the Small-Mart Revolution is led by determined consumers, investors, and entrepreneurs will the legislators follow.

Several years back I sat with a half-dozen people in the office of the mayor of Annapolis, Maryland, to convince her that she should declare a "Buy Local Day." Also in the room were several activists, the head of economic development, and two LOIS businessmen. The mayor was a good listener but cautious—she clearly did not want to offend anyone.

The economic development person denounced the proposal. Despite his earlier enthusiasm for our work, he thought that overt city support for local business would alienate chain stores and complicate his TINA recruitment efforts. The activists then reacted angrily, reminding the mayor of how many numbskull projects the economic development department had sponsored that wound up hurting local business, spawning sprawl, and draining municipal coffers. Into the fray of rising tempers entered the local businesspeople as voices of moderation, reason, and mediation. They suggested ways of wording the campaign and the resolution so that they were least offensive to TINA advocates. The mayor was relieved and swayed, and once the head of economic development realized the campaign was going to happen, he, too, backed down.

Had the activists not been involved, the meeting never would have happened. Had the mayor not been involved, the formal declaration would have been impossible. Had the small businesspeople not been present, the win-win solutions never would have been placed on the table. Everyone played an indispensable role—except, of course, the economic developer, whose outdated views had to be circumvented. But once the diverse stakeholders started working together, the Small-Mart Revolution began to materialize.

# Thirty Items for Policymakers

## DAILY MANTRA

Remove *all* public support, including anything that requires city staff time and energy, from nonlocal business and refocus it instead, laser-like, on local business.

## LOCAL STUDIES

1. **Indicators.** Prepare quantifiable measures of the community's quality of life (economic, environmental, social, and political) that hold economic development policies accountable. Conduct public hearings in which residents decide which indicators are most relevant, then put together an annual report on the best ones, distribute it widely, and place it on a website.

2. **Assets Analysis.** Gather data on assets in the region, especially unused or underused economic inputs like unemployed labor, abandoned lots and buildings, and idle machinery, all to clarify what's available for new or expanded small business.

3. **Imports Analysis.** Prepare an annual measure of imports and dependencies, especially in basic goods and services, to underscore where local consumer demands already exist for new locally owned businesses.

4. **Subsidy Inventory.** Perform a full evaluation of all subsidies given in the last ten years to business (grants, loans, guarantees, tax abatements, capital improvements, TIFs, and bond issues), and catalogue which, if any, went to local businesses.

5. **State of the Region Report.** Prepare an annual booklet with the latest assessments of indicators, assets, and imports, as well as other inventories noted below, all to strategically identify business opportunities that offer the greatest benefit for your community.

6. **Community Reinvestment Report.** Study which local depository institutions—and, if any exist, which investment institutions—are reinvesting more than 90 percent of their savings/investments locally.

7. **Pension Fund Analysis.** Identify which pension funds, whether public or private, specialized or mutual, might be capable of reinvesting locally.

8. **Good Community-keeping Seals.** Evaluate the performance of all businesses in the region and award a special seal to any firm that is not only locally owned but also a good performer with respect to workers, consumers, and the environment.

## LOCAL TRAINING

1. **Entrepreneurship Programs.** Revitalize entrepreneurship programs in public schools, community colleges, and local universities to emphasize local and small business. Allocate municipal funds to help other institutions like churches, civic groups, and small business associations set up entrepreneurship study groups.

2. **Mentorship Programs.** Link established businesspeople (especially retirees with extra time) with young and aspiring entrepreneurs.

3. **Place-based Scholarships.** To retain the best and brightest, create a scholarship fund that extends no-interest loans to college-bound kids. (If they return to and settle in the community after graduation, they enjoy no- or low-interest provisions; otherwise, interest rates kick up to market levels.)

4. **Incubators.** Limit public support to incubators that house only locally owned businesses, and link them to local entrepreneurship programs and business mentors.

## LOCAL PURCHASING

1. **The Homegrown Directory.** Prepare a directory of local businesses organized by product or business type that could help residents buy local. This could then be distributed in hard copies and over the Internet to consumers.

2. **Regional Directory.** Combine your homegrown directory with neighboring towns around a regional theme.

3. **Selective Public Contracting.** Give a 5 to 10 percent bidding advantage to local businesses. Better still, demand that all bidders estimate anticipated multiplier benefits.

4. **Small Business Bidding Assistance.** Set up an office that helps local business compete more effectively for public contracts.

5. **Broker B2B Deals.** Consider replicating the model of the Oregon Marketplace, which in the 1980s and early 1990s helped local businesses buy cost-effective inputs from local suppliers.

6. **Buy-Local Campaigns.** Support private efforts to create local credit, debit, loyalty, or gift cards, perhaps by providing them to public employees.

7. **Time Dollars.** Help coordinate a city-wide Time Dollar program, and provide tax credits for each Time Dollar earned to promote volunteerism and to lower public expenditures on social services.

8. **Local Currency.** Support or create a local scrip, since only businesses and service providers committed to respending locally will be interested in accepting the currency. Pay bonuses or raises to public employees in the scrip, and accept the scrip for partial payment of taxes, both of which Philadelphia did during the Great Depression.

## LOCAL INVESTING

1. **Bank Local.** Make sure the city uses a local bank or credit union to conduct business and handle payroll.
2. **Invest Local.** Begin moving municipal investment, including surplus revenues and pension funds, into local business either directly or indirectly through local-business venture, hedge, or mutual funds.
3. **Bond Finance.** Limit the use of industrial revenue bonds to projects involving locally owned business.
4. **Subsidies.** Remove as many business subsidies as possible, and sunset the rest. Subject those remaining to a fair bidding process open to local business. Never pay subsidies, including tax abatements, before the promises of jobs and other benefits are fulfilled.

## LOCAL PUBLIC POLICY

1. **Smart Growth.** Revamp zoning to permit most kinds of uses in most places, especially home-based businesses. More fully use developed land and buildings before grinding up green space or farms.
2. **Smart Zoning.** Use local zoning powers to prevent gigantic chain-store clusters that can destroy existing small business (though beware the legal and economic ramifications of total bans on outside competition).
3. **Smart Schools.** Refurbish older, smaller school buildings instead of building newer, bigger ones. Make it easy and safe for children to walk or bicycle to school.
4. **Smart Taxes.** Phase out all taxes on business, income, sales, and property, and phase in revenue-neutral taxes on energy, nonrenewable resources, pollution, and nuisances. If more revenue is ever needed, use Henry George property taxes (on land, not on improvements) to spur business.
5. **Smart Wages.** Create a living wage ordinance to eliminate most working poverty in the community. Use savings in local welfare programs to ease the transition for burdened small business. Celebrate, don't lament, how these scare away chain stores.
6. **Smart Politics.** Invest in serious, professional lobbyists to press for reforms of various national laws concerning subsidies, corporations, banking, and trade that are currently biased against local business.

# eight

\*\*\*\*\*\*\*\*\*\*\*\*\*\*\*\*\*\*\*\*\*\*\*\*\*\*\*\*\*\*\*\*\*\*\*\*\*\*\*\*\*\*\*\*\*\*\*

# COMMUNITY BUILDERS

Bucksport, Maine, is a quaint coastal town halfway between Bangor and Bar Harbor. Historically it was a shipbuilding center "eighteen miles from everywhere," but over the past generation, the backbone of its economy has been a mill run by the International Paper Company. Every year the city council dutifully reviews and updates its emergency plans if, God forbid, a fire, explosion, hurricane, or some other disaster were to destroy the mill. Elaborate preparations are made for routes of escape, entry points for fire and police vehicles, and requisition spots for airlifts of the injured. And yet for the one disaster most likely to occur and most likely to destroy Bucksport, there is no planning whatsoever. What happens if International Paper does what it has done in towns across the United States and moves operations elsewhere?

What's missing in Bucksport, and in practically every community in America, is a serious plan for escaping from TINA. How can the Small-Mart Revolution be accelerated so that the inevitable exit of a big TINA business does not lead to a regional catastrophe? As consumers, investors, entrepreneurs, and policymakers, we can help spread and strengthen LOIS businesses and diversify our local economy. And yet, ultimately, success depends on removing these hats and realizing that we are all members of the same community. The fundamental building block of participatory democracy is community, and each of us, irrespective of our wealth, color, gender, or even age (at least once we're adults), has an equal say as a *citizen* in the future. How can we come together as community builders and assemble the jigsaw pieces of the Small-Mart Revolution into a more compelling action plan?

Wonderful examples abound of community builders taking control of their economy's future. A grassroots group called Sustainable Seattle, for example, pioneered the concept of indicators so that they, not just the economists and economic developers, could define the meaning of progress. Following the ideas in the workbook *Building Community from the Inside Out*, with seventy thousand copies in circulation, communities across the country have prepared comprehensive inventories of assets available for new or expanded business.[1] They tally both economic assets like labor, land, and capital, and noneconomic assets like schools, civic groups, and churches. Using materials prepared by the Rocky Mountain Institute, many small rural communities have studied leakages of dollars from inefficient handling of energy, water, or garbage, and devised grassroots plans to plug the leaks and pump up the local multiplier.[2]

Five building blocks are essential for the Small-Mart Revolution: local planning, local training, local investing, local purchasing, and local policymaking. *Local planning* means analyzing *all* the leaks in the economy, and identifying the precise opportunities for new or expanded LOIS business. *Local training* requires no longer recruiting outside talent and, instead, nurturing a new generation of LOIS entrepreneurs. *Local investing* demands rerouting bank savings and pension investments into LOIS businesses. *Local purchasing* means localizing the buying done by consumers, businesses, and government purchasing agents. And *local policymaking* means, at a minimum, eliminating the vast range of TINA subsidies, zoning, and other government initiatives that currently disadvantage LOIS firms.

We have seen examples of each, yet it is impossible to point to a single community that has woven all five kinds of action into a coherent plan. Consequently, it is easy to ridicule any initiative—an ESCO here, a farmers market there—as being tiny, superficial, and symbolic. We might feel good in our righteous behavior as consumers, investors, or entrepreneurs, but we should be concerned that the community is still marching over a cliff. Standing in isolation and compared to what's possible, these initiatives *are* insignificant. The real power of the Small-Mart Revolution comes when a community engages many parallel activities that reinforce and strengthen one another. When neighbors work together to identify leaks, create leak-plugging business, finance them with their savings, support them with their purchasing, and nurture them with friendly public policies, then the real power of the Small-Mart Revolution can be unleashed.

Over the past three years I have helped design three such efforts at community building: a national network of Local First campaigns, a community planning-and-action process in St. Lawrence County in upstate New York, and a similar process in the Katahdin Region in mid-Maine. All three have only begun to take the kinds of comprehensive steps suggested here. But they offer clues about what community-building might look like in your own town or city.

## Local First

There is a long and rich tradition of social change movements in the United States mobilizing purchasing power. The Founding Fathers dumped British tea in the Boston harbor, the antislavery movement boycotted plantation products, the civil rights movement refused to ride segregated buses, and the antiapartheid movement convinced state and local governments to boycott South African imports. Even contemporary buy-local campaigns have deep historical roots. For more than a century local banking and credit union networks encouraged consumers to keep their savings local to facilitate investment in local business and housing. After the first oil shock in the 1970s, environmental groups organized consumers to use local energy resources like wood, ethanol, small-scale hydropower, and wind. In recent years efforts by farmers to get nearby consumers to buy their fruits, vegetables, and meats have gathered momentum, with grassroots groups promoting local food purchasing in almost every state. A national nonprofit called Food Routes Network (on whose board I sit) distributes packages of marketing materials encouraging residents to "Buy Local, Buy Fresh."

While meeting in Portland, Oregon, in May 2003, the Business Alliance for Local Living Economies (BALLE) decided to lead a national campaign that would encourage chapters to bring together these buy-local campaigns. The hard-headed pragmatism of BALLE's business leaders rallied around the slogan "Local First." "Buy Local" *per se* seemed too focused on just purchasing (and not equally vital local planning, training, investing, and policymaking). "Buy Local" also seemed too rigid. Local First means buy local whenever it's sensible. It recognizes that most of us occasionally will shop at Office Max, Home Depot, and Sam's Club. Local First is not about boycotting these stores and feeling guilty about our transgressions. Local First is about helping consumers do the right thing, not denouncing those who, out of ignorance, indifference, habit, or necessity, continue to engage in business as usual. It aims only to encourage consumers, businesses, and government purchasing agents to buy local. They key word is *encourage*. If you cannot find a local good or service you're looking for at the right price, by all means buy the nonlocal ones.

The first campaign to get off the ground was in Bellingham, Washington, north of Seattle in the fall of 2003. At the time a husband and wife team, Derek and Michelle Long, were directing both the national BALLE network and organizing their own business community in Whatcom County (which contains Bellingham) under the name Sustainable Connections. It made sense for them to undertake market research and framing for their own Local First Campaign as a model for what might be seeded nationally.

Fast-forward three years, and Sustainable Connections now has five hundred local businesses involved. The week before Thanksgiving is "Buy Local Week," when Christmas shoppers are encouraged to do their spending at local stores. The best-selling item at Village Books is the organization's coupon book called *Where The Locals Go*, now in its fourth edition and featuring discounts from 160 member businesses. Throughout the rest of the year Sustainable Connections distributes a "Retail Kit" that arms local businesses with a window poster, a "Think Local First" decal, a "Tip Sheet for Making the Campaign a Success," frequently asked questions and answers, a CD with monthly marketing materials, "The Top Ten Reasons to Think Local," as well as a sheet of logos for public display and print advertisements. It also prints seasonally appropriate promotional materials, like "Be a Local Lover" for Valentines' Day and "Make Mom Proud" on Mothers' Day. One of its July 4th posters says to "Celebrate Your Independents!" and shows sepia pictures from another Bellingham buy-local campaign one hundred years earlier. The Longs have synthesized their work into a fabulous handbook called *Think Local First: A How-To Manual*.[3]

The wordsmith talent evident on the bumper stickers and ads is quite entertaining: "Buy Local or Bye-Bye Local" or "Buy Fresh: There's No Taste Like Home." "Think Local, Buy Local, Be Local" has become the slogan of the movement, coupled with the image of nearby Mount Baker its image. Both are emblazoned on the chest of their "Be Local" bee mascot, which has appeared on T-shirts, pins, and window posters, and has been riding a giant trike around the commercial district. Participants in the "buy fresh" campaign are connecting local farmers with local restaurants and have advertised their work by participating in local races dressed up as produce—two potatoes in a canoe, an eggplant mountain biker, and a running carrot. Sustainable Connections also has deployed a big bingo wheel at community events, occasionally spun by the mayor, who hands out prizes from local stores.

Everyone is starting to notice. The head of the local community foundation calls Sustainable Connections the community's most important nonprofit. The mayor of Bellingham considers it one of his most important economic development agencies. After the Longs presented their work to the newly elected governor of Washington, Christine Gregoire, she proclaimed that she wanted to see the Local First vision replicated across the state. "And," adds Michelle Long, with justifiable pride, "we're only three-and-a-half years old."[4]

"Three years ago," says John D'Onofrio, owner of Northwest Computer, "being 'local' was a nonissue. Now there isn't a day that goes by that someone doesn't say they are supporting our business because we are local and that it is important to them. In the fifteen years that I have owned my business, I have found Sustainable Connections to be the most effective, most rewarding, and most cost-effective organization I have encountered."[5]

Local First campaigns usually find that the local paper will publish an editorial supporting local businesses, which amplifies and spreads the message more quickly. Occasionally, however, a troglodyte economist, economic developer, or business reporter will take to the op-ed page to oppose the effort. When the Greater Philadelphia Sustainable Business Network (SBN) proclaimed May 2005 "Buy Local Philly Month," they received unexpected publicity when Andrew Cassel, a business writer with the *Philadelphia Inquirer*, wrote a column poohpoohing the campaign.[6] "A community that truly practiced SBN's idea of 'local exchange,'" he wrote, "would be a very poor community indeed. In fact, no matter where you look, the healthiest, richest cities and nations are those that do precisely the opposite: Open commerce and investment, and connect with the rest of the world."

Cassel's piece provided a fabulous opportunity to discuss the advantages of LOIS and the problems with TINA, and to clarify that Local First is the opposite of protectionism. Judy Wicks, proprietor of the White Dog Café, where SBN has its office, wrote a long letter to the editor rebutting Cassel, which prompted Cassel to write another column against Local First, which precipitated a devastating rebuttal by a writer in the *Philadelphia City Paper.*[7] At SBN's conference celebrating "Buy Local Philly Month," I offered to turn my hour of plenary speaking time into a debate with Cassel, but he declined. So instead, with his photo projected on the wall, I happily engaged his arguments without him:

- *Is an economy with a strong base of local exchange "poor"?* Not at all. As Jane Jacobs has long argued, local exchange is the basis for a strong economy, especially for a strong exporting economy.
- *Is Local First "protectionist?"* Hardly. Local First actually celebrates free and robust consumer choices made by smart individuals and businesses armed with the best information possible.

- *Why should consumers have to spend more?* "If you save $1 buying at Home Depot rather than your corner hardware store," argues Cassel, "that's $1 you can use to help the local economy in other ways." But who said anything about spending more? Even though many Americans are willing to spend more on local goods, Local First doesn't advocate that. Local First simply suggests that you ask the question, as I did in the introduction, about what kind of bargains you're really getting. If I want to avoid wasting my hard-earned money on Wal-Mart's "cheap goods" because they have high transaction or overcharge costs, because they are of poor quality, because they perpetuate worker oppression in China, because they turn my Main Street into ghost towns, no pointy-headed economist is going to tell me I have to do otherwise. I should be free to spend my resources any way I damn please.

- *Is Local First discriminatory?* Cassel felt "troubled by the idea of singling out certain firms for promotion based on who their owners are. What makes SBN's campaign so different from one urging people to patronize businesses owned by Christians, or heterosexuals, or white people?" Hmmm. Maybe the answer is that the word "discriminating" has two different meanings. Local First promotes discriminating shopping, in the sense of choosing wisely, while the other form of discrimination is immoral and illegal.

There's a smart aleck like Andrew Cassel lurking in every community, just waiting to come out swinging. We should be grateful! This is what real public education in a democracy is all about. The choices ahead of us—between TINA and LOIS, between Wal-Marts and Small-Marts— are real, and an engaged citizenry should debate the pros and cons of each. Once you have the public's attention, all kinds of other tools become plausible: local credit and debit cards, local stock, LOIS incubators, you name it. And then real debate over the future of local public policy can begin.

## "Not That Far Out"

This was the slogan economic developers in St. Lawrence County, New York, thought would be a catchy way to attract new business and talent from outside the community. That was the bad news. The goods news was that in 2002 an entirely new grassroots economic development constituency took charge. St. Lawrence University (SLU) received an endowment from the family of Ellen C. Burt, an alumna of the college, to create an "Annual Symposium on Education, Environment, and Economic Vitality." Her husband, Stewart, chaired the Anchor Hocking Corporation that made brands like Rubbermaid and Intercraft, and together with their children insisted that the endowment not be structured as a typical tenured professorship. Grateful for how much the region had given to their own early lives, the Burts wanted to give a gift that might slow or even reverse the region's steady economic decline.

St. Lawrence County is located in the North Country in New York. It can be reached most easily by flying into Ottawa, the capital of Canada, and driving due south for a little more than an hour, then over an old, metallic bridge at Ogdensberg. The St. Lawrence Seaway, of course, was once a busy artery for the industrializing United States, but today it is mostly littered with the remnants of shipping, logging, textile, and other industries that have long since moved on.

Of the fifty-seven counties in New York, St. Lawrence has the largest area and the smallest population (about 111,000). It is endowed with huge natural assets, including minerals, forests, and waterways. It has large government and university sectors that insulate the region from the ups and downs of the business cycle and produce a relatively well-educated workforce. And it has a remarkably low crime rate and cohesive family structures. Yet, despite these strengths, the county has chronically high levels of unemployment and poverty. One result is that top-flight universities in the area, including Clarkson University, St. Lawrence University, and SUNY-Potsdam, often see their best students skip town after graduation.

The Burt Symposium Committee decided to use the first annual event as a platform for countywide action. The committee was made up of high-level representatives throughout the county's government, commerce, and university sectors. It was led by two SLU education professors, Jim Shuman (no relation) and Jim Waterson, and enjoyed the imprimatur of SLU President Daniel Sullivan. It included Karen St. Hilaire, head of the county's chamber of commerce, an unusual visionary who in turn was able to secure the involvement of multiple local chambers of commerce representing one city, thirteen villages, and thirty-two towns in the county. It also included Ellen Rocco, the head of North Country Public Radio, and Ann Heidenreich, a grassroots community organizer working on local energy issues. And it had a budget, which it used to hire a half-time, spirited organizer named Susan Kramer.

The symposium committee decided to create a set of research teams organized around specific sectors of the economy, linked to the categories of available national and state data: Agriculture & Food, Education, Energy, FIRE (finance, insurance, and real estate), Health, Housing and Construction, Manufacturing, Retail and Wholesale, Tourism and Entertainment, and Transportation. Each team was to be made up of a combination of business people and activities, thinkers and doers, professors and students, who would be asked to come up with the best list of promising LOIS business opportunities.

My role was to prepare a report filled with facts and figures that could get the teams started. I assembled a list of twenty indicators from three principal sources: the U.S. Census Bureau, the annual "Social-Economic Profile of the North County" performed by the Merwin Rural Services Institute, and the annual "New York State Statistical Yearbook" compiled by the Nelson A. Rockefeller Institute of Government. The economic indicators were not encouraging. The unemployment rate in SLC had recently been nearly double the national and state rates. Per capita income, while rising in nominal terms, had been stagnant once inflation was factored out. SLC workers were steadily losing ground vis-à-vis their New York State and U.S. counterparts. In 1999, for example, workers in SLC earned 83 percent what U.S. workers did (they had been even in 1973). The cost of living in SLC, while relatively high in some categories, did not deviate far from the national average, underscoring the significance of the erosion of earnings.

Next, I analyzed the asset base: What exactly does St. Lawrence County have available for new or expanded LOIS businesses? Three assets stood out. Because of recent farm bankruptcies, the county had 225,000 acres of vacant land. An unused or underused asset like this, of course, is also potentially usable by new businesses. Second, unemployment in the county hovered around four thousand over the past decade. Again, unemployed workers are, from an asset standpoint, potentially employable workers. Finally, in June 2000 there was approximately $1 billion on deposit in FDIC-insured institutions in SLC. At the same time the total amount deposited in all New York State banks was $444 billion, nearly *three times* as much per capita as in SLC. That year for every dollar in an FDIC-insured institution, a typical American had about six dollars in savings elsewhere (see chapter 5), which implies that SLC residents had roughly $6 billion in pension funds, mutual funds, stocks, bonds, and insurance funds.

The last step was to analyze dollar leakages. The organizers didn't have hundreds of thousands of dollars to commission an economics think tank to analyze the economy, nor did they have the human resources required to survey hundreds of consumers and businesses in the county to ascertain how money was moving around. So I developed a quick and dirty methodology for getting a handle on leakages using widely available data from the U.S. Bureau of Economic Analysis.[8] Some of the biggest categories of the economy that were net importers were forestry and fishing; fabricated metal products; wholesale trade; retail furniture and clothing stores; finance, insurance, and real estate (FIRE); and virtually all service sectors except health care, education, and social services. Clearly there were many possible places to create new LOIS businesses.

I then calculated how much extra wealth St. Lawrence County could have if it were as self-reliant as the average county in the United States. The bottom line was that a comprehensive effort at import replacement could result in $1.8 billion in new output each year, $634 million in new earnings, and more than fourteen thousand new jobs. In other words, *import replacement in SLC could double the size of the local economy and put all the unemployed people in the county back to work.* Of course, realizing this potential is a significant challenge and will require many years of assiduous attention to indicators, assets, economies of scale, and LOIS expansion strategies. It also will require educating local consumers and businesses to redirect some of their purchases, savings, and investments toward local enterprise. But the numbers caught people's attention.

Given my poultry passion, I asked members of the Food and Agriculture Team to consider "meat leakages." (Vegans, please skip this paragraph.) Despite the long and rich history of agriculture in the region—*Dairy Today* still considers St. Lawrence one of the top three counties in the United States for raising dairy cows—residents import eleven thousand beef cows each year, thirty-six thousand pigs and hogs, and nearly two million chickens. Recall that the county has 225,000 acres of vacant land, four thousand unemployed workers, and $7 billion of potentially investable capital. Does anyone see a business opportunity?

Every team turned out to have plenty of dollar leaks like these begging to be plugged. The timber industry was sending 60 percent of all locally cut trees to saw mills outside the county. While the educational institutions were areas of economic strength, none was buying local food, even local milk and dairy products. The county's prodigious hydroelectric resources made it nearly energy self-reliant on paper, but four out of five households were actually heating themselves with imports of oil and natural gas. All kinds of financial services—banking, investment, insurance, and real estate—were being imported, denying the locals not only a robust FIRE industry but also making it inevitable that local finance was being invested nonlocally. The health sector was strong because of several hospitals, but residents had to go outside the county to find pharmacists, dentists, doctors, and speech pathologists. Although a few manufacturing plants remain in the county, one of its largest industries, electronics assembly, was mostly owned by Canadians. Retail trade was superficially strong but largely dominated by chain stores like Wal-Mart. The county had many tourist attractions, but once visitors showed up they would not be able to find much in the way of local restaurants, motels, clubs, and movie theaters to accommodate them.

The symposium opened with Karen St. Hilaire delivering a brilliant vision for the region excerpted in the adjacent box (see pp. 200–201), and then I presented my report. The teams worked diligently for two days and sketched a compelling road map for expanding the local economy. Over the months that followed, however, some of the enthusiasm dissipated. About a third of the teams lost steam, victims of distracted leadership, unengaged members, and the typical pause of activity that occurs in universities during the summer recess. Another third continued to do interesting pieces of work, though these "teams" really each comprised only one or two engaged people. The Education Team published a resource guide on partnerships in the county promoting economic development. The Manufacturing Team helped set up a locally owned wireless Internet company. The Housing Team did some groundbreaking work on the economic potential of replacing mobile homes, almost all imported, with homegrown new houses. And the Retail Team did preliminary work to convert an abandoned building into a community marketplace.

Two of the teams wound up being superstars. The Energy Team established an energy service company that performed energy audits in ninety-two buildings (a prerequisite for comprehensive energy savings plans for each), carried out preliminary work for a local wind farm, and worked with a private company to build the county's first biodiesel plant. The Food and Agriculture Team decided to promote farm-to-school programs (including setting up vending machines dispensing local milk), develop a North County label for all locally produced foodstuffs, and prepare guides to local farmers and food producers.

## Remarks for Burt Symposium
*Karen St. Hilaire, 5/6/03*

Today I have the privilege of sharing with you my ideas and observations about a little spot on the earth called St. Lawrence County.

This speck of land—totaling 2,846 square miles—is a place, where in a world filled with conflict, one can live a life in relative peace and harmony.

It is a place where farmers and professors live side-by-side sharing space and ideas.

It is a place that, at first glance appears to be homogeneous . . . and then, you discover that one community has people who come from forty different countries.

It is a place where your nearest neighbor can be right next door or . . . a half-mile away.

It is a place where you can canoe for three days and never see another soul.

It is a place that has two hundred lakes, rivers, and ponds bustling with activity or alive with stillness.

It is a place where you can cross-country ski into the deep woods and hear only the sound of your skis sliding on the snow.

It is a place where over three thousand people gather in one spot any winter weekend to watch the best of NCAA hockey.

It is a place where you can see a solar car cruising down the highway at the same time you are passing a horse and buggy.

It is a place which borders two nations—one, to the north and one comprised of those who were here long before our ancestors.

---

Karen St. Hilaire later received an award from Senator Hillary Clinton for her chamber's work, and the two women forged a relationship that opened doors to several hundred thousand dollars of assistance from eBay and Hewlett-Packard to form the St. Lawrence Marketplace. The county is now helping a dozen or so LOIS businesses master eBay: it gives them computer equipment and classroom instruction that enable them to prepare listings, add catchy language and visuals, process orders expeditiously, and build customer loyalty.

It is a place where castles hold the lure of another era . . . and islands total many more than the thousand their name suggests.

It is a place where one out of every two music teachers in New York State is trained.

It is a place where people with ideas can start new businesses and be applauded for their success.

It is a place where ice storms bring communities together and the welfare of your neighbor is very much your concern.

It is a place where the population density of one town is 1.2 people per square mile.

It is the birthplace of a world-renowned artist whose works are on display for all to see.

It is a place that has educated astronauts, scientists, corporate leaders, opera singers, actors, politicians, and entrepreneurs.

It is a place where people from around the world travel to catch fish that we discard.

It is a place which attracts bird-watchers from throughout the Northeast and a place which has one of two important bird areas for bank swallows in the country.

It is a place where you can dive in crystal clear waters to explore shipwrecks from another century.

It is a place where you can raise buffalo, elk, emu, llamas, alpacas and still be in the top three dairy counties in the state.

It is a place where the sunshine of the summer drives you to seek shade and the ice and snow of the winter drive you to seek shelter.

For many of us, St. Lawrence County is Shangri-La.

A third North Country Symposium has now come and gone, and the organizers are still tinkering with its mission. Some folks want to work regionally, others want to be more attentive to specific towns and villages. There's much discussion about next stages of implementation. Perhaps the most positive sign is that the county's planners and economic developers, who didn't participate in the first year, are insisting on a more central role. They, too, want a piece of the LOIS action. "It's a promising development," says Jim Shuman, "and it is safe to say that the symposium has helped community leaders throughout the county to think in terms of LOIS far more than they did before its inception."

## The Worksphere Initiative for the Katahdin Region

Shortly after the first Burt Symposium, I received a telephone call at five in the morning from Richard Schweppe, Senior Vice President of the Training & Development Corporation (TDC). What was once the premier paper mill in the world had shut down around Christmas and put fourteen hundred people out of work in an area of mid-Maine known as the Katahdin Region (because of the proximity to Mount Katahdin, in the middle of Baxter State Park). The Department of Labor had just given TDC an extraordinary grant of $8 million to help the workers find new employment, and TDC wanted to make sure that the same old economic development mistake—getting some big, outside firm to come in, reopen the mills, and save the day—was not made again. Could I help?

So began two years of continuous travel to Maine to improve and ex-pand the methodology we used in St. Lawrence County. Let me begin, though, by digressing. Ever since I was six years old, I've been obsessed with moose. I have drawn them compulsively, collected moose para-phernalia, periodically worn antlers on my head, and even, during my student years in California, encouraged friends and acquaintances to call me "Moose." That I should be enlisted to serve a community so well-endowed with these majestic creatures seemed providential. I soon learned, however, that my passions did not exactly coincide with those of the residents of Millinocket. When I asked a storekeeper on my first visit where I might find a moose, she responded with absolute disdain, probably how I would have reacted had a visitor to Washington asked me where he could spot rats or crack dealers: "Why would you want to see one of those?" To the locals, the moose were nuisances that wandered too many times into the front ends of their cars.

But I also learned that moose were not highly regarded because they were but another symbol of seemingly out-of-control environmental-ism believed to be destroying the way of life of hard-working people. The typical Maine citizen fancies him or herself as a radical independent and eschews orthodoxies of both mainstream political parties. The state currently has two moderate Republican senators (talk about an endangered species!), and recently had an independent, Angus King, as its governor. The earthy residents have contended with a harsh climate and managed to tap the forests for paper and lumber, the rivers for electricity, the lobsters and salmon for food exports, and the blueberries and potatoes for food. Just don't mess with their property, their guns, or their fishing runs along bitterly contested Canadian boundaries.

Over the past generation, of course, the lumber and paper have gone the way of other global industries. Processing plants now make less sense in the United States than in regions abroad with low-cost labor (though this may change as oil prices rise), and to the extent that these plants are kept open, new technology is rendering growing numbers of American workers obsolete. The pace of change is disorienting, and many, desperate to point fingers, blame environmentalists for driving the paper business out and bringing in their place dubious, low-wage, humiliating tourist jobs. For a century, families in Millinocket and East Millinocket expected their sons to go to work at high-wage union jobs in the mills, their daughters to marry mill workers, and their grandchildren to do the same. That way of life, that sense of security, has vanished.

These kinds of changes are occurring throughout Maine. Forget about Portland, the biggest city in the southern part of the state, which culturally and economically is really part of greater Boston. But travel north and you find a gorgeous landscape, verdant forests, and a lively rural society that is delivering fewer jobs, with lower wages, than much of the rest of the country. In the last three years Maine has lost the greatest percentage of its manufacturing jobs per capita of any state in the country.

The founder of TDC, Chuck Tetro, had come to many of the same views about community economies that I had but through a totally different route. For years TDC has been a national innovator in workforce development through Job Corps Centers, One-Stop Shops for career advancement, case-management software systems, and even a research institute on work. But Tetro gradually concluded that even the best programs in workforce education, skill building, and job placement were not enough for communities in crisis like Millinocket. A healthy work-force requires a healthy local economy in which all residents are indis-pensable participants, architects, and leaders. To describe a community that had both sustainable employability and sustainable production, Tetro invented the word "Worksphere." Millinocket, Tetro hoped, would be the first testing ground for his Worksphere ideas.

One immediate challenge came from the strictures of TDC's grant from the Department of Labor. Many government programs are rooted in old-fashioned distinctions between workers and management, with the former falling under the jurisdiction of the Department of Labor and the latter falling under the Department of Commerce. Worker training grants like this one cannot be used for economic develop-ment. You can offer unemployed workers extra salary support, medical benefits, classes, and job leads, but you cannot train them to become entrepreneurs and take control of their lives. Go figure.

Anyway, TDC decided that the best response to the regulations was to use 95 percent of the grant for old-style worker support, and 5 per-cent on the acquisition of "fugitive jobs," all those jobs that should be locally available but are not because of an inadequate level of local spending. The mission of the Worksphere Initiative of the Katahdin Region, or WIKR, was to organize teams, like those in St. Lawrence County, that could identify, target, and capture fugitive jobs.

Again, I prepared a background paper and discovered that the Katahdin Region was in some ways similar to St. Lawrence County. Both areas view themselves as part of the North County, a vast region stretching across the northeast U.S.–Canadian border, with similar timber and water resources, similar resource-based economies that have passed their peak, similarly long winters and short summers, and a similar frontier-like culture. But the differences were equally striking. While the economy in St. Lawrence County has been balanced over the years by public spending on universities and prisons, the economy in mid-Maine had no diversification whatsoever. While St. Lawrence County was seeking a steady course toward economic renewal, mid-Maine was seeking a way to avoid plunging more deeply into crisis.

The hunt for fugitive jobs began with an alliance with the Milli-nocket Area Growth and Investment Council, or MAGIC. The head of MAGIC was a smart, soft-spoken man named Bruce McLean. Having

served in the U.S. Air Force for many years in deep bunkers prepared
to launch nuclear missiles, McLean now reaches for the wild blue yon-
der in his private plane, which he flies several times a week through various local river valleys and over Mount Katahdin. Being homegrown
gives McLean enough legitimacy to do his job (if you're "from away,"
watch out), but he is not an uncontroversial figure. MAGIC is a local
institution attempting to seed regional initiatives, at a time when the
three constituent towns—Millinocket, East Millinocket, and Medway—
still curse one another at high school basketball games. Despite deep
conservative political convictions, he had enough belief in environmental stewardship to take a small grant from The Wilderness Society,
which some of the locals (who view green policies as part of a secret,
UN-led conspiracy to dupe freedom-loving Americans) as an act of
treason.

TDC and MAGIC organized action teams and brought them
together at a conference held, fittingly, in the old mill. Senator Susan
Collins welcomed the hundred participants—many recently unemployed mill workers—and I then presented data on indicators, assets,
and leakages.

None of the trends in the Katahdin Region, even before the mill closure, were encouraging. According to the U.S. Census, between the
years 1970 and 2000 the population dropped from 11,800 to 8,520.
Most young people were fleeing the region after high school graduation, leaving an aging and less productive population in place. Over two
decades the mills have had a series of layoffs, closures, and reopenings,
steadily eroding job security and per capita income. Millinocket Council Member Gail Fanjoy had likened it to a "death by a thousand paper
cuts." Compared to the United States, or even Maine, a greater percentage of residents in the region smoke and are in "fair to poor"
health. Nearly half the residents are officially obese. Retail sales were
steadily declining, and even tourist traffic, which many thought might
bring new life into the economy, was decreasing, in part because fewer
people were visiting Baxter State Park.

And yet, from an import replacement standpoint, the Katahdin
Region had staggering potential. The study I performed for the region
showed that, collectively, the residents of Millinocket, East Millinocket,
and Medway spend $78 million per year. If they spent as much money

locally as the average American did, there would be fourteen hundred more jobs in the region—coincidentally the same number as were laid off at the mill in Christmas 2002!

The region is also rich in many assets that could provide the foundation for a revival. It has a huge low-cost housing stock, with nearly a fifth vacant, and a huge trained, educated, and talented workforce ready for new employment. Because most residents had their savings in local banks or credit unions, more than a hundred million dollars in finance was available.

The results of the leakage analysis were eye-popping and revealed business opportunities in almost every sector of the economy. There were opportunities for farmers markets, new restaurants, and hydroponics. If supplemented with better local hotels and entertainment (there are no movie theaters in the region, for example) and perhaps some kind of theme ("Moose Capital of the World"?), tourists could be drawn back. Oil imports could be displaced through wind power, wood burning, and biofuels. The local hospital, one of the biggest employers in the region, could begin to source supplies like uniforms and stationary locally. Local pension funds could dramatically expand the availability of capital for new enterprises.

One of the first questions after my presentation came from Charlie Cirame, a scruffy former mill worker who was once very active in the mill's union. What were the prospects for buying back the mill and getting things back to normal? My heart sunk. Can't they see that the old era is over? I explained that it would be extremely difficult to put together the tens of millions of dollars needed to buy out the mill, and even if we could, there was no reason that the market forces that made large-scale paper production uneconomic for Great Northern Paper would be any less true for the new owners. I tried to convince Charlie and others that their future depended, not on new mill jobs, but on new forays into the businesses they've been dreaming about all their lives.

Over the following year, the teams met periodically, refined the indicators, and came up with a list of recommended business opportunities in their sector. The results of their work—some fifty business ideas—were presented in a colorful booklet called *Katahdin First: Resources and Opportunities Guide*. During this same period, we also began publishing a monthly supplement in the *Community Press* called *Local First*. Each issue contained a list of locally owned businesses, profiles of interesting entrepreneurs, and editorials about why residents should buy local.

Because the region has about 350 identifiable businesses and all but a couple dozen are locally owned, those who did not make the list screamed bloody murder. The manager of Hannaford Brothers, the chain grocery store, threatened to pull his advertising from the *Community Press*. Why should he be punished with a boycott, he fumed, just because he was part of a chain? He did everything he could to support the community with charitable giving, fair prices, and good corporate behavior. We sat down with him, and tried to explain that Local First did not mean that we were encouraging residents to boycott Hannaford, only to buy more from the locally owned grocer down the street. Okay, this might mean lower sales in the short-term, but he should understand the larger picture. This is a region fighting for its life, and to the extent that the regional economy can be pumped up through local purchasing, all businesses, even the nonlocal ones, will benefit. It's fair to say that he still wasn't happy with the campaign, but ultimately he decided not to go to war against us.

Slowly the community began to pull itself back together. Many old-timers have decided to stick around and find new work. MAGIC began a campaign to lure back "native sons and daughters," all those high school graduates who had drifted away over the years. New businesses have opened on Main Street, such as the Katahdin Coffee Shop, Angelo's, and the Army-Navy Store. The next generation of businesses, like Fat Cat Advertising, is being incubated in MAGIC's Business Resource & Innovation Center (BRIC). Thirty young people have banded together to manage their own public television station, the KAT. Their broadcasts of the Millinocket City Council meetings have become among the most watched shows in the community, boosting civic engagement and landing Bruce McLean a city council seat. For the first time in a long time, the community has marginalized the naysayers and rallied around the entrepreneurs.

Everywhere you look there are new signs of vitality. The JJ Newberry Building, once boarded up, was finally sold to the soon-to-be inaugurated Katahdin Cultural Center. The Katahdin Fund is cranking up a

major capital campaign that will finance myriad community development projects. A new map now shows tourists and other visitors the
rich cultural, historical, and business resources in the region. Festivals,
hunting, snowmobiling, boating, shooting photos, fishing, moose
watching, rafting, fine dining, attending conferences—there's a growing list of reasons for people to visit, spend a little money, and pump
up the economy.

It needs to be said that many of the residents, while doing their part
in the Worksphere Initiative, were not entirely satisfied with the results. Yes, there's a great list of business ideas and a few got started, but
how can more be done faster? It did not help that for a hundred years,
two bureaucratic behemoths—the mill and the union—controlled the
town's economic agenda, leaving residents with little experience in
entrepreneurship and leadership. But we continued to remind the
Katahdin residents—and ourselves—that change comes slowly.

On the last day of our grant from the Department of Labor, we held
a dinner for a dozen of the most promising new entrepreneurs. We
also invited four of the top financiers in the region, in the hope that the
"meet and greet" would open new spigots of loan capital. As the
evening was ending I finally recognized one of the entrepreneurs who
up to that point had looked only vaguely familiar. It was Charlie, the old
mill worker, who had cut his hair, bought a suit, and now was developing his own ice cream business.

The efforts in St. Lawrence County and in the Katahdin Region have
made it clear that once a community completes the process of identifying leak-plugging businesses, they need the tools to train entrepreneurs and to mobilize capital for them. I wish I could say that all these
tools are proven and ready to be deployed in your own town. Some are,
many aren't. There's no mystery about what citizens in a community
must do to bring about the Small-Mart Revolution. Find and plug the
leaks. Train leak-plugging entrepreneurs. Invest and buy local. And
remind the cynics of what Thomas Edison told a reporter who once
snidely asked him how it felt to have failed at inventing the light bulb
nine thousand times: "I never failed; I just found nine thousand ways
not to invent the light bulb. I knew I would eventually run out of things
that didn't work!"

★★★★★★★★★★★★★★★★★★★★★★★★★★★★★★★★★★★★★★★★★★★★

# Five Items for Community Builders

★★★★★★★★★★★★★★★★★★★★★★★★★★★★★★★★★★★★★★★★★★★★

1. **Education.**  Help key members of the community (including business-people, politicians, civil servants, civic activists, and academics) understand the virtues of the Small-Mart Revolution.

2. **Local First.**  Undertake grassroots education about which businesses are local and how best to support them with local planning, training, purchasing, investing, and public policy.

3. **Identify Leaks.**  Identify economic leaks (all those places where goods and services are being imported unnecessarily) that suggest opportunities for new or expanded local businesses. Use this, along with an analysis of local assets, to assess specific businesses most promising for the community's future.

4. **Vision.**  Organize key stakeholders to study the leakage analysis and craft a unified, coherent vision of the community's economic future.

5. **Implementation.**  Develop a set of consistent, reinforcing Small-Mart programs and policies that enable the community realize its vision.

# nine

★★★★★★★★★★★★★★★★★★★★★★★★★★★★★★★★★★★★★★★★★★★

# GLOBALIZERS

Martin Luther King, Jr., once invoked the words of the prophet Micah to say that the ultimate measure of a society was how it treated its most powerless members. With this principle in mind, I found the most horrifying event of 2004 to be when Chechen terrorists took over School Number One in Beslan, holding hostage a thousand young children on their first day of school. How the shooting began, no one knows for sure, but by the time the carnage was over 344 people were dead, 186 of them children. I don't have an opinion on whether the Chechens should or should not be a part of Russia, but every civilized person in the world knows that the last people you ever put in the line of fire are children. It's the fate of the world's children that should inform everything we, their guardians, do in their name, and by any standard, we, the residents of planet Earth, are failing our children miserably. According to the 2005 *State of the World's Children*, prepared by UNICEF, about half the world's children—more than a billion— "are denied a healthy and protected upbringing. . . ."[1] About 90 million children are "severely food-deprived," 140 million have never gone to school, 270 million have no health care, 400 million lack access to safe water, 500 million live without proper sanitation, and 640 million are essentially homeless. Millions of children now have HIV, and 15 million are orphans from parents who have died of AIDS. Even the slaughter in School Number One was not an isolated incident. Since 1990, 3.6 million have been killed in wars, many deliberately targeted.

It's easy to see the numb in numbers like these, and I only recite them as a reminder about why any worthy revolution ultimately must alleviate global suffering. I therefore take very seriously skeptics who suggest that LOIS is really only suitable for well-off communities in well-off countries. Americans, they say, perhaps can afford to pay more for local goods and services, but most of the world cannot. Plus, won't a philosophy emphasizing self-reliance sentence every poor community in the world that supplies America's consumer needs to lives of misery? Doesn't every act of import replacement deny an exporter in the developing world the opportunity to grow economically? Isn't self-reliance another way of saying let's freeze the status quo and rich countries win and the world's children lose? And doesn't the continuation of global poverty set the stage for more wars, more human rights violations, and more environmental degradation?

Fortunately, the Small-Mart Revolution does have a global vision. And it holds much more promise than TINA's does in improving the lot of all of the world's people, especially its children.

## Revolutionary Poverty Alleviation

Let's begin by reiterating a point made throughout this book: *The Small-Mart Revolution is not about spending more on any goods or services.* It's about consumers shopping carefully, weighing quality as well as price, being more attentive to the expense of travel and time, and accounting wisely for the costs to their community exacted by nonlocal purchases. It's about each of us placing our savings in competitive local banking institutions and keeping our loans local, so that the stream of interest and principal payments build local wealth rather than drain them. It's about investors putting our retirement funds in profitable local business, either directly through stock purchases or indirectly through local pension and mutual funds. It's about LOIS entrepreneurs seizing the new efficiencies generated through the eight trends, shrinking economies of scale, and local businesses deploying the expanding arsenal of ways to compete effectively against global firms. It's about policymakers ending the massive subsidies to TINA and removing the countless biases in law and policy that suppress viable local business. It's about everyone in the community coming together to envision a better economic future for all of its members, including the poor, the elderly, the infirm, and the young; identifying leaks and new business opportunities; and systematically mobilizing talent, capital, and technology to plug those leaks.

TINA offers benefits to the poor, but they are all superficial, short-lived, and double-edged. A nation of Wal-Mart buyers cannot possibly afford even shoddy discount goods if they are also Wal-Mart workers who lack decent incomes and benefits. A TINA auto manufacturer may provide those jobs, but it is also setting your community up for a catastrophe if—no, when—the firm suddenly departs, especially if the community's former ability to improve labor and environmental standards has been compromised and much of the wealth generated is ultimately sucked out by outsiders. Remember the words of the guardian of the Holy Grail: "choose wisely."

The examples throughout this book underscore that LOIS is not a luxury indulged in by a few well-off communities but a survival strategy embraced most readily by those left behind by the failings of mainstream development, in such struggling locales as St. Lawrence County and the Katahdin Region in Maine. Communities like these are poor because of the absence not just of wealth but also of strong multipliers. Poor communities typically have hollow economies, where money earned or invested flies in and out quickly and has virtually no significant economic impact. They are the maquiladora export platforms, where half-fabricated products are brought in, along with the workers, managers, and machinery, and final products hastily shipped out for distant markets. They are casino towns, where outsiders flock to new jobs, only to find that the larger labor pool brings down average wages and that their prospects lie in ruins when the boom ends. They are the forgotten rural outposts, where downtown has been decimated by a box store and where the most imaginable businesses are tourist traps to reminisce about the past rather than cutting-edge factories to secure a prosperous future. They are the dangerous inner-city neighborhoods, where outsiders run heavily barricaded convenience stores and filling stations that charge twice what competitors do in the suburbs.

The sad truth is that we all live in economies with poor multipliers; it's just a matter of degree. We all are buying too many goods from chain stores without seriously considering local alternatives. We all are carelessly sending away most of our savings, through our banks, pension plans, and insurance policies, to the far corners of the planet. We all are unnecessarily importing oil, electricity, food, and clothing. We all are needlessly outsourcing our lives.

Put positively, every community, rich and poor, can benefit from LOIS. Local goods and services already make up most of the U.S. economy, and if economies of scale shrink, their proportion will expand. Enormous new wealth is possible by nurturing those businesses with greater multipliers, better environmental and labor standards, deeper ties to the community, and more robust records of innovation. Every community has rich gushers of wealth waiting to be tapped in its backyard.

But what about outside our own country? What about the argument that every step toward localization here displaces a marginal farmer or worker somewhere else? There is a grain of truth in this criticism, and that's why I believe it essential for every Small-Mart community to use its new-found wealth to help seed the revolution in other communities worldwide. As my colleague Colin Hines in the United Kingdom proclaims: We must spread the local, globally.

One of the worst ways to bring new wealth into poor countries is to keep buying their plantation-grown bananas and coffee. Given how little of each import dollar actually winds up in the hands of the workers most in need—probably less than a penny—this is, at best, an extremely inefficient antipoverty strategy. It perpetuates domination of the poor by TINA corporations, and justification of this arrangement in the name of ending poverty is a delusion.

If we really want to help the poor, it's far smarter to help poor countries, poor communities, and the poorest residents living in them to achieve the same level of local self-reliance we seek for ourselves. Mohandas Gandhi argued that the way to defeat British power was to restore self-reliance, especially in basics like textiles and salt. He did not suggest that India embark on a campaign to attract nicer British factories or to expand exports to London.

This isn't going to be easy. It requires that we do much more than just buy from the right store, sign off on the right trade agreement, or flick the right election lever once every four years. Serious global antipoverty work requires ongoing, long-term partnerships between North and South in which we help *one another* reorganize every element of our economies. As we in the North create community food systems, we might help partners in the South transform their food systems, away from the plantations and export crops and toward the cultivation of enough healthy fruits, vegetables, rice, and beans to feed their own families. As we strengthen and spread our own local banks, credit unions, stock markets, and mutual funds, we can help partners create these institutions as well, so that local savings everywhere increasingly support local housing, local education, and local entrepreneurship. As we deploy new technologies to become more energy efficient, we can share our know-how with renewable resource innovators in the South. For nearly a generation, the city-state of Bremen in Germany has been spending about one million dollars per year to help its partners in the South—in Pune, India, for example—become more energy efficient by giving away digesters that convert local waste products and plant matter into burnable biogas. Every Small-Mart step we take can, if we are prepared to share and spread it, provide another piece to the puzzle of global poverty relief.

"Help" can come in many ways. You might set up sister-community relationships, fortified by sister-farmers, sister-bankers, and sister-utility managers. Bremen is part of a network of two thousand northern cities and towns that have their own North-South development policies.[2] Judy Wicks set up sister restaurant relationships between the White Dog Café and a half-dozen similar restaurants around the world, including Cabbages & Condoms, a restaurant in Thailand that funnels its profits into preventing AIDS. The Internet makes ongoing communication among such partners easy and cheap and can facilitate the exchange of good ideas, technology, and policy that will enable both partners to become more self-reliant. You might send technical support people to work with your partners' communities, or bring their leaders here for training.

The spirit of the Small-Mart vision of globalization is to assist one another in becoming more self-reliant without charge, with participants keenly aware that everyone will benefit from an open-source approach. In 1992 Richard Jefferson used his U.S. training in biosciences to found CAMBIA, a nonprofit agricultural research center based in Australia. A new website, BioForge.net, provides a forum for scientists from North and South to openly share information, research, projects, and innovations in fields like agriculture and pharmaceuticals. "The idea that we should feed the world is paternalistic, patronizing silliness," says Jefferson. "The world can feed itself it we can lower the cost of innovation."[3]

As these activities proceed, even the richest partners should remember that they have as much to learn as to teach. Microfinance was pioneered by the Grameen Bank in Bangladesh. Some of the best mass-transit innovations have come from Curitaba, Brazil. The wireless telecommunications networks in Asia, which skipped the "wired" phase of industrialization, are among the best in the world. One of the world's finest examples of a self-reliant community is Gaviotas, a two-hundred-person village in Colombia, which has pioneered several solar and wind technologies, developed a particularly effective and environmentally benign means of extracting resin from pine trees, and set up organic farms, social service programs, and reforestation efforts that have drawn worldwide attention.[4]

As more and more communities join in the Small-Mart Revolution, trade will of course continue, but it will be in goods and services less and less vital to day-to-day survival. If we're trading primarily art, music, and wine instead of oil, wheat, and water, our local economies will be healthier through self-reliance in the basics, less vulnerable to unpredictable global calamities, and we will all be less inclined to go to war over real or perceived needs. Because LOIS can expand local economies, especially the world's poorest, global movement toward LOIS will grow the entire planet's economy. A reasonable expectation, noted earlier, is that every participating community's economy expands in absolute terms, while the *relative* role of exports (compared to local production) declines.

The Small-Mart Revolution is not about ducking globalization but about redefining it. Millions of critically important tasks for helping communities embrace LOIS have yet to begin on a global scale, and none of them have anything to do with perpetuating self-destructive trade patterns. Instead, these tasks include preparing promising small-scale business plans, designing appropriate technology, training LOIS entrepreneurs, providing communities with the capacity to measure and plug economic leaks, and implementing tools that promote local purchasing and investment. For the shrinking number of industries where local scale is not practical or competitive, there are wonderful transnational opportunities to reorganize business sectors. Global retailing networks can be made out of independent businesses that, like True Value Hardware, blend global distribution with locally owned retail. Flexible manufacturing networks of locally owned entities can be put together across national borders to produce complex goods and services. It's not unthinkable that powerful networks like these could buy out chain stores and reorganize them into global networks of locally owned businesses. A network of locally owned banks might take over a failing global giant and recharter each branch into an independent entity owned by its depositors, each committed to reinvesting locally while remaining part of a larger global network that can compete in every other respect with Bank of America. How about a "Global Fund of Rural Communities" that holds small pieces of local hedge funds that specialize in local, small-stock issues and yet provides investors with geographic diversification?

As the Small-Mart Revolution takes hold, corporations like Wal-Mart will still exist, though their market share will shrink, their tight grip on our investment portfolios will loosen, and their ability to buy politicians and public policy will diminish. As the problems afflicting TINA businesses intensify, a growing number may think seriously about dividing into smaller, regional units, perhaps even restructuring themselves as networks of locally owned businesses to take full advantage of the growing number of consumers embracing Local First. Those that do not adapt to this new environment favoring place-based enterprises may well become extinct.

## The Revolutionarily Peaceful Future

The Small-Mart Revolution is about much more than economics. A community that has learned how to meet most of its own needs with its own resources is an essential building block for solving many of the world's most pressing problems.

Consider issues of war and peace. History is littered with examples of countries deploying their militaries to get or protect strategic waterways, trade routes, fertile farmland, fishing waters, gold, diamonds, and—of course—oil. A country made up of self-reliant communities will have very little rational reason to invade or coerce another country for resources. It will not, for example, need to import oil from unstable, unreliable, and undemocratic sheikdoms in the Middle East, nor deploy battleships, troops, or nuclear weapons to protect access to those oil resources.

As we know, leaders wage wars for many other reasons: to protect human rights, to spread democracy, to distract from domestic problems, to satisfy whims. And yet an enormous body of historic and theoretical evidence underscores that mature democracies rarely go to war with one another. While it's possible to imagine self-reliant countries that are dictatorships—the old Albania or contemporary Burma and North Korea come to mind—they are hardly made up of self-reliant communities or embrace the free-market principles of the Small-Mart Revolution. Self-reliance through starvation, as practiced by Kim Il Jong in North Korea, is really not self-reliance at all—it's self-destruction. As one thinks through the specifics of community self-reliance, where many small businesses control the nation's economic power, where localities maintain more power, responsibility, and money than national authorities, the country today that most readily comes to mind is Switzerland, which has assiduously avoided military entanglements for several hundred years and whose residents enjoy the seventh highest per capita income in the world (the United States is number two, after Luxembourg).

Spreading LOIS worldwide provides a new tool for spreading democracy, not through threats or violence, but through opportunity and collaboration. There are examples of non-democracies with robust small-business sectors, like Singapore and China, but sooner or later, the growing economic power at the grassroots will demand commensurate political power. Economic self-reliance confers the power to become more autonomous and to delink from unjust higher authorities. Once regions have the technological and economic ability to delink from their national authorities, and localities can delink from their regions, dictatorships are going to have a very rough time maintaining absolute power over much of anything.

A world of self-reliant communities is also a world that begins to move seriously toward sustainability. As noted earlier, LOIS is a necessary, if insufficient, condition for environmental stewardship. Only by having an economy made up primarily of locally owned businesses can a community ratchet up ecological standards. And spreading technologies and business designs that enable other communities to do likewise will have many positive consequences on the global environment.

The 1987 report of a commission chaired by Norwegian Prime Minister Gro Harlem Brundtland offered a definition of sustainability that has endured for two decades.[5] Sustainability means the ability to meet the needs of all people today without compromising the ability of future generations to meet their own needs. A community embracing LOIS might recast this principle in the following way: Sustainability requires that every community meet the needs of all its members (including plants and animals), present and future, without compromising the needs of other communities meeting the needs of their members, present and future. LOIS places responsibility on a community to operate within the constraints of its ecosystem: to minimize the use of nonrenewable resources; to use renewable resources like solar energy, water, crops, trees, wildlife, and fish to the extent that nature can renew them each year; to produce no more waste than local ecosystems can safely assimilate; and to import goods and services from only those communities attentive to the same ecological principles.

But won't communities, left to their own devices, turn inward, dump their messes on other communities, practice "not in my backyard" (NIMBY) policies? Perhaps. No political institution, whether national or local, automatically does the right thing. The embrace of LOIS globally will require concerted, global action. Fortunately, there is ample precedent in the growing number of communities practicing policies that might be called "begin in my backyard," or BIMBY.

Despite national leaders who are not yet convinced that climate disruption is a serious problem and have tried to scuttle the Kyoto Accords and other significant global efforts to cut carbon dioxide emissions, more than 170 BIMBY-oriented communities in the United States have pledged to adopt the Kyoto targets.[6] By mid-2005 seventeen cities had already reduced emissions below 1990 levels and estimated that they had already saved $600 million. Mayor Richard Daley has launched an all-out effort to green Chicago by planting trees, building bike paths, cutting energy use, and requiring box stores to have "green roofs." Governor Arnold Schwarzenegger in California has bucked the national

Republican Party and signed legislation that demands that automakers improve fleet efficiency, essentially setting new national standards.

Pick almost any global problem, and you will find intriguing connections with the spread of LOIS. Overpopulation? For years, demographers have pointed out that the best way to reduce a family's size is to raise its income security, which can come from greater self-reliance. Avian flu? Cultivating our own food systems, rather than relying on imports, will substantially slow and lessen the impact of global epidemics, nearly all of which, as Jared Diamond has pointed out in *Guns, Germs and Steel*, are accelerated by global exchange of cattle, pigs, or chickens.[7] Species destruction? Moving toward the sustainable management of local food and timber systems preserves critical habitats for plants and animals worldwide. Immigration? Only by spreading successful models of community economy can we hope to convince millions of potential migrants to stay put. LOIS alone cannot solve any of these problems, but it's a critical piece of any coherent global agenda.

## Community-Lifting Revisited

It has now been about a year since my fateful visit to Wal-Mart. Much has happened nationally and personally. A hurricane named Katrina flooded New Orleans, and the once-majestic city is now engaged in community reconstruction on an almost unprecedented scale. Sure, it's dangerous to live below sea level, but then again, the Dutch have lived this way for hundreds of years with a quarter of their country's land mass protected by an intricate series of dikes. With global warming and rising seas looming ahead, thousands of seaside communities will have to follow suit and learn how to reengineer their levies and flood controls to Dutch standards.[8] What is impressive is the stand many of the victims of Hurriane Katrina have taken: damn the costs, damn the risks, and damn the waters, we are staying put.[9]

Betsy Lewis is coming back to the Lower Ninth Ward of New Orleans, despite its poverty, because in her mind it was a neighborhood that worked. It's a place where more than half the homes are resident owned, where Fats Domino came from and now lives, and where he built a house for his ex next door. Says Lewis: "You couldn't get in trouble in this neighborhood without someone telling your mom. In front of whoever's house you were at lunch time is where you went to eat."[10]

Karen Edwards lived in Eastern New Orleans for twenty-seven years. After more than a few days of pumping the several feet of swamp water out of her house, she said, "I'm getting used to it. Now there is some hope."[11] State Representative Austin Badon, Jr., came back to eight feet of water, with his life's belongings scattered in mildewed piles. "I'm not letting some little storm run me away from my home," he insists.[12] City Councilwoman Cynthia Hedge Morrell proclaims, "Pontchartrain Park may have crumbled under the floodwaters, but it will not wash away from the city's landscape."[13] Outside the Eastover Country Club, the golf course of which is now a vast sea of mud, a banner says: "It Ain't Over—It's East Over. We Are Rebuilding."[14]

The determination of the New Orleans residents to tough it out, to save their neighborhoods and history, to make sure that the rhythmic sounds of Jazz Fest and the kaleidoscopic craziness of Mardi Gras continue should inspire all of us to take a stand against the global flood of allegedly cheap goods. We will not be put out of work by distant TINA managers who think no further than their next quarterly report and then flee elsewhere. We will not abandon our neighborhoods. We will rebuild our LOIS businesses.

Personally, I've been fighting a collapse of my own biological levies over the past year. Two decades of intermittent back pain worsened considerably and I could no longer walk. For several months, I was stuck in bed, belly down, virtually immobile. The up side, if there was any, was a long, uninterrupted stretch to write the first draft of this book. I wiggled to get my head over the side of the bed, and my wife Deborah kindly stuck the laptop on a milk carton just below me, allowing me to create a new micro-office. I wound up having surgery at a local hospital, and then undergoing physical rehabilitation several times a week.

As my therapist was finalizing my post-rehab exercise regimen, she stared at my feet and said, "You know, those sneakers have got to go." Yep, she meant those cheap sneakers from Wal-Mart, where our journey began. She pointed out to me how their shoddy design failed to give my arches any support and allowed my foot to roll over the sides. If my back was to get better, she said, I would need to invest in a better quality pair. Finding a locally made sneaker, of course, is almost impossible these days. But this time, I will shop carefully and at least buy them from a local vendor I trust. This time every fiber of my body will know that community lifting does not pay.

The biggest obstacle to the Small-Mart Revolution is apathy—the belief that *there is no alternative*. But we need not settle for insecure jobs or schlock chain stores. Every one of our decisions as consumers, as investors, as entrepreneurs, as voters, as organizers has a profound impact on our future. Obviously, if we continue to buy cheap nonlocal goods, invest in nonlocal business, concede potential niches for local enterprise, and vote for politicians who embrace elephant-mouse casserole, our future is grim. But these choices are not inevitable and are increasingly irrational. Educating ourselves and our neighbors about the real alternatives can go a long way.

A close cousin of apathy is the tendency to blame someone or something else. This is why contemporary politics are so sickening. Liberals think we need more national government, conservatives think we need less, while few focus on revolutionary reforms needed at the local level in the private and public sectors. No law, no expenditure, no gift from the U.S. government can possibly give any community what it needs to revitalize itself. A truly revolutionary premise of the Small-Mart Revolution is that each of us has the power, skill, and resources to take charge of our own destiny and restore vitality to our communities. No longer need our communities turn to federal agencies for more handouts, to large global corporations for new jobs, or to philanthropists for more grants. In fact, every success in begging—rather than empowering ourselves through wise purchasing, investing, entrepreneurship, and policymaking—makes the needed task of achieving self-reliance more difficult.

The Small-Mart Revolution can be the beginning of a new grassroots declaration of independence, and across the United States there are powerful signs of its taking hold. When recently asked about which institutions had a positive impact on society, four out of five Americans mentioned small business (the second highest score), while fewer than two in five mentioned big business.[15] The movement against Wal-Mart has gotten so fierce that the company is now sponsoring conferences to engage and listen to its critics. New BALLE and AMIBA chapters, bringing together local businesspeople, are being formed at a rate of one per month. There is hardly a commercial district in the United States that doesn't have some sign encouraging people to buy local. Once most of us understand that LOIS businesses are the best contributors to our community well-being, that most of our own goods and services can be competitive with the global alternatives, and that our own public policies are unnecessarily killing our own businesses, we will be able to make our stand against TINA's vision of globalization. And we will build.

SMALL-MART REVOLUTION CHECKLIST

# Eight Items for Promoting the Local, Globally

★★★★★★★★★★★★★★★★★★★★★★★★★★★★★★★★★★★★★★★★★★★★★★★★

1. **Revamp Trade Agreements.**  Lobby national and global decision makers to reform, revamp, and rethink current global trade agreements so that they are community friendly.

2. **Intermunicipal Agreements.**  Link up with Small-Mart cities worldwide and formulate agreements on key issues ignored (or squelched) by existing trade agreements regarding environmental protection, corporate responsibility, worker rights, human rights, and community rights.

3. **Global Technical Assistance.**  Help poorer communities become more self-reliant by providing them, without charge, your best Small-Mart technology, training, business, and policy ideas.

4. **Global Boycotts.**  Work in concert with sympathetic communities worldwide to boycott countries and global corporations who oppose the Small-Mart Revolution.

5. **Global Investment Funds.**  Set up global "funds of funds" that can provide geographic diversification of local business investment funds.

6. **Global Banks.**  Finance a Small-Mart World Bank that provides targeted loans to local business development in poor communities.

7. **Global Currency Exchanges.**  Create a Small-Mart International Monetary Fund that facilitates exchanges of local currencies.

8. **Global Business Networks.**  Weave global networks of related businesses together so that they can support one another against multinational enterprises. Like U.S. producers cooperatives, these networks could facilitate bulk purchases, mutual credit, large-scale marketing, and technical assistance.

# APPENDIX A

# The Fall and Rise of
# Small-Scale Competetiveness

One way to get a handle on the "optimal" scale of any business is to analyze data in the North American Industry Classification System (NAICS). For each of its thousand-plus industry categories, NAICS presents aggregate data on the location, branching, employment, and payroll of member firms. The U.S. Bureau of the Census collects these data every five years, most recently in 2002. There are twenty broad categories with two digits, starting with 10 ("Agriculture, Forestry, Fishing, and Hunting") and going up to 30 ("Unclassified"). Each of these two-digit categories breaks out into subcategories, with each additional digit representing another level of detail. The calibration of some industry categories can go as fine as six digits.

It's possible to calculate for each of these thousand-plus NAICS sectors a number that indicates its propensity toward larger scale. Table A1 compares these numbers for each sector between the years 1998 and 2002, and shows which sectors are undergoing the greatest consolidation. Table A2 performs the same exercise, this time highlighting those sectors decentralizing most rapidly. I discuss some of the implications of these findings in chapter 2.

## Table A.1
### Fastest consolidating business sectors

| Business Sector | Small Business Jobs | | |
| --- | --- | --- | --- |
| | 1998 | 2002 | % Change |
| Securities Intermediation and Related Activities | 31.88% | 25.40% | –20.31% |
| Broadcasting and Telecommunications | 17.26% | 13.78% | –20.20% |
| Rental and Leasing Services | 51.54% | 41.85% | –18.80% |
| Warehousing and Storage | 61.90% | 51.68% | –16.50% |
| Clothing and Clothing Accessories Stores | 33.17% | 28.68% | –13.55% |
| Couriers and Messengers | 15.13% | 13.09% | –13.49% |
| Building Material and Garden Equipment and Supplies Dealers | 62.80% | 56.55% | –9.95% |
| Support Activities for Transportation | 57.72% | 52.13% | –9.68% |
| Electronics and Appliance Stores | 54.76% | 49.68% | –9.27% |
| Support Activities for Mining | 50.29% | 45.81% | –8.91% |
| Publishing Industries | 39.31% | 35.95% | –8.54% |
| Administrative and Support Services | 42.73% | 39.16% | –8.36% |
| Hospitals | 8.99% | 8.24% | –8.33% |
| Sporting Goods, Hobby, Book, and Music Stores | 49.74% | 45.74% | –8.03% |
| Heavy Construction | 74.27% | 68.75% | –7.43% |
| Credit Intermediation and Related Activities | 34.63% | 32.14% | –7.19% |
| Performing Arts, Spectator Sports, and Related Industries | 77.11% | 71.97% | –6.67% |
| Transit and Ground Passenger Transportation | 60.94% | 57.02% | –6.44% |
| Gasoline Stations | 67.63% | 63.84% | –5.59% |
| Amusement, Gambling, and Recreation Industries | 67.15% | 63.46% | –5.50% |
| Health and Personal Care Stores | 34.84% | 33.10% | –4.99% |
| General Merchandise Stores | 3.13% | 2.97% | –4.99% |
| Plastics and Rubber Products Manufacturing | 44.98% | 42.79% | –4.87% |
| Nursing and Residential Care Facilities | 55.50% | 52.93% | –4.64% |
| Nonstore Retailers | 57.71% | 55.19% | –4.37% |

| Business Sector | Small Business Jobs | | |
|---|---|---|---|
| | *1998* | *2002* | *% Change* |
| Wholesale Trade, Durable Goods | 69.12% | 66.26% | −4.15% |
| Special Trade Contractors | 92.13% | 88.49% | −3.95% |
| Motor Vehicle and Parts Dealers | 82.97% | 79.79% | −3.83% |
| Wholesale Trade, Nondurable Goods | 60.10% | 57.84% | −3.75% |
| Furniture and Home Furnishings Stores | 69.52% | 67.22% | −3.30% |
| Professional, Scientific, and Technical Services | 66.28% | 64.19% | −3.15% |
| Social Assistance | 81.12% | 78.71% | −2.97% |
| Truck Transportation | 60.90% | 59.14% | −2.89% |
| Miscellaneous Store Retailers | 73.79% | 71.73% | −2.79% |
| Food Manufacturing | 32.75% | 31.86% | −2.70% |
| Museums, Historical Sites, and Similar Institutions | 81.22% | 79.61% | −1.98% |
| Foodservices and Drinking Places | 65.39% | 64.16% | −1.89% |
| Information Services and Data Processing Services | 34.27% | 33.67% | −1.75% |
| Building, Developing, and General Contracting | 86.63% | 85.28% | −1.55% |
| Waste Management and Remediation Services | 51.71% | 51.00% | −1.37% |
| Real Estate | 82.53% | 81.53% | −1.21% |
| Repair and Maintenance | 86.63% | 85.68% | −1.10% |
| Religious/Grantmaking/Civic/Professional and Similar Organizations | 91.48% | 90.75% | −0.79% |
| Printing and Related Support Activities | 68.07% | 67.83% | −0.35% |
| Miscellaneous Manufacturing | 57.73% | 57.57% | −0.28% |
| Accommodation | 43.00% | 42.91% | −0.22% |
| Fabricated Metal Product Manufacturing | 65.80% | 65.70% | −0.16% |
| Nonmetallic Mineral Product Manufacturing | 48.76% | 48.69% | −0.14% |
| Wood Product Manufacturing | 59.39% | 59.35% | −0.07% |

*Source:* Raw data is available from the U.S. Census Bureau, at censtats.census.gov/cgi-bin/cbpnaic/cbpsel.pl. The chart presents the three-digit SIC industries that have consolidated the most between 1998 and 2002. The percentage in the first two columns refers to the number of jobs represented by small business (<500 employees) in each year. The third column shows the change between the two years.

## Table A.2
### Fastest decentralizing business sectors

| Business Sector | Small Business Jobs | | |
| --- | --- | --- | --- |
| | 1998 | 2002 | % Change |
| Funds, Trusts, and Other Financial Vehicles | 34.91% | 49.23% | 41.02% |
| Primary Metal Manufacturing | 27.74% | 32.85% | 18.43% |
| Apparel Manufacturing | 58.80% | 69.29% | 17.84% |
| Management of Companies and Enterprises | 11.25% | 12.95% | 15.09% |
| Textile Mills | 31.09% | 35.59% | 14.48% |
| Leather and Allied Product Manufacturing | 49.60% | 56.57% | 14.06% |
| Utilities | 15.17% | 17.06% | 12.44% |
| Pipeline Transportation | 5.05% | 5.58% | 10.62% |
| Transportation Equipment Manufacturing | 17.83% | 19.53% | 9.50% |
| Scenic and Sightseeing Transportation | 75.85% | 82.98% | 9.41% |
| Beverage and Tobacco Product Manufacturing | 27.78% | 30.04% | 8.15% |
| Lessors of Intangible Assets, Except Copyrighted Works | 63.04% | 67.87% | 7.65% |
| Electrical Equipment, Appliance, and Component Manufacturing | 28.18% | 30.03% | 6.59% |
| Computer and Electronic Product Manufacturing | 27.13% | 28.99% | 6.88% |

| Business Sector | Small Business Jobs | | |
|---|---|---|---|
| | *1998* | *2002* | *% Change* |
| Water Transportation | 39.56% | 41.92% | 5.96% |
| Chemical Manufacturing | 25.84% | 27.34% | 5.83% |
| Oil and Gas Extraction | 46.59% | 48.83% | 4.79% |
| Mining (except oil and gas) | 38.05% | 39.76% | 4.51% |
| Textile Product Mills | 51.75% | 54.04% | 4.43% |
| Petroleum and Coal Products Manufacturing | 21.38% | 22.28% | 4.18% |
| Air Transportation | 6.79% | 7.06% | 4.04% |
| Ambulatory Health Care Services | 71.10% | 73.43% | 3.28% |
| Furniture and Related Product Manufacturing | 56.32% | 57.56% | 2.19% |
| Motion Picture and Sound Recording Industries | 42.87% | 43.73% | 2.00% |
| Forestry and Logging | 90.36% | 91.95% | 1.76% |
| Personal and Laundry Services | 75.78% | 76.97% | 1.56% |
| Machinery Manufacturing | 46.69% | 47.30% | 1.31% |
| Paper Manufacturing | 28.28% | 28.64% | 1.29% |
| Food and Beverage Stores | 34.84% | 35.16% | 0.92% |
| Insurance Carriers and Related Activities | 30.72% | 30.91% | 0.62% |
| Educational Services | 47.03% | 47.20% | 0.36% |

*Source:* Raw data is available from the U.S. Census Bureau, at censtats.census.gov/cgi-bin/ cbpnaic/cbpsel.pl. The chart presents the three-digit SIC industries that have decentralized the most between 1998 and 2002. The percentage in the first two columns refers to the number of jobs represented by small business (<500 employees) in each year. The third column shows the change between the two years.

# APPENDIX B

# The Scale of Existing Business by Payroll

In chapter 3 the point was made that in nearly all the thousand-plus categories in the North American Industry Classification System (NAICS) (see appendix A for a description), there are more small firms than large ones, even if a small business is defined as having fewer than one hundred employees (the SBA uses the criterion of fewer than five hundred employees). This means, significantly, that there are compelling examples of successful small-scale enterprise in almost every nook and cranny of the economy.

But skeptics can point out, quite rightly, that this does not tell us much about the *typical* scale characteristics of an industry. Because more than 99 percent of all firms are small, it should not be surprising that small firms dominate most industry categories *in terms of the sheer number of firms.* By employment or by payroll, the character of each industry will look very different. Take the six-digit code 451211 for "Book Stores."

There are 5,790 bookstore companies, and only forty-three of these firms have five hundred or more employees. This hardly means the book industry is decentralized. Those forty-three firms, like Borders and Barnes & Noble, actually account for two-thirds of the industry's jobs and payroll. So the distribution of payrolls between small and large firms in each industry turns out to be a better measure of its overall scale.

Table B.1 shows the percentage of payrolls in each business category paid by small businesses. With respect to firms with fewer than one hundred employees, only two industries have negligible payrolls:

"Utilities," which are publicly protected monopolies; and the "Management of Companies and Enterprises," which by definition involves only larger firms. In a few other industries such as "Information Processors" (software companies, for instance) and "Finance and Insurance," the payrolls of the smaller firms are between 10 percent and 20 percent of the entire industry. In "Manufacturing" and "Transportation and Warehousing," small firm payrolls are just over 20 percent. In four categories small businesses dominate, and in eight of the twenty categories small businesses account for at least 40 percent of all payrolls. Under the SBA criterion, small businesses dominate eight categories, and account for at least 40 percent of the payrolls of twelve categories. These data suggest that even by payroll, successful small businesses are major players, not just in retail and services, but in most sectors of the economy.

Inside every two-digit category, moreover, even those in which large firms pay most of the payrolls, are six-digit industries in which small businesses are doing very well. Look at manufacturing in table B2, where globalization seems to have put small business at a major disadvantage. By the SBA criterion, small businesses actually dominate the production of clothing, textiles, leather, wood, printing, fabricated metals, and furniture. In some categories, like textiles, this result may indicate how many of the biggest companies have moved operations overseas. But it also highlights how much small-scale manufacturing still remains in the country, and suggests the possibilities for a small-business revival as the other trends shrinking economies of scale, noted in chapter 3, begin to take hold. Those trends will nudge smart entrepreneurs in every industry to scour the existing universe for small success stores (whether they are typical or special), study their business plans, and "borrow" the best elements for their own business plans.

## Table B.1
### Percentage of payrolls in each industry
### paid by small business in 2002

| NAICS Description | <100 employees | <500 employees |
|---|---|---|
| Agriculture, Forestry, Fishing, and Hunting | 71.13% | N/A |
| Mining | 24.27% | 37.18% |
| Utilities | 6.18% | 11.99% |
| Construction | 64.09% | 81.99% |
| Manufacturing | 20.80% | 36.51% |
| Wholesale Trade | 41.53% | 57.25% |
| Retail Trade | 37.39% | 48.97% |
| Transportation and Warehousing | 24.37% | 35.06% |
| Information | 13.86% | 22.59% |
| Finance and Insurance | 17.64% | 27.45% |
| Real Estate and Rental and Leasing | 51.24% | 66.66% |
| Professional, Scientific, and Technical Services | 46.03% | 61.74% |
| Management of Companies and Enterprises | 2.54% | 9.71% |
| Administrative and Support and Waste Management and Remediation Services | 25.46% | 40.20% |
| Educational Services | 22.58% | 41.75% |
| Health Care and Social Assistance | 31.93% | 46.54% |
| Arts, Entertainment, and Recreation | 42.94% | 69.70% |
| Accommodation and Foodservices | 42.80% | 56.03% |
| Other Services (except public administration) | 69.13% | 82.95% |
| Auxiliaries, Corporate Executives, Subsidiary, and Regional Managing Offices | N/A | N/A |
| Unclassified | N/A | N/A |
| TOTAL | 31.48% | 45.07% |

*Source:* Raw data comes from the U.S. Census Bureau, at censtats.census.gov/cgi-bin/
cbpnaic/cbpsel.pl . The chart shows the relative role of small-business payrolls in each
two-digit NAICS business category. The middle column shows the result if a small business
is defined as fewer than 100 employees, and the right column if the SBA definition
(<500 employees) is used.

## Table B.2
### Percentage of payrolls in each manufacturing sector
### paid to small business in 2002

| NAICS Description | <100 employees | <500 employees |
|---|---|---|
| All Manufacturing | 20.80% | 36.51% |
| Food Manufacturing | 14.01% | 29.71% |
| Beverage and Tobacco Product Manufacturing | 12.05% | 22.97% |
| Textile Mills | 17.24% | 36.92% |
| Textile Product Mills | 35.04% | 53.60% |
| Apparel Manufacturing | 41.14% | 67.71% |
| Leather and Allied Product Manufacturing | 30.16% | 53.59% |
| Wood Product Manufacturing | 33.12% | 55.68% |
| Paper Manufacturing | 10.25% | 24.64% |
| Printing and Related Support Activities | 44.94% | 65.54% |
| Petroleum and Coal Products Manufacturing | 9.52% | 18.03% |
| Chemical Manufacturing | 10.65% | 21.91% |
| Plastics and Rubber Products Manufacturing | 20.05% | 39.89% |
| Nonmetallic Mineral Product Manufacturing | 27.76% | 45.14% |
| Primary Metal Manufacturing | 11.68% | 27.74% |
| Fabricated Metal Product Manufacturing | 43.22% | 64.04% |
| Machinery Manufacturing | 26.52% | 44.73% |
| Computer and Electronic Product Manufacturing | 12.03% | 25.09% |
| Electrical Equipment, Appliance, and Component Manufacturing | 15.00% | 29.45% |
| Transportation Equipment Manufacturing | 5.99% | 13.66% |
| Furniture and Related Product Manufacturing | 35.98% | 56.62% |
| Miscellaneous Manufacturing | 31.99% | 52.18% |

*Source:* Raw data comes from the U.S. Census Bureau, at censtats.census.gov/cgi-bin/
cbpnaic/cbpsel.pl. The chart shows the relative role of small-business payrolls in each
three-digit NAICS category of manufacturing. The middle column shows the result if
a small business is defined as fewer than 100 employees, and the right column if the
SBA definition (<500 employees) is used.

# Acknowledgments

Critical to completion of this book have been my colleagues at the Training & Development Corporation, where I have worked over the past two years. Literally hundreds of hours of dialogue involving Charles Tetro, Richard Schweppe, Kathy Coogan, Bruce Vermeulen, Jon Farley, and others are reflected in these pages. I appreciate their willingness to tolerate my using company time to write about the Small-Mart Revolution and to carry out real-world experiments around its implementation.

I'm deeply grateful to Tom Elliott, with whom I collaborated in developing CommunityFood.com, a Web business linking small farmers with food purchasers, and who provided critical support at a moment when I might otherwise have had to get a real job.

I would like acknowledge my many colleagues at the Business Alliance for Local Living Economies (BALLE ) who have inspired, informed, and nurtured my thinking, especially the co-chairs and co-founders Laury Hammel (Boston) and Judy Wicks (Philadelphia), and David and Fran Korten (Bainbridge Island), all of whom administered equal doses of praise and guilt to get this book done. Other important BALLE colleagues—as well as non-BALLE community organizers, thinkers, and practitioners, who have informed much of the Small-Mart analysis—are best identified by their communities:

Abingdon (VA): Anthony Flaccavento;

Albuquerque: Michael Castro, Teresa Cordoba, Michael Guerrero, Richard Moore;

Ames (IA): Lorna Michael Butler, Fred Kirshenmann, Rich Pirog, Ricardo Salvador, Ann Schultz;

Annapolis (MD): Dick Lahn, Erik Michelsen, Anne Pearson;

Ann Arbor (MI): Lisa Dugdale;

Arlington (VA): Cecilia Cassidy, Paul Hughes, Kit Johnston, Charlie Rinker;

Atlanta: Chris Johnson;

Baltimore: Brad Johnson, Ted Rouse;

Bangor (ME): Bjorn Claeson, Geoff Gratwick;

Berea (KY): Jeanne Marie Gage;

Bellingham (WA): Derek and Michelle Long;

Bloomington (IN): Jeff Isaac;

Bonn: Lutz Frenzel;

Boston: Simon Billinness, Rich Cowan, Al Nierenberg;

Boulder: Eric Doub, John Steiner;

Burlington (VT): John Bloch, Peter Clavelle, Edward Delhagen, Wayne Fawbush, Robbie Harold, Don Jamison, Ellen Kahler, Nancy Nye, Gerald Schorin, Richard Schramm;

Charlottesville (VA): William Lucy;

Chicago: Bruno Bottarelli, Suzanne Keers, Ellen Shepard, Jim Slama;

Cooperstown (NY): Teresa Winchester;

Davis (CA): Judy Corbett, Gail Feenstra;

Detroit: Grace Boggs;

East Lansing (MI): Deborah Davis, Laura DeLind, Pat Hudson, Terry Link, Phil Shepard, Tom Stanton;

El Paso (TX): Margarita Calderon, Frank Lopez;

Eugene (OR): Mel Bankoff, Pat Fagan;

Lehigh Valley (PA): Alan Jennings;

Flint: Guy Bazzani, Ellie Fry, Rob McCarthy;

Great Barrington (MA): Chris Lindstrom, Nancy and John Root, Susan Witt;

Hudson Valley (NY): Ann Davis, Melissa Everett, Ajax Greene, Judith LaBelle, Meredith Taylor;

Indianapolis: Steve Bonney;

Irvine (CA): Larry Agran, Will Swaim;

Laramie (WY): Debbie Kay Popp, Kim Vincent;

Lexington (KY): Lori Garkovich, Betty King;

Lisbon: Carlos Medeiros;

London: Peter North, Anja Mia Lorenz;

Los Angeles: Suzanne Biegel, Andy Fisher;

Madison (WI): Margaret Krome, Josie Pradella, Steve Stevenson;

Maine (statewide): Larry Dansinger, Auta Main, John Moore, Sanna McKim, Richard Rockefeller, Davis Taylor;

Mendocino County (CA): Patty Bruder, Alan Falleri, Johanna Schultz;

Minneapolis: Frank Altman, Mitra Milani Engan, Joel Hodroff, Emily Hoover, Christian Isquierdo, Claudette Konola, Kevin Lynch, Ken Meter, Nina Utne, Vonda Vaden;

Montana (statewide): Jonda Crosby, Brian Kahn, Jeff Milchen;

Moscow (ID): Colette DePhelps;

Mountclaire (NJ): Ken Brook, Richard Franke, Gerald Kloby;

Nagoya: Tetsuro Inaba, Katsuya Kodama;

Napa Valley (CA): Celine Haugen;

New Jersey (statewide): Michael Hozer, Miriam MacGillis, Peter Montague, Dana Silverman, Harold Simon;

New York City: Amanda Birnbaum, Wendy Brawer, Premilla Dexit, Stephanie Greenwood, Allen Hunter, Charlie Komanoff, Chuck Lief, Richard Perl, Cliff Rosenthal, Jose Sanchez, Martha Williams;

Oneonta (NY): Carlena Ficano;

Pennyslvania (statewide): Thomas Linzey;

Philadelphia: Alan Barak, Lynn Cutler, Dale Hendricks, Leanne Krueger-Braneky, John Smith;

Portland (ME): Christina Feller, Auta Main;

Portland (OR): John Blatt, Stuart Cowan, Janet Hammer, Deborah Kane, Lee Lancaster, Matt Lounsberry, Sophia McDonald, Dan Meek, Paul Needham, Derrell Ness, Bryan Redd, Don Sayre;

Prince George's County (MD): Peter Shapiro;

Princeton (NJ): Fran McManus, Wendy Rickard;

Ramapo (NJ): Trent Schroyer, Tula Tsalis;

Rochester: Hank Herrera, Rhonda Vaccaro;

Salt Lake City: Betsy Burton, Kinde Nebeker, David Nimkin;

San Francisco Bay Area: Ann Bartz, Larry Bensky, Channing Chen, Deb Nelson, Randy Hayes, Terry O'Keefe, Micha Peled, Don Shaffer, Mal Warwick;

Santa Cruz (CA): Bruce Cooperstein, Barbara Meister;

Santa Fe: Bill Althouse, M. Carlota Baca, Lynwood Brown, Tarby Bryant, Randy Burge, Craig Fiels, Sarah Laeng-Gilliatt, David Kaseman, Russell Means, Dan Pierpont, Rob Rikoon, Mark Sardella, Cathie Zacher;

Seattle: Jill Bamberg, Walt Blackford, Victor Bremson, Eugene Cahn, Brian Gershon, Heather Nordell, Gifford Pinchot III, Nick Licata, Mark Pomerantz, Ron Sher;

Sonoma County (CA): Jan Ballard;

Spokane: Sheri Barnard, Susanne Croft, Glen Lanker, Jim Wavada;

Tokyo: Takashi Ebashi;

Vancouver (BC): Penny Isbell, Carol Newell, Joel Solomon;

Washington (DC): Larry Bohlen, Sally Fallon, Mary Fehlig,
Naomi Friedman, Ian Fisk, Carol Iverson, Tosha Link, Larry Martin,
Leonard Minsky, Margaret Morgan-Hubbard, Patty Rose,
Rick Ryback, Jim Schulman, Sam Smith, Marc Weiss;

Western Massachusetts: Karen Christiansen, Tim Cohen-Mitchell,
Daniel Finn, Doug Hammond, Ed Maltby, Terry Molner, Eric Muten,
Nora Owen, Richard Sclove, Joe Sibilia.

Western Slope (CO): Connie Harvey, Colin Laird;

Yellow Springs (OH): Pat Murphy, Megan Quinn.

I asked a number of people for brutally honest readings of the man-
uscript, and they didn't let me down. For trying to save me from my
worst instincts, special thanks to Jamie Curtismith, Deborah Epstein,
Louis Freedberg, Thomas Hernandez, Doug Hoffer, Melissa Houghton,
H. Thomas Johnson, John Lee, Ted Nace, Perla Ni, Thomas Michael
Power, Rob Rikoon, Ellen Shepard, Jack Shuman, Jim Shuman, Tim
Size, and Jonathan Weiss. How well they succeeded, of course, is ulti-
mately my responsibility.

I was blessed with three very able research assistants. Evelyn Wright
performed background research in the spring and summer of 2005,
assisted by Lily Scott. In the final phases of completion of the book,
Merrian Fuller performed the heroic task of helping me check literally
hundreds of facts, large and small.

I have had several opportunities to teach local-economy workshops
to groups of professionals, and they always wind up being the real
teachers. I'm especially grateful to the twenty-two "students" I had for
eight days at the Whidbey Institute, near Seattle, during July 2005.

Bits and pieces of various chapters are from projects supported by
foundations over the past ten years. The analysis of urban farming was
underwritten by the Ford Foundation (Roland Anglin, James Spencer)
and the Village Foundation (Bobby Austin); the discussion of small-
business equities market by the Pond Foundation of Santa Fe (John

Daw); and the linkages between smart growth and public education and the analysis of rural finance by the Kellogg Foundation (Winnie Hernandez-Gallegos, Oran Hesterman). Other important intellectual colleagues in the philanthropic community have been Carl Anthony, Rupert Ayton, Harriet Barlowe, Paul Brest, Andre Carothers, Susan Clark, Harriet Crosby, Ellen Dorsey, Jed Emerson, Gale Emrich, Wendy Emrich, Jim Epstein, Betsy Feder, Diane Feeney, Anne Fitzgerald, Rick Foster, Jeff Furman, Ellen Furnari, Tracy Gary, Denis Hayes, Eric Heitz, Henry Holmes, John Hunting, Gail Imig, Ned Kasouf, Jenny Ladd, Donna Lartigue, Thomas Layton, Lance Lindblom, Owen Lopez, Josh Mailman, Doug Malcolm, Doug Ogden, Larry Ottinger, Maurice Paprin, Richard Perl, Drummond Pike, Ed Skloot, Daniel Solomon, Peggy Spanel, Cathy Sutton, Marge Tabankin, Stephen Viederman, and Ann Zill.

My colleagues in Bay Friendly Chicken have been great teachers regarding the world of entrepreneurship. Special thanks to Michael Heller, David Barnes, Chris Bedford, Rico DiMattia, Jim Lewis, Karina Lundahl, Carole Morrison, Simon Nadler, and Jerry Wunder.

The two community-building projects described in Chapter 8 provided invaluable laboratories for Small-Mart ideas. I'm grateful for the support of the organizers in St. Lawrence County, particularly Jim Shuman, Ann Heidenreich, Jim Waterson, Susan Kramer, Karen St. Hilaire, Daniel Sullivan, Anne Sullivan, and the Burt Family, who funded the effort. In the Katahdin Region of Maine, I worked with a fabulous team of organizers, led by Guilds Hollowell, Bruce McLean, Ron Brown, and Judy Holt.

At some cosmic level, there's no such thing as an original idea, and everything I've written in here has built on a community of living mentors (some of whom may not know it). Many thanks to: Chad Alger, Neil Allison, Gar Alperovitz, Autumn Alvarez, John Anner, Catherine Austin-Fitts, Kenny Ausubel, Robert Baron, David Barsamian, John Barton, Medea Benjamin, John J. Berger, Tim Bowser, Jeremy Brecher, Anne Claire Broughton, Peter Brown, Jeb Brugmann, Edgar & Christine Cahn, David Callahan, Mike Callicrate, Scott Campbell, John Cavanagh, Ralph Cavanagh, Ilan Chabay, Don Chen, Bill Collins, Chuck Collins, Lance Compa, David Corn, Jim Crowfoot, Herman Daly, Kevin Danaher, John Dorrer, Richard Douthwaite, Mark Dowie,

Fiona Dove, Valentine Doyle, William Drayton, Steve Dubb, Ronnie Dugger, Nick Dunlop, Ann & Paul Ehrlich, Richard Falk, David Fenton, Dietrich Fischer, John Fisk, Gil Friend, Anthony Garrett, Jeff Gates, Varun Gauri, Susan George, Mark Gerzon, Ron Goldfarb, Christopher Gunn, Fred Halliday, Hal Hamilton, Don Harker, Hal Harvey, Paul Hawken, Richard Healey, Hazel Henderson, Oran Hesterman, Gunther Hilliges, Colin Hines, Jochen Hippler, Dee Hock, Doug Hoffer, John Holdren, June Holley, Eric Horvitz, Dan Houston, Katrina Howell, Evelyn Hurwich, John Ikenberry, John Ikerd, David Imbroscio, Robert Johansen, Si Kahn, David Kallick, Hal Kane, Jenny Kassan, Greg Kats, Eric Kaufman, Will Keepin, Robert Keohane, John Kincaid, Michael Kinsley, Linda Kleinschmit, Joanne Kliejunas, Jane Knight, Dominic Careri Kulik, James Howard Kunstler, Lucinda Kurtz, Anna Lappé, Frances Moore Lappé, Eleanor LeCein, Greg LeRoy, Bernard Lietaer, Amory Lovins, Hunter Lovins, Neil Liebowitz, Nancy Lindborg, Thomas Lyson, Jim Lutz, Robert McIntyre, Jerry Mander, John McLaughrey, Russell Mechem, Charles William Maynes, Stacy Mitchell, Elizabeth Mueller, Dan Meek, David Morris, Eric Nelson, Toni Nelson, Helena Norberg-Hodge, David Orr, Kathy Ozer, Richard Perl, Janice Perlman, Mark Perlmutter, Ron Peterson, Peter Plastrik, Brenda Platt, Danny Postel, Mary-Beth Raddon, James Ranney, Jamin Raskin, Marcus Raskin, Joan Roelofs, Dorothy Rosenberg, Karen Rothmyer, Kirkpatrick Sale, Mark Satin, Max Sawicky, Trent Schroyer, Richard Sclove, Neil Seldman, Dan Siegel, Ken Silverstein, Nina Simons, Jaq Smit, Joshua Smith, Kennedy Smith, Sam Smith, Stewart Smith, Mark Sommer, Greg Steltenpohl, Dan Swinney, Charles Tansey, Nicholas Targ, Woody Tasch, Betsy Taylor, Amy Ting, Andrea Torrice, Lidia Usami, Paul van Tongeren, Dion van den Berg, Katrina van den Heuvel, William Ury, Sarah Vogel, Jay Walljasper, Joani Walsh, BR Walton, Debby Warren, Greg Watson, Betty Weiss, Romona Taylor Williams, Susan Witt, Michael Wood-Lewis, Jenny Yancy, and Simon Zadek.

Every day, I offer praise to the spirits of the world that Berrett-Koehler exists. After years of being treated like a cog in the publishing world, it is almost miraculous to find a publishing staff that cares so much about ideas and authors. Johanna Vondeling, the acquisitions editor and Mother Superior at BK, delivered just the right combination of faith, persistence, and tough love to get the job done. Katherine Silver and Dave Peattie performed an unusually meticulous effort at copyediting.

Finally, I appreciate all the love, support, and patience my family—especially my wife, Deborah—has shown for the countless hours of travel and work required for this project. If you like this book, please send her roses (locally grown, if possible).

# About the Author

Michael Shuman, an attorney, economist, and writer, is Vice President for Enterprise Development for the Training & Development Corporation (TDC) of Bucksport, Maine. Since publication of his previous book, *Going Local: Creating Self-Reliant Communities in the Global Age* (Routledge, 2000), he has been considered one of the nation's foremost experts on locally owned business.

After growing up in the suburbs in Long Island and St. Louis, Shuman entered Stanford University, where he received a bachelors' degree with distinction in international relations and economics in 1979 and a law degree in 1982. In 1980 he won First Prize in the Rabinowitch Essay Competition of the *Bulletin of the Atomic Scientists* on "How to Prevent Nuclear War."

He cofounded the Center for Innovative Diplomacy, an international advocacy organization representing several thousand mayors and city council members. He was also director of the Institute for Policy Studies, a progressive think tank, and head of the Institute for Empowerment and Entrepreneurship, a division of the Village Foundation, serving African-American men and boys. He was a Kellogg National Leadership Fellow between 1987 and 1990.

Among Shuman's most recent efforts to promote local economies are: the start-up of a community-owned poultry company in Salisbury, Maryland, called Bay Friendly Chicken; the organization of university-government-business collaborations in St. Lawrence County, New York, and in the Katahdin Region of Maine to study opportunities for new local business; an analysis of the impact of devolution in the former Soviet Union for the United Nations Development Program; and the development of a website (www.CommunityFood.com) to support marketing by family farmers. He has also served as a senior editor for the recently published *Encyclopedia of Community* and helped cofound the Business Alliance for Local Living Economies (BALLE).

He has written seven books and published nearly one hundred articles for such periodicals as the *New York Times, Washington Post, Nation, Weekly Standard, Foreign Policy, Parade,* and *Chronicle on Philanthropy.* He has given an average of a talk a week for 25 years to communities and universities throughout the world.

He currently lives in Washington, DC, with his wife, Deborah Epstein, and his two children, Adam and Rachel.

# Notes

## Introduction

1. Simon Head, "Inside the Leviathan," *New York Review of Books*, 16 December 2004, 80.

2. Wal-Mart's website boasts, "Global Insight, an independent economic analysis firm, concluded that Wal-Mart saved working families over $2,300 per household last year." See www.walmartfacts.com/community. This factoid—repeated uncritically in op-ed pages across America—is a classic case of misrepresentation by the corporate giant.

Even taking the Global Insight study at face value, the *net* savings per household—after accounting for depressed wages—is $1,046, less than half the number Wal-Mart uses. "The Economic Impact of Wal-Mart," monograph (Global Insight, 2 November 2005): 18.

But the deception turns out to be greater, because Global Insight is making claims for the *average* household in the United States. It duly notes that consumer expenditures totaled $8.2 trillion and that Wal-Mart's prices saved 113 million households $263 billion. The average consumption per household is $73,000. *Median* household consumption—that is, the level below which half of all households are at—is about $44,000. For the lower half of all U.S. households, the "working" families who are the main customers at Wal-Mart, the average savings are under $630 per year. Wal-Mart's website thus overstates its case fourfold. (Thanks to Stacy Mitchell for pointing this out.)

Whether the Global Insight study, underwritten by Wal-Mart, is credible is another question. Its economic model is proprietary and its assumptions therefore cannot be reviewed. One underlying assumption that seems particularly dubious is that many of the efficiency gains in retail over the past fifteen years would never have occurred but for Wal-Mart. In fact, Wal-Mart is continuously learning from other retailers and vice versa.

Global Insight also never grapples with the direct costs of displaced small retailers, nor the lost community multiplier benefits when these high-multiplier retailers are replaced by low-multiplier Wal-Marts. As chapter 2 suggests, the multiplier benefits of a typical local business can be two to four times greater than that of a chain store. In chain-store dependent communities, the $1,046 saved by a household could cost the same household $1,000 to $3,000 in terms of lost community income, wealth, jobs, and taxes. Jason Furman's provocative paper, "Wal-Mart: A Progressive Success Story," contains the same oversight. Monograph (New York, NYU Wagner Graduate School of Public Service, 28 November 2005).

3. "Maine Drug Pricing Survey—2002," Maine Department of Public Health, Bureau of Elder and Adult Services.

4. Stacy Mitchell reports, "As Barnes & Noble and Borders Books have gained market share—the two companies account for about half of bookstore sales—they've sharply reduced the number of books offered at a discount. Blockbuster's rental fees are higher in markets where it has a near monopoly." See Stacy Mitchell, "10 Reasons Why Maine's Homegrown Economy Matters: And 50 Proven Ways to Revive It," monograph (Maine Businesses for Social Responsibility, Belfast, ME, June 2004): 9.

5. The 10 percent savings are in line with the observations of several pro-Wal-Mart analysts. Pankaj Ghemawat and Ken A. Mark write, "According to one recent academic study, when Wal-Mart enters a market, prices decrease by 8 percent in rural areas and 5 percent in urban areas." "The Price Is Right," *New York Times*, 3 August 2005. The report by Global Insight discussed in note 2 also says "The expansion of Wal-Mart over the 1985–2004 period can be associated with a cumulative decline of 9.1% in food-at-home prices, a 4.2% decline in commodities (goods) prices, and a 3.1% decline in overall consumer prices . . ." "The Economic Impact of Wal-Mart": 1.

6. Bill Quinn, *How Wal-Mart Is Destroying America (and the World): And What You Can Do About It* (Berkeley: Ten Speed Press, 2000), 96.

7. "Attorney General Launches Investigation into Accuracy of Wal-Mart Pricing," press release, Connecticut Attorney General's Office, 21 November 2005.

8. "Everyday Low Wages: The Hidden Price We All Pay for Wal-Mart," monograph (Democratic Staff of the House Committee on Education and the Workforce, 16 February 2004).

9. Head, "Inside the Leviathan," 88.

10. Ibid.

11. Kenneth E. Stone, "Impact of the Wal-Mart Phenomenon on Rural Communities," in *Proceedings: Increasing Understanding of Public Problems and Policies* (Chicago: Farm Foundation, 1997), 12.

12. Mitchell, "10 Reasons Why Maine's Homegrown Economy Matters," 1.

13. Ibid. For an in-depth analysis of the problems with chain stores, see Stacy Mitchell, *The Big-Box Swindle: The True Cost of Mega-Retailers and the Fight for America's Independent Businesses* (Boston: Beacon Press, 2006).

14. For state and local subsidies, see Alan Peters and Peter Fisher, "The Failures of Economic Development Incentives," *Journal of the American Planning Association*, 70, no. 1 (Winter 2004): 28. See chapter 1 for further details.

For national subsidies, see Stephen Slivinski, "The Corporate Welfare Budget Bigger Than Ever," Policy Analysis, no. 415 (Cato Institute, Washington, DC, 10 October 2001). Slivinski notes seventy-nine items that total $87 billion. Of these, only five programs—Rural Community Advancement, Rural Business-Cooperative Service, Appalachian Regional Commission, Small Business Administration, and Small Business Innovation Research Programs—target small business. They total $2.8 billion. Assume generously that as much as a quarter of the other programs benefit a few lucky small businesses, and the total level of subsidization for nonlocal business is about $63 billion. Since Slivinski's analysis excludes tax breaks and trade barriers, $63 billion enormously underestimates the full extent of government distortion of markets.

15. Francis Fukuyama, "The End of History?" *The National Interest*, Summer 1989.

16. Colin Hines, *Localization: A Global Manifesto* (London: Earthscan, 2000), 171.

17. For a review of recent innovations in cooperatives, see Michelle Bielik, "New Generation Cooperatives on the Northern Plains," monograph (Winnipeg, University of Manitoba Department of Agricultural Economics & Farm Management, 2000). For a review of cutting-edge nonprofit enterprises, see Christopher Gunn, *Third-Sector Development: Making Up for the Market* (Ithaca, NY: Cornell University Press, 2004).

For an encyclopedic overview of the wide range of community enterprise alternatives to large corporations, see Steve Dubb, *Building Wealth: The New Asset-Based Approach to Solving Social and Economic Problems* (Washington: Aspen Institute, April 2005).

18. Michael H. Shuman, *Going Local: Creating Self-Reliant Communities in a Global Age* (New York: Routledge, 2000).

19. Kirkpatrick Sale, *Human Scale* (New York: J.P. Putnam, 1980).

20. See e.g., Michael H. Shuman and Merrian Fuller, "Profits for Justice," *The Nation*, 24 January 2005; Michael H. Shuman, "Why I Won't Sign," *The Progressive*, November 2001; Michael H. Shuman, "Going Local: Devolution for Progressives," *The Nation*, 12 October 1998; and Michael H. Shuman, "Why Progressive Funds Give Too Little to Too Many," *The Nation*, 12–18 January 1998.

21. My earliest writings were on citizen diplomacy and municipal foreign policy. See, e.g., Gale Warner and Michael H. Shuman, *Citizen Diplomats* (New York: Continuum, 1985); Michael H. Shuman "Local Foreign Policy v. Courts," *Foreign Policy*, Spring 1992; and Michael H. Shuman, "Local Foreign Policies," *Foreign Policy*, Winter 1986–87.

## Chapter 1

1. Between 1973 and 2003, real wages in the bottom three deciles grew between 6.4 percent and 7.0 percent over the entire thirty-year period. Lawrence Mishel, Jared Bernstein, and Sylvia Allegretto, *The State of Working America 2004–2005* (Ithaca, NY: Cornell University Press, 2005), Table 2.6.

2. Elise Gould, "Prognosis Worsens for Workers' Health Care: Fourth Consecutive Year of Decline in Employer-Provided Insurance Coverage," EPI Briefing Paper no. 167 (Economic Policy Institute, Washington, DC, October 2005).

3. Thomas Friedman, *The Lexus and the Olive Tree* (New York: First Anchor Books, 2000), xviii and 329.

4. "The Economic Impact of BMW on South Carolina" (Division of Research, Moore School of Business, University of South Carolina, May 2002): 2 (hereafter cited as *Moore School Report*).

5. Ibid., 22 (emphasis in original).

6. Beth Van-Spanje, "What Is Economic Development: A Primer" (National Council for Urban Economic Development, Washington, DC, 1996): 3. Since this was published, the National Council has merged with another organization and been renamed the International Economic Development Council.

7. Ibid., 1.

8. This story is drawn from Timothy Egan, "U.S.: Towns Hand Out Tax Breaks, Then Cry Foul as Jobs Leave," *New York Times*, 20 October 2004.

9. Ibid.

10. Ibid.

11. Ibid.

12. Louis Uchitelle, "When Subsidies to Lure Business Don't Pan Out," *New York Times*, 9 November 2003.

13. Sydney P. Freedberg and Connie Humburg, "Risky Business," *St. Petersburg Times*, 10 April 2005.

14. Philip Mattera and Anna Purinton, "Shopping for Subsidies: How Wal-Mart Uses Taxpayer Money to Finance Its Never-Ending Growth," monograph (Good Jobs First, Washington, DC, May 2004).

15. See Greg LeRoy, *The Great American Job Scam* (San Francisco: Berrett-Koehler, 2005).

16. Uchitelle, "When Subsidies to Lure Business Don't Pan Out."

17. Peters and Fisher, "The Failures of Economic Development Incentives": 28.

18. Robert B. Reich, "Who Is Them?" *Harvard Business Review*, March–April 1991, 77 and 85.

19. *Moore School Report*, 24.

20. This megasubsidy included a gigantic tax break, a state-funded employment center, and a municipally funded deep-water port. Neal Peirce, "Public Subsidies: Going, Going, Boeing?" 21 July 2003, www.stateline.org; and Paul Jacob, "What Is Seen and What Is Obscene," posted 14 March 2004, www.Townhall.com.

21. Uchitelle, "When Subsidies to Lure Business Don't Pan Out."

22. A living wage of $10 per hour yields an annual salary of $20,800. This could be paid by a portfolio of U.S. savings bonds equal to $480,000, currently paying 4.35 percent per year. Slightly riskier stock investments—but not necessarily riskier than investing in a TINA enterprise—would compare favorably to subsidies of even $250,000.

23. Jay Hancock, "South Carolina Pays Dearly for Added Jobs," *Baltimore Sun*, 12 October 1999.

24. Ibid. BMW, of course, is no longer just a German company.

25. Ibid.

26. *Moore School Report*, 24.

27. Robert M. Ady, "Discussion" (of other articles in the issue by Ronald Fisher and Michael Wasylenko) *New England Economic Review*,

(Federal Reserve Bank of Boston) (March–April 1997): 79. Thanks to Doug Hoffer for bringing this to my attention.

28. Peters and Fisher, "Failures of Economic Development Incentives," 35.

29. That's not to say that LOIS businesses never move or never sell out to others who have less regard for community. But these are rare occurences for small businesses. For TINA, mobility is the norm.

30. Thomas Friedman, *The World Is Flat: A Brief History of the Twenty-First Century* (New York: Farrar, Straus & Giroux, 2005).

31. Hancock, "South Carolina Pays Dearly."

32. Richard Florida, *The Rise of the Creative Class* (New York: Basic Books, 2002).

33. Freedberg and Humburg, "Risky Business."

34. Ibid.

## Chapter 2

1. See Hoover's database on "Companies and Industries," www.hoovers.com. See also www.hersheytrust.com and Michael D'Antonio, *Milton S. Hershey's Extraordinary Life of Wealth, Empire, and Utopian Dreams* (New York: Simon & Schuster, 2006).

2. "Wrigley Challenges Confectionery Giants," *Confectionery News*, 14 September 2005; "Hershey Trust Bows to Pressure over Future Sale," *Confectionery News*, 27 September 2002; and "Hershey Kisses Company Sale Goodbye," 18 September 2002, www.isa.org.

3. *Jacobellis v. Ohio*, 378 U.S. 184, 197 (1964).

4. U.S. Census Bureau, *Statistical Abstract of the United States: 2004–2005*, Table No. 732, 494.

5. U.S. Department of Commerce, Bureau of Economic Analysis, Table 1.3.5 on "Gross Value Added by Sector," available on the web at www.bea.doc.gov/bea/dn/nipaweb.

6. Edgar S. Cahn, "Nonmonetary Economy," in *Encyclopedia of Community*, eds. Karen Christensen and David Levison (Thousand Oaks, CA: Sage, 2003), 1001–04. Cahn quotes, for example, estimates made by the think tank Redefining Progress.

7. Ibid. See also P.S. Arno, C. Levine, and M.M. Memmott, "The Economic Value of Informal Caregiving," *Health Affairs* 18, no. 2: 182–88.

8. "The Underground Economy," Brief Analysis no. 273 (National Center for Policy Analysis, 13 July 1998).

9. Ibid.

10. Brian Headd, "Redefining Business Success: Distinguishing Between Closure and Failure," *Small Business Economics* 21 (2003): 51–61.

11. U.S. Census Bureau, *Statistical Abstract*, Tables No. 733–34, 495. It is worth pointing out the limits of these data: "Although the data sources mentioned . . . put great effort into finding new firms promptly, determining when new firms close, dealing with unreported data, and identifying mergers and spin-off, they still imperfectly represent the universe of firms that is their target." Catherine Armington, "Development of Business Data: Tracking Firm Counts, Growth, and Turnover by Size of Firms," monograph (SBA Office of Advocacy, Washington, DC, December 2004): 34.

12. The choices of years for comparison may seem arbitrary, but they reflect: (a) that federal accounting of sectors made a major change in 1998, from Standard Industrial Codes (SIC) to the North American Industry Classification System (NAICS); and (b) that 2002 is the most recent data available.

13. Sherri Burri McDonald and Christian Wihtol, "Small Businesses: The Success Story," *The Register-Guard*, 10 August 2003. The calculation per TINA job is based on the gross number of total jobs the six companies were providing in mid-2003. Were the measurement done on the basis of net increases in jobs after the subsidies, the cost per TINA job would be $67,220—or thirty-three times greater than the cost per LOIS job. See also Michael H. Shuman, "Go Local and Prosper," *Eugene Weekly*, 8 January 2004.

14. The Austin study is "Economic Impact Analysis: A Case Study," monograph (Civic Economics, Austin, Texas, December 2002). The Andersonville study is "The Andersonville Study of Retail Economics" (Civic Economics, Austin, Texas, October 2004). Both can be downloaded free of charge at www.civiceconomics.com.

"The Economic Impact of Locally Owned Businesses vs. Chains: A Case Study in Midcoast Maine," monograph (Institute for Local Self-Reliance and Friends of Midcoast Maine, September 2003).

15. See, for example: David Morris, *The New City-States* (Washington, DC: Institute for Local Self-Reliance, 1982), 6 (showing that two thirds of McDonald's revenues leak out of a community); Christopher Gunn and Hazel Dayton Gunn, *Reclaiming Capital: Democratic Initiatives and Community Control* (Ithaca, NY: Cornell University Press, 1991) (finding that 77 percent of a typical McDonald's "social surplus" leaves the community); Gbenga Ajilore, "Toledo-Lucas County Merchant Study," monograph (Urban Affairs Center, Toledo, OH, 21 June 2004)(calculating an

economic impact of a local bookstore more than four times greater than that of a typical Barnes & Noble); Justin Sachs, *The Money Trail* (London: New Economics Foundation, 2002) (spelling out a multiplier methodology used by communities throughout the United Kingdom, and documenting case studies showing how local businesses double or triple the economic impact of nonlocal competitors).

16. For a more extensive discussion of the Packers, see Shuman, *Going Local*, 3–6.

17. This does not mean *conventional* economic growth can continue *ad infinitum*, because ultimately the world will run up against finite energy and mineral resources and limits to how much waste its ecological sinks can absorb. It is possible, however, to imagine the infinite growth of ingenuity if it's also accompanied by reductions in the consumption of physical resources and energy.

18. Thomas Michael Power, *Environmental Protection and Economic Well-Being* (Armonk, NY: M. A. Sharpe, 1996), 125. (References omitted.)

19. See Amory B. Lovins and L. Hunter Lovins, *Brittle Power: Energy Strategy for National Security* (Andover, MA: Brickhouse, 1982).

20. Brian Halweil, *Home Grown: The Case for Local Food in a Global Market*, Worldwatch Paper no. 163 (Washington, DC: Worldwatch, November 2002).

21. David Wessell, "Capital: Decentralization and Downtowns," *Wall Street Journal*, 25 October 2001.

22. Power, *Environmental Protection and Economic Well-Being*, 133.

23. Mitchell, "Maine's Homegrown Economy Matters," 8.

24. Matissa N. Hollister, "Does Firm Size Matter Anymore? The New Economy and Firm Size Wage Effects," *American Sociological Review*, 69 (October 2004): 659–76.

25. Jim Hightower, "Whose Town Is It?" *The Austin Chronicle*, 20 February 2004.

26. Quoted in Thomas A. Lyson, "Big Business and Community Welfare: Revisiting a Classic Study," monograph (Cornell University Department of Rural Sociology, Ithaca, NY, 2001): 3.

27. Ibid., 12–13.

28. Ibid., 14.

29. Thad Williamson, David Imbroscio, and Gar Alperovitz, *Making A Place for Community: Local Democracy in a Global Era* (New York: Routledge, 2003), 8.

30. For a description of how BSR mutated into a Fortune 500 enclave in recent years, see Russell Mokhiber and Robert Weissman, "Hijacked:

Business for Social Responsibility," 3 November 2005, www.common dreams.org.

31. Since 1990, during the era of Wal-Mart expansion, American consumers have increased their driving for all retail an estimated 95 billion automobile miles per year. Stacy Mitchell, "Will Wal-Mart Eat Britain," speech to the New Economics Foundation, 26 May 2005, at www.newrules.org.

32. Dan Swinney, "Building the Bridge to the High Road," monograph (Midwest Center for Labor Research, Chicago, Illinois, 1998).

33. Jon Gertner, "What Is a Living Wage," *New York Times Magazine*, 15 January 2006.

34. See, for example, Bruce T. Herbert's insistence on asking Weyerhaeuser tough questions, forcing the board to rescind its no Q&A policy at a recent shareholder meeting. Gretchen Morgenson, "Managers to Owners: Shut Up," *New York Times*, 24 April 2005. For examples of creative institutional shareholder activism, see Marjorie Kelly, David Smith, and Nicholas Greenberg, "Transforming Economic Power: State and Local Approaches to Corporate Reform," monograph (New York: Demos, 2005): 8–11.

## Chapter 3

1. Paul R. La Monica, "Bank Merger Mania Is Back," *CNN/Money*, 27 October 2003.

2. John H. Boyd and Stanley L. Graham, "Investigating the Banking Consolidation Trend," *Quarterly Review* (Federal Reserve Bank of Minneapolis) (Spring 1991): 4.

3. Tom Schlesinger, "Nationwide Banking: An Analysis of the Treasury Proposal," monograph (Southern Finance Project, Philamont, VA, March 1991). The Southern Finance Project has since changed its name to the Financial Markets Center (www.fmcenter.org).

4. Amory B. Lovins et al., *Small Is Profitable: The Hidden Economic Benefits of Making Electrical Resources the Right Size* (Snowmass, CO: Rocky Mountain Institute, 2002), 53.

5. Sale, *Human Scale*.

6. Bruce Greenwald and Judd Kahn, "All Strategy Is Local," *Harvard Business Review*, September 2005, 96.

7. Susan Warren, "Texas Grocer Thrives by Catering to Locals," *Wall Street Journal*, 1 December 2004.

8. Niraj Dawar and Tony Frost, "Competing with Giants: Survival

Strategies for Local Companies in Emerging Markets," *Harvard Business Review*, March–April 1999, 119.

9. John King, "Bay Area Farmers' Future," *San Francisco Chronicle*, 24 September 1998, updated with data from the California County Agricultural Commissions, "Agricultural Production Value Without Timber," www.nass.usda.gov/ca/bul/agcom/indexcav.htm.

10. Paul T. Kidd, "Summary of Book: Agile Manufacturing," www .knowledge.hut.fi/projects/itss/kidd_agile.htm.

11. H. Thomas Johnson, "Confronting the Tyranny of Management by Numbers: How Business Can Deliver the Results We Care Most About," *SOL Journal of Knowledge, Learning, and Change* 5, no. 4 (2004): 6–9.

12. Peter Schwartz, personal communication, November 2000. Even mainstream automakers are beginning to apprehend the shift in optimal scale. See Micheline Maynard, "Carmakers' Big Idea: Think Small," *New York Times*, 12 February 2006.

13. Stewart Smith, personal communication, 2 December 2005. These data update his earlier work, "Sustainable Agriculture and Public Policy," *Maine Policy Review* 2, no. 1 (April 1993): 68–78.

14. Rich Pirog, "Calculating Food Miles for a Multiple Ingredient Food Product," monograph (Leopold Center for Sustainable Agriculture, Ames, IA, March 2005). See also Halweil, "Home Grown," 17–22.

15. Good data are kept by the Agriculture Marketing Service of the U.S. Department of Agriculture. See www.ams.usda.gov/farmersmarkets/FarmersMarketGrowth.htm.

16. The movement's members exceeded eighty-three thousand by mid-2005, organized in eight hundred "convivia" in fifty countries. Heike Mayer and Paul Knox, "Slow Cities: Sustainable Places in a Fast World," monograph (Urban Affairs and Planning Dept., Virginia Tech, Blacksburg, VA, 2005).

17. See www.farmersdiner.com.

18. "Adding Values to Our Food System: An Economic Analysis of Sustainable Food Systems" (Integrity Systems Cooperative Co., Everson, WA, February 1997).

19. Anne C. Bellows, Katherine Brown, and Jac Smit, "Health Benefits of Urban Agriculture," monograph (Community Food Security Coalition, Venice, CA, 2004), www.foodsecurity.org.

20. "National Community Gardening Survey," monograph (American Community Gardening Association, New York, 1996), www.community garden.org.

21. Bruce Butterfield, National Gardening Association, personal communication, 30 December 2005.

22. Katherine Brown and Anne Carter, "Urban Agriculture and Community Food Security in the United States: Farming from the City Center to the Urban Fringe," monograph (Community Food Security Coalition, Venice, CA, October 2003): 13; available at www.foodsecurity.org.

23. Michael Abelman, *On Good Land: The Autobiography of an Urban Farm* (San Francisco, CA: Chronicle Books, 1998). For an update, see www.fairviewgardens.org.

24. Mohammed Nuru, "Community Food Security, Urban Agriculture and Economic Development Perspectives on a Model from the San Francisco League of Urban Gardeners," in Gail Feenstra, David Campbell, and David Chaney, eds., "Community Food Systems: Sustaining Farms and People in the Emerging Economy," conference proceedings (Division of Agriculture and Natural Resources, University of California, Davis, CA, September 1997): 48.

25. Brown and Carter, "Urban Agriculture and Community Food Security in the United States," 5.

26. These numbers have grown each of the last five years. Mark Nord, Margaret Andrews, and Steven Carlson, "Household Food Security in the United States, 2004," Economic Research Report no. 11 (Economic Research Services of the USDA, Washington, DC, 2005).

27. Brown and Carter, "Urban Agriculture and Community Food Security in the United States," 7.

28. "Growing Food on City Roofs," *USA Today* (publication of the Society for the Advancement of Education), June 1993. Also see "Lightweight Soil for Green Roofs," www.gaia-inst.org.

29. Lovins, et al., *Small Is Profitable*, 26.

30. Ibid., 29.

31. Ibid.

32. "Taking a Battering Worth $6B," *Newsday*, 19 August 2003.

33. Lovins, et al., *Small Is Profitable*, xv.

34. John Vidal, "Analyst Fears Global Oil Crisis in Three Years," *The Guardian* (UK), 26 April 2005.

35. James Howard Kunstler writes, "Now we are faced with the global oil-production peak. The best estimates of when this will actually happen have been somewhere between now and 2010. In 2004, however, after demand from burgeoning China and India shot up, and revelations that Shell Oil wildly misstated its reserves, and Saudi Arabia proved incapable of goosing up its production despite promises to do so, the most

knowledgeable experts revised their predictions and now concur that 2005 is apt to be the year of all-time global peak production." James Howard Kunstler, "The Long Emergency: What's Going to Happen as We Start Running Out of Cheap Gas to Guzzle," *Rolling Stone*, 13 April 2005. The piece is adapted from his provocative and important book, *The Long Emergency: Surviving the Converging Catastrophes of the Twenty-First Century* (New York: Atlantic Monthly Press, 2005).

36. Vidal, "Analyst Fears Global Oil Crisis."

37. *International Energy Outlook 2005*, DOE/EIA–0484 (2005), Energy Information Agency, July 2005.

38. Some have suggested this number is as high as 70 percent. See Paul Craig Roberts, "Private Accounts: Right Idea, Wrong Time," *Business Week*, 7 March 2005, 39. This seems unlikely. Wal-Mart's annual report for 2004 states that the "cost of sales" were about $219 billion. In a recent PBS Frontline episode on Wal-Mart, Ray Bracy, the company's vice president for federal and international public affairs, said that Wal-Mart imports approximated $15 billion in goods from China each year. That's about 7 percent of the total cost of sales.

39. Julie Osborn, Chuck Goldman, Nicole Hopper, and Terry Singer, *Assessing U.S. ESCO Industry: Results from the NAESCO Database Project* (Environmental Energy Technologies Division, Lawrence Berkeley Labs, Berkeley, CA, August 2002): 5.

40. "Balancing Natural Gas Policy—Fueling the Demands of a Growing Economy," vol. 1, Summary of Findings and Recommendations (National Petroleum Council, 25 September 2003): 23.

41. Ibid., 15.

42. The use of electricity from *any* source for household heating or transportation, even through an intermediary like hydrogen for example, will necessarily be more expensive because of the thermal and physical losses that occur from generating electricity and then converting it into another form of energy.

43. See Michael H. Shuman and Hal Harvey, *Security without War: A Post Cold-War Foreign Policy* (Boulder, CO: Westview, 1993), 206–9.

44. See Lundahl's various speeches and newsletters at www.culture change.org.

45. For example, the catastrophe school of thought is carelessly reviving myths about the lack of viability of oil substitutes—for example, that the manufacture of windpower requires great quantities of steel that in turn require coal-polluting production—that used to be propagated a generation ago by the nuclear power industry. See the similar claims made in

a much-publicized report by Herbert Inhaber, from the Canadian atomic energy establishment. That report—*Risk of Energy Production*, AECB-1119/REV-2 (Ottawa: Atomic Energy Control Board, November 1978)—is demolished by John P. Holdren et al., "Risks of Renewable Energy Sources: A Critique of the Inhaber Report," ERG 79-3 (Energy Resources Group, University of California at Berkeley, CA, June 1979).

46. See David Morris, "The Carbohydrate Economy, Biofuels, and the Net Energy Debate," monograph (Institute for Local Self-Reliance, Washington, DC, August 2005).

47. Amory B. Lovins et al., *Winning the Oil Endgame: Innovation for Profits, Jobs, and Security* (Snowmass, CO: Rocky Mountain Institute, 2004), x and 104.

48. Ibid., x.

49. Ibid., 105–6. See also David Luhnow and Geraldo Samor, "As Brazil Fills Up on Ethanol, It Weans Off Energy Imports," *Wall Street Journal*, 9 January 2006.

50. Paul R. Krugman and Robert Z. Lawrence, "Trade, Jobs and Wages," *Scientific American*, April 1994, 44–49.

51. U.S. Census Bureau, *Statistical Abstract*, Table 641, 425.

52. Paul Krugman, *Pop Internationalism* (Cambridge, MA: MIT Press, 1997), 213.

53. Joseph Asher, "Will You Be There When I Need You," *ABA Banking Journal* (April 1999): 30.

54. Friedman, *The World Is Flat*.

55. Bureau of Economic Analysis, Selected NIPA Tables, September 2005, Table 1.1.5 "Gross Domestic Product," D-3.

56. "U.S. Current-Account Deficit Decreases in Second Quarter 2005," press release, Bureau of Economic Analysis, 16 September 2005.

57. Not all Indians are thrilled with these call centers either. One of the best-selling novels in India in late 2005 was Chetan Bhagat's *One Night at the Call Center*, which takes a dim view of the high human toll and low business value of outsourcing. "Bestselling Indian Author Paints Grim View of Outsourcing Jobs," Yahoo News, 29 December 2005.

58. Friedman, *The World Is Flat*, 11–15. Thanks to Aaron Spector, a lifelong certified accountant, for pointing this out.

59. Greenwald and Kahn, "All Strategy Is Local," 104.

60. This number comes from the 1997 Current Population Survey, discussed in Jeffrey J. Kuenzi and Clara A. Reschovsky, "Home-Based Workers in the United States–1997," Current Population Report P70-78 (Washington, DC: U.S. Census Bureau, December 2001): 2.

61.  Michael Porter, *The Competitive Advantage of Nations* (New York: Free Press, 1990).

62.  Eric D. Larson, "Trends in the Consumption of Energy-Intensive Basic Materials in Industrialized Countries and Implications for Developing Regions," paper presented at the International Symposium on Environmentally Sound Energy Technologies in Milan, Italy, 21–25 October 1991.

63.  Ibid., 2.

64.  For a good introduction to the topic, see "Internet Sales Tax Fairness" at www.newrules.org . Given the regressive nature of sales taxes and the desirability of replacing all sales tax with taxes on pollution and nonrenewable resources (see chapter 7), it's hard to get too worked up about this.

65.  "Employment Briefs," *Detroit News*, 13 December 1998.

66.  Thomas J. Peters and Robert H. Waterman, Jr., *In Search of Excellence* (New York: HarperCollins, 1982), 31–32. One hypothesis that enjoys some empirical support about why workers in large firms are paid more than those in small ones is that the insecure, mind-numbing, and unpleasant nature of the work requires higher compensation. See, e.g., Jonathan Gardner, "Can Worker Distaste for Employer Size Explain the Employer Size-Wage Differential?" monograph (Watson Wyatt LLP, Reigate, Surrey, United Kingdom, May 2003).

67.  "Communicating Change," *Harvard Business Review*, May–June 1996, 97.

68.  Quoted in Douglas Wolk. "The New Crop," *Workforce Management Online*, June 2005.

69.  Greenwald and Kahn, "All Strategy Is Local," 100.

70.  Peters and Waterman, Jr., *In Search of Excellence*, 31–32.

71.  Wolk, "The New Crop."

72.  *Green Scissors 2003: Cutting Wasteful & Environmentally Harmful Spending* (Washington, DC: Green Scissors Coalition, 2003).

73.  Slivinski, "The Corporate Welfare Budget Bigger Than Ever."

74.  James MacKenzie, Roger Dower, and Donald Chen, "The Going Rate: What It Really Costs to Drive" (World Resources Institute, Washington, DC, 1992).

75.  See the debt clock maintained by Ed Hall at www.brillig.com/debt_clock/.

76.  "Three Out of Five Cities Are Less Able to Meet Fiscal Obligations," press release, National League of Cities, 10 October 2005.

77. Paul Craig Roberts, "Collapsing Case for Free Trade," *The American Conservative*, 6 December 2004, 16.

78. Paul A. Pautler, "The Effects of Mergers and Post-Merger Integration: A Review of Business Consulting Literature," monograph (21 January 2003), www.ftc.gov.

79. Gretchen Morgenson, "What Are Mergers Good For?" *New York Times Magazine*, 5 June 2005.

80. Boyd and Graham, "Investigating the Banking Consolidation Trend," 12.

81. Ibid.

82. Rich Karlgaard, "Carly Fiorina's Seven Deadly Sins," *Wall Street Journal*, 11 February 2006.

## Chapter 4

1. Also in the next minute, government agencies will shell out $4 million in various purchasing contracts. Two out of three of these dollars will be spent by fifty state and thirty-six thousand local governments. The rest will go for investment and net imports. The U.S. economy is made up of $12 trillion worth of final transactions every year.

2. U.S. Department of Labor, Bureau of Labor Statistics, "Consumer Expenditures in 2002," Report 974, February 2004, 3. Note that the Consumer Expenditure Survey excludes investment. When I buy a car, I'm usually investing about half my money in the vehicle itself, and spending the other half on the interest on the loan to buy it. National accounting of consumption looks only at your payment of interest, plus the depreciation of your car each year—that is, how much of your car's worth you use each year. (When you try to resell your car and realize how quickly the blue book value plummets in the years after manufacture, you get a sense about how depreciation works.) Chapter 5 focuses on the challenges of localizing investment.

3. Amory B. Lovins, "Natural Capitalism: The Next Industrial Revolution," 21 Annual E. F. Schumacher Lectures, October 2001 (E. F. Schumacher Society, Great Barrington, MA, 2003): 7.

4. This number is higher than total household energy expenditures because it includes non-household efficiency savings and transportation efficiency savings that show up elsewhere in consumer expenditures.

5. See www.eatingfresh.com.

6. The most recent report of the World Health Organization (WHO) finds, for example, that in 2002 the Netherlands spent 8.8 percent of its

GDP on health care, while the United States spent 14.6 percent. Yet, in 2003, the Dutch outperformed us in terms of life expectancy by two years, child mortality by 33 percent, and adult mortality by 24 percent for women and 49 percent for men. See *World Health Report* (World Health Organization, Geneva, 2005): 174–81, and 192–99.

7. According to Surgeon General Richard H. Carmona, "There is no greater imperative in American health care than switching from a treatment-oriented society to a prevention-oriented society. Right now we've got it backwards." Richard H. Carmona, "Reshaping America's Health Care for the Future," Remarks before the Joint Economic Committee of the U.S. Congress, 1 October 2003, www.hhs.gov/surgeongeneral.

8. I learned about the huge possibilities for local entertainment on my first real job, when I was Film Programs Coordinator for the Palo Alto Cultural Center, which regularly put on programs, classes, competitions, and festivals involving local actors, producers, teachers, concessionaries, and audiences. Many California cities, at that time, were investing 1 percent of city budgets in the arts, a policy that became one of the victims of Proposition 13 but now deserves renewed attention.

9. Florida, *The Rise of the Creative Class.*

10. *Our Built and Natural Environments: A Technical Review of the Interactions between Land Use, Transportation, and Environmental Quality,* EPA 231-R-01-002 (Environmental Protection Agency, Washington, DC, January 2001), 27.

11. Laura J. Henze, Edward Kirshner, and Linda Lillow, "An Income and Capital Flow Study of East Oakland, California," monograph (Community Economics, Oakland, CA, 30 November 1979): 1. See chapter 7 for further discussion of this and similar studies.

12. My apologies for the imprecise nature of these estimates. I am not aware of any coherent way to estimate how much of each line item in the Consumer Expenditure Survey is currently localized, though I welcome suggestions from readers.

13. A survey of businesses participating in Philadelphia's buy local month found that a fifth enjoyed increased sales, 57 percent experienced a "positive impact," and 90 percent would participate again. Carolyn Said, "Main Street Fights Chain Street Campaign Hopes to Persuade People to Shop at Local Stores before Heading to the Big Retailers and Regional Malls," *San Francisco Chronicle,* 29 November 2005.

14. For a fuller explanation of local money, including its legality, see Michael H. Shuman, *Going Local,* 133–38. See also Lewis D. Solomon,

*Rethinking Our Centralized Monetary System* (Westport, CT: Praeger, 1996).

15. During the Great Depression John Maynard Keynes urged national governments to stimulate aggregate demand, either through deficit spending or through lower interest rates. These short-term public policy tools restore consumer and producer confidence and thereby set the economy back on a sound footing. See John Maynard Keynes, *General Theory on Employment, Interest, and Money* (Orlando, Florida: First Harvest/Harcourt, 1964) (originally published in 1936).

16. Paul Glover, personal communication, 30 January 2006.

17. See www.lets-linkup.com.

## Chapter 5

1. U.S. Census Bureau, *Statistical Abstract,* Table No. 429, 499.

2. Ibid., Table 1169, 741. If you expand this analysis to include all U.S. financial assets, which totaled $101 trillion in 2003, you will find that those placed either indirectly in banks or held by banks, credit unions, and savings and loans themselves still constitute about the same fraction of the asset universe. Table 1158, 736.

3. Ibid., Table 1168, 740.

4. Ted Nace, personal communication, 16 November 2005.

5. Since 1977 the CRA has required that banks seeking permission to merge or open new branches demonstrate a record of reinvesting adequately in the poor living in the towns where the banks do business. Community activists have successfully wielded the CRA to extract from the bankasaurs more than $1.5 trillion of community-friendly lending. "CRA Sunshine Reveals Benefits of Bank-Community Group Partnerships" (National Community Reinvestment Coalition, Washington, DC, 2002).

6. According to the Small Business Administration, small businesses tapping lines of credit turn first and foremost to personal credit cards (46 percent) and business credit cards (34 percent). "Finding Funding: Breaking Down the Basics of Small-Business Borrowing," *Wall Street Journal,* 29 November 2004.

7. Interest rates of 20 to 30 percent are not uncommon. Marcella Bombardier, "Gift to Tufts Will Aid World's Smallest Firms," *Boston Globe,* 4 November 2005.

There are several reasons U.S. microloan funds have fared less well than their global counterparts. One of the key features of the funds—

groups of peers in which each member does not receive a tranche of funding until the previous tranche is paid—works better in Third World contexts because peer members in a village have known one another for a lifetime. U.S. participants, in contrast, often have just met. Also, for many Third World entrepreneurs, the microloan programs are the only loans around. First World microloan recipients, in contrast, are those rejected by a much more open and finely tuned system. Finally, fifty dollars goes a lot further in a Third World economy than five thousand dollars goes in a First World economy. Even LOIS businesses usually have significantly higher startup costs. See John Buntin, "Bad Credit," *The New Republic*, 31 March 1997.

8. U.S. Census Bureau, *Statistical Abstract*, Table 1161, 738.

9. See www.trfund.com.

10. See www.upstream21.com.

11. This is the best one can do given how little state and local financial data exists. National household asset data are adjusted to New Mexico by income.

12. Of the $9.4 billion assets held by PERA, $2.2 billion are in government bonds, $4.3 billion in stocks, $0.7 billion in corporate bonds, and $1.8 billion in international securities. The fund does hold a tiny $15 million investment in an office building that it and other state agencies use. Public Employees Retirement Association of New Mexico, *Standing the Test of Time: Comprehensive Annual Financial Report, Year Ended June 30, 2004* (Santa Fe, NM, 2004).

13. Kelly, et al., "Transforming Economic Power."

14. See "Investment Performance: Third Quarter 2005," monograph (New Mexico State Investment Council, Santa Fe, NM, 2005): 2.

15. For information about the various investment funds, see www.state.nm.us/nmsic.

16. See note 7.

17. There are exceptions, of course. One of the most important concerns founding investors, who are free to risk their own capital in an enterprise, even if they have little or no personal wealth.

18. Rule 501 of Regulation D of the Securities and Exchange Act of 1933. See www.sec.gov.

19. See www.sfmicroangels.com.

20. Allison Batdorff, "Powell Mercantile Serves as Model for Others," *Casper Star Tribune*, 15 November 2004; Sharon Earhart, "Making Merc Work," *Headwaters News* (Center for the Rocky Mountain West, University of Montana), 2 March 2005.

21. 29 U.S.C. 1001 et seq. For a good overview, see Thomas R. Hoecker, "ERISA and the 401(k) Plan Fiduciary," monograph (Snell & Wilmer LLP, Phoenix, AZ, 2005), www.swlaw.com.

22. Kelly, et al., "Transforming Economic Power," 10. See also Gilbert Chan, "Urban Projects Pay Off for CalPERS," *The Sacramento Bee*, 4 September 2005.

23. U.S. Census Bureau, *Statistical Abstract*, Table 718, 484.

24. Sinclair Stewart and Paul Waldie, "Safety Device or Ticking Time Bomb?" *The Toronto Globe and Mail*, 1 June 2005.

25. James Tobin, "A Proposal for International Monetary Reform", *Eastern Economic Journal* 4 (1978): 153–59. See also Harlan Cleveland, Hazel Henderson, and Inge Kaul, *The United Nations: Policy and Financing Alternatives* (New York: Apex Press, 1995).

26. Rob Rikoon, president of Rikoon-Carret Wealth Managers, personal communication, 9 August 2003. See also the comments of David Malizia, managing director at Florida Capital Partners, a Tampa-based private equity firm ("I'm a three- to five-times cash flow valuation man") in Jim Melloan, "What's Your Company Worth Now? How, and By Whom, Valuations Are Established," *Inc. Magazine*, August 2004, 64.

## Chapter 6

1. "Industry at a Glance," *Poultry USA*, January 2004, 18c.

2. Dan Fesperman and Kate Shatzkin, "The Plucking of the American Chicken Farmer," *Baltimore Sun*, 28 February 1999.

3. See www.bellandevans.com.

4. Amy Chozik, "As Malls Think Small, Boutiques Get Their Chance," *Wall Street Journal*, 24 June 2005.

5. Paul H. Ray and Sherry Ruth Anderson, *The Cultural Creatives: How 50 Million People Are Changing the World* (New York: Harmony Books, 2000); and Paul H. Ray, "The New Political Compass," monograph version 7.3 (April 2002).

6. Kelly L. Giraud, Craig A. Bond, and Jennifer J. Keeling, "Consumer Preferences for Locally Made Specialty Products Across Northern New England" (Department of Resource Economics and Development, Durham, NH): 20.

7. Ibid., 4.

8. Rich Pirog, "Ecolabel Value Assessment," monograph (Leopold Center for Sustainable Agriculture, Ames, IA, November 2003): 8.

9. Lori Bird and Blair Swezey, *Green Power Marketing in the United*

*States*, 8th ed., NREL/TP-620-38994 (National Renewable Energy Laboratory, Golden, CO).

10. Cited at www.esw.org/earthpage/archives/2005_05.html

11. R.W. Beck, Inc. "U.S. Recycling Economic Information Study" (National Recycling Coalition, July 2001).

12.. David Morris and Irshad Ahmad, *The Carbohydrate Economy: Making Chemicals and Industrial Materials from Plant Matter*, summary (Washington: Institute for Local Self-Reliance, 1992), 1.

13. Lovins et al., *Winning the Oil Endgame.*

14. Ezio Valentini, "Switzerland's WIR System and Barter Worldwide," monograph (2000), www.appropriate-economics.org/materials.html.

15. Mitchell, "10 Reasons Why Maine's Homegrown Economy Matters," 36–37.

16. Jeff Bailey, "Co-ops Gain as Firms Seek Competitive Power," *Wall Street Journal*, 15 October 2002.

17. Mitchell, "10 Reasons Why Maine's Homegrown Economy Matters," 36.

18. Ibid.

19. Alberto Rinalda, "The Emilian Model Revisited: Twenty Years After," *Business History*, 47, no. 2 (April 2005): 244. Two thirds of Italy's manufacturing firms overall are small, while only a third of Germany's and the United States' firms are. "Structurally Unsound," *The Economist*, 24 November 2005.

20. The examples that follow are drawn from Paul Kalomiris, "Innovative State Policy Options to Promote Rural Economic Development," monograph (National Governors Association Center for Best Practices, Washington, DC, February 2003).

21. Alexander von Hoffman, "Small Businesses, Big Growth," *New York Times*, 4 September 2003.

22. See the various documents at www.interraproject.org.

23. Alana Probst, one of the founders of the Oregon Marketplace, in an interview with Merrian Fuller, 5 October 2005.

24. Barbara C. Bellows, Rex Dufour, and Janet Bachmann, "Bringing Local Food to Local Institutions," monograph (National Sustainable Agriculture Information Service, Fayetteville, AR, October 2003).

25. Chozick, "As Malls Think Small, Boutiques Get Their Chance."

26. Kenneth Stone of Iowa State University argues that most chain stores, like Wal-Mart and Home Depot, destroy as much economic activity as they create. "Competing with the Discount Mass Merchandisers," monograph (Iowa State University Economics Department, Ames,

1995). See also: Thomas Muller and Elizabeth Humstone, "What Happened When Wal-Mart Came to Town? A Report on Three Iowa Communities with a Statistical Analysis of Seven Iowa Counties" (National Trust for Historic Preservation, Washington, DC, May 1996); and Thomas Muller, "The Fiscal and Economic Impact of a Proposed Shopping Center Project on the City of Leominster," August 2003.

27. Kevin Helliker and Shirley Leung, "Counting Beans: Despite the Jitters, Most Coffeehouses Survive Starbucks," *Wall Street Journal*, 24 September 2002.

28. "Look What the Poultry Industry Is Doing for Delmarva: 2004 Facts about Delvarma Broiler Chicken Industry," fact sheet (Georgetown, DE, Delmarva Poultry Industry, 2004).

29. For an excellent recent overview, see Steve Striffler, *Chicken: The Dangerous Transformation of America's Favorite Food* (New Haven, CT: Yale University Press, 2005).

30. It's hard to see how the animal welfare goals can be met with many of the "free range" methods. How superior is the life of a chicken penned up, for example, in a movable cage?

31. Anne Fanatico and Holly Born, "Label Rouge: Pasture-Based Poultry Production in France," monograph (National Sustainable Agriculture Information Service, Fayetteville, AR, November 2002).

## Chapter 7

1. The studies done by Oakland, Chester, and other communities are summarized in Gunn and Gunn, *Reclaiming Capital: Democratic Initiatives and Community Development*, 37–53.

2. Michael J. Kinsley, *Economic Renewal Guide: A Collaborative Process for Sustainable Community Development* (Snowmass, CO: Rocky Mountain Institute, 1997).

3. Doug Hoffer and Ellen Kahler, "The Leaky Bucket: An Analysis of Vermont's Dependence on Imports," monograph (Vermont Peace & Justice Center, Burlington, Vermont, 2000).

4. The full range of discounted benefits was $27 million to $1.14 billion. Michael H. Shuman, "Economics of Proposed Biomass-fired District Heating System for Santa Fe, New Mexico," monograph (Local Energy, Santa Fe, NM, November 2005).

5. Greg LeRoy, "No More Candy Store," monograph (Grassroots Policy Project/Federation for Industrial Retention and Renewal, Washington, DC, 1994).

6. LeRoy, *The Great American Job Scam*.

7. See, e.g., Rob Gurwitt, "Edge-ucation," *Governing*, March 2004.

8. This includes funds transferred from the federal government and then spent. U.S. Census Bureau, *Statistical Abstract*, Table 429, 272.

9. Kelly, et al., "Transforming Economic Power," 7; and "Local Purchasing Preferences," at www.newrules.org.

10. Kelly, et al., "Transforming Economic Power," 5.

11. "Local Purchasing Preferences," on www.newrules.org.

12. Consider, for example, two identical bids to sell $1 million of paper towels to the city. Vendor A, locally owned, winds up spending $400,000 of the contract on inputs of labor, paper, and technology inside the city. Vendor B, from outside the city, spends only $100,000 inside the city. Further assume that the economic multiplier is two and the city has a sales tax rate of 5 percent. With Vendor A, the city's total output is increased $1.8 million—$1 million of new local production, plus $400,000 times two. The sales tax revenue is $90,000. With Vendor B, the city's output is increased $200,000—no new local production, except the $100,000 subcontract times two. The sales tax revenue is $5,000. Were these numbers presented transparently, the city would still award the contract to local Vendor A even if its bid were $85,000 higher. In this particular example an 8.5 percent bidding advantage to local bidders is economically justified.

Doug Hoffer applies this logic to suggested reforms of Vermont's procurement rules. "Targeted State Purchasing as a Tool for Economic Development" monograph (Montpelier, Vermont, Vermont Democracy Fund, 2004).

13. Jeff Yost, President and CEO of the Nebraska Community Foundation, personal communication, 2 February 2006.

14. Price elasticity of demand refers to the sensitivity of a consumer purchase to a price increase or decrease. When demand has a high level of elasticity, a small change in price leads to a big change in demand. When demand has a low level of elasticity, a big change in price leads to a small change in demand. The concept is important for tax shifting: if the demand for "bads" like pollution is elastic, rising taxes will lead to very little increased government revenue.

15. My preferred alternatives would be Henry George property taxes and wealth taxes. See Shuman, *Going Local*, 144–49.

16. Roughly three quarters of the price is government taxation. Peter Ford, "Gas Prices Too High? Try Europe," *Christian Science Monitor*, 26 August 2005.

17. For a good summary of the case for abolishing corporate taxes, see Chris Edwards, "State Corporate Income Taxes Should Be Repealed," Tax and Budget Bulletin no. 19 (Washington DC, Cato Institute, April 2004).

18. U.S. Census Bureau, *Statistical Abstract*, 272.

19. For good examples of cutting-edge local ordinances, see www.newrules.org.

20. Thomas Linzey, "Factory Farms, Corporations, and Democracy," on the website of the Community Environmental Legal Defense Fund, www.celdf.org.

21. See also Haya El Nasser, "Cities Put Shackles on Chain Stores," *USA Today*, 21 July 2004.

22. Thomas Linzey, interviewed on *NOW*, PBS, 18 February 2005.

23. Property rights advocates are particularly infuriated by the recent five to four Supreme Court decision of *Kelo et al. v. City of New London*, which held that a city can take one person's land and award it to another person in the name of economic development and the public good. Case No. 04-108, decided June 23, 2005. In my view, the conservative position, which would limit takings to truly public projects and insist on market-rate "just compensation," would benefit LOIS enormously. The current *Kelo* holding makes it easier for communities to continue their TINA subsidization practices.

24. Owe Courreges, "Wal-Mart Skirts Building Restriction by Building Two Stores Side-by-Side," *Lone Star Times*, 7 March 2005.

25. Rob Wooley, "Honey, We Shrunk the Big Box!" *Great Lakes Bulletin News Service*, 30 November 2005.

26. See Economic Policy Institution, "General Information on the Minimum Wage," Table 4, at http://www.epi.org/content.cfm/issue guides_minwage_minwage.

27. Ibid.

28. Miguel Bustillo, "State Sees Conflict in Trade Pact," *Los Angeles Times*, 18 July 2005.

29. Liz Figueroa and Jesse Colorado Swanhuyser, "Trade Tribunals Must Not Trump State, Local Laws," *San Francisco Chronicle*, 23 August 2005.

30. Ibid.

31. Center for Strategic and International Studies, "Dispute Over Aircraft Subsidies Back on WTO Docket," www.globalization101.org, posted 2 June 2005.

32. Emad Mekay, "Brazil Triumphs over U.S. in WTO Subsidies Dis-

pute," InterPress News Service, 4 March 2005, www.commondreams.org; and Patrick Baert, "WTO Acts in Jet Giants Row, *The Standard* (Hong Kong), 21 July 2005.

33. "States' Rights vs. Free Trade: As Trade Pacts Proliferate, States Start to Howl About Lost Sovereignty," *Business Week*, 7 March 2005.

34. Figueroa and Swanhuyser, *Trade Tribunals.*

35. For information about Portland's Metro Regional Government, see www.metro-region.org.

36. See, e.g., William R. Barnes and Larry C. Ledebur, *The New Regional Economies: The U.S. Common Market and the Global Economy* (Thousand Oaks, CA: Sage, 1998)

37. Scott Campbell, assistant professor of Urban Planning, University of Michigan, personal communication, 3 November 2005.

38. See, e.g., Barnes and Ledebur, *The New Regional Economies.*

## Chapter 8

1. John P. Kretzmann and John L. McKnight, *Building Communities from the Inside Out* (Chicago: ACTA Publications, 1993).

2. See, e.g., Kinsley, *Economic Renewal Guide.*

3. Michelle and Derek Long, *Think Local First: A How To Manual* (San Francisco: Business Alliance for Local Living Economies, 2005)

4. Michelle Long, personal communication, 7 December 2005.

5. Ibid.

6. Andrew Cassel, "Sure, Act Locally, But Buy Globally," *Philadelphia Inquirer*, 1 May 2005.

7. Bruce Schimmel, "The Blonde and the Blowhard," *Philadelphia City Paper*, May 26–June 1, 2005.

8. The starting place is the Regional Economic Information System (REIS), an annual model produced by the U.S. Bureau of Economic Analysis (BEA) of all the income-producing sectors of the economy. The most recent data available are for the year 2000. The raw data in the model show the personal income and earnings for each two-digit-SIC (standard industrial code) sector. Because the United States is a relatively self-reliant country (only about a sixth of our GDP is spent on imports), a "typical" county also should be self-reliant. Significant earnings deviations from the norm reveal net imports or exports.

If the United States were made up of self-reliant, regional economies, their consumption patterns would be similar to the nation as a whole. In different parts of the country, there are some differences in what Americans consume, but they typically range by only a few percentage points for most goods and services. The differences are larger when it comes to consumption by businesses, since a region with a large mining sector will purchase very different inputs than, say, one with a large fishing sector. But a self-reliant American region would have both a modest mining and fishing sector and equal representation of all industries, so again, tending toward the average is a reasonable indicator of a high degree of self-reliance.

This methodology actually understates the potential for import replacement. It assumes that sectors similar to the average U.S. region are self-reliant, when, in fact, they may simply be importing and exporting the exact same amount of a commodity. Even a net exporting sector may be importing for local demand, which means it still could hold opportunities for import replacement.

## Chapter 9

1. See report's summary and press release at www.unicfusa.org.

2. Michael H. Shuman, *Towards a Global Village: International Community Development Initiatives* (London: Pluto, 1994).

3. Karen Lowry Miller, "Juggling Two Worlds," *Newsweek International Edition*, 29 November 2004.

4. See www.friendsofgaviotas.org; and Alan Weisman, *Gaviotas: A Village to Reinvent the World* (White River, VT: Chelsea Green, 1999).

5. World Commission on Environment and Development, *Our Common Future* (Oxford: Oxford University Press, 1987), 8.

6. Amanda Griscom Little, "The Revolution Will Be Localized," www.grist.org, 14 July 2005. See also Eli Sanders, "Rebuffing Bush, 132 Mayors Embrace Kyoto Rules," *New York Times*, 14 May 2005.

7. Jared Diamond, *Guns, Germs, and Steel: The Fates of Human Societies* (New York: W.W. Norton, 1997).

8. The Dutch engineer their dikes to prepare for the worst event imaginable in ten thousand years. The Army Corps of Engineers, in contrast, built the New Orleans flood controls to outlast an event projected to come every one hundred years, and wound up employing faulty designs that failed to achieve even that standard.

9. Many of these costs, of course, are being carried by all Americans through massive congressional appropriations, so all Americans can take some credit for the decision to rebuild.

10. Roberta Brandes Gratz, "In New Orleans' Mud, a War Determined Not to Slip Away," Elm Street Writers Group, posted on 7 November 2005 at www.commondreams.org.

11. Bruce Hamilton, "Hope, Despair in Eastern New Orleans; Some Vow to Rebuild, Others Bid Farewell," *Times-Picayune*, 14 October 2005.

12. Ibid.

13. Gwen Filosa, "Rebuilding the Park: Residents of a Ruined Pontchartrain Park Plot a Strategy to Rebuild the Historic Area," *Times-Picayune*, 30 October 2005.

14. Hamilton, "Hope, Despair in Eastern New Orleans."

15. "Small Business Gets High Marks in Opinion Poll," *Wall Street Journal*, 5 October 2004.

# Index

# ORGANIZATIONS

## Training & Development Corporation (TDC)

Over its 30-year lifetime, TDC, based in Bucksport, Maine, has been innovating in the field of workforce development. Its New England Institute became an important center for professional development and technical assistance providing services in thirty-eight states and the UK. Its Automated Case Management System was implemented in 300 sites around the country enabling a degree of personalized service and program accountability that has not yet been surpassed. Its Career Advancement Center informed the development of DOL's One-Stop Career Centers, embraced by the first Bush Administration's Department of Labor as a national model for serving dislocated workers and later by the Clinton Administration, as a systems approach to the provision of labor market services.

TDC's programs today include a Job Corps Center in Loring, Maine; Career Advancement Centers in Bangor, Maine, and Richmond, Virginia; and Media WORKS Enterprise®, also in Bangor and Richmond. For more information about these programs, visit www.tdc-usa.org .

TDC also is launching a new generation of work under the banner of Worksphere®, which blends workforce development with community and economic development. *The Small-Mart Revolution* is TDC's first publication on the philosophy, programs, and policies associated with Worksphere. Over the coming years, TDC plans to help communities in Maine and beyond implement these ideas. If you are interested in learning more about Worksphere or in deploying TDC's programs in your own community, please visit www.small-mart.org. There you will also be able to sign up for TDC's e-zine providing the latest information, news, references, stories, and programs about the issues covered in this book.

## CommunityFood.com

CommunityFood.com is an internet-based organization designed to promote the production and sale of fresh, wholesome food, homemade gifts, and other products direct from sustainable growers, coops and community-friendly rural businesses. Through a network of thousands of suppliers and other community-food resources, CommunityFood seeks to support a food system that promotes the health of land, workers, and communities. CommunityFood supports the Small-Mart Revolution because every local economy is first and foremost about food.

For further information, please visit www.communityfood.com.

## Business Alliance for Local Living Economies (BALLE)

BALLE was founded in 2001 to mobilize the small-business owners and civic leaders to create more humane and sustainable local economies. Today, in communities across North America—in places like Bellingham, Washington; Grand Rapids, Michigan; San Francisco, California; Portland, Oregon; and Vancouver, British Columbia— BALLE is offering competitive alternatives to global corporations financed by Wall Street-driven capital markets and controlled by absentee owners.

BALLE is made up of 26 networks composed of over 4,500 entrepreneurs in the U.S. and Canada. These networks are putting together the "building blocks" of local living economies—offering food, clothing, shelter, energy, healthcare, media, finance, and manufacturing to customers, while influencing public policy, encouraging community-based entrepreneurship, and educating citizens about more sustainable purchasing choices.

Among the current projects:

- In Bellingham, Washington, business leaders created a "Local First" campaign that encourages citizens to buy from local businesses as a way to keep money circulating within the community.
- Members of Vermont Businesses for Social Responsibility, a BALLE network whose members employ 8 percent of the state's workforce, are pushing for a greater state commitment for renewable energy and healthcare.
- The Philadelphia BALLE network trains new social entrepreneurs in the business skills they need to be successful through their Social Venture Institute.

BALLE is pleased to support projects like *The Small-Mart Revolution*, which prove that coordinated groups of locally owned companies can stand up to some of the harmful forces of globalization and foster the health and vitality of a region.

For more information about BALLE visit: www.livingeconomies.org .

# ABOUT BERRETT-KOEHLER PUBLISHERS

Berrett-Koehler is an independent publisher dedicated to an ambitious mission: Creating a World that Works for All.

We believe that to truly create a better world, action is needed at all levels—individual, organizational, and societal. At the individual level, our publications help people align their lives with their values and with their aspirations for a better world. At the organizational level, our publications promote progressive leadership and management practices, socially responsible approaches to business, and humane and effective organizations. At the societal level, our publications advance social and economic justice, shared prosperity, sustainability, and new solutions to national and global issues.

A major theme of our publications is "Opening Up New Space." They challenge conventional thinking, introduce new ideas, and foster positive change. Their common quest is changing the underlying beliefs, mindsets, and structures that keep generating the same cycles of problems, no matter who our leaders are or what improvement programs we adopt.

We strive to practice what we preach—to operate our publishing company in line with the ideas in our books. At the core of our approach is *stewardship,* which we define as a deep sense of responsibility to administer the company for the benefit of all of our "stakeholder" groups: authors, customers, employees, investors, service providers, and the communities and environment around us.

We are grateful to the thousands of readers, authors, and other friends of the company who consider themselves to be part of the "BK Community." We hope that you, too, will join us in our mission.

## A BK Currents Book

This book is part of our BK Currents series. BK Currents books advance social and economic justice by exploring the critical intersections between business and society. Offering a unique combination of thoughtful analysis and progressive alternatives, BK Currents books promote positive change at the national and global levels. To find out more, visit www.bkcurrents.com.

# BE CONNECTED

## Visit Our Website

Go to www.bkconnection.com to read exclusive previews and excerpts of new books, find detailed information on all Berrett-Koehler titles and authors, browse subject-area libraries of books, and get special discounts.

## Subscribe to Our Free E-Newsletter

Be the first to hear about new publications, special discount offers, exclusive articles, news about bestsellers, and more! Get on the list for our free e-newsletter by going to www.bkconnection.com.

## Participate in the Discussion

To see what others are saying about our books and post your own thoughts, check out our blogs at www.bkblogs.com.

## Get Quantity Discounts

Berrett-Koehler books are available at quantity discounts for orders of ten or more copies. Please call us toll-free at (800) 929-2929 or email us at bkp.orders@aidcvt.com.

## Host a Reading Group

For tips on how to form and carry on a book reading group in your workplace or community, see our website at www.bkconnection.com.

## Join the BK Community

Thousands of readers of our books have become part of the "BK Community" by participating in events featuring our authors, reviewing draft manuscripts of forthcoming books, spreading the word about their favorite books, and supporting our publishing program in other ways. If you would like to join the BK Community, please contact us at bkcommunity@bkpub.com.